Women and Reiki
Energetic/Holistic Healing in Practice

Gender, Theology and Spirituality

Series Editor
Lisa Isherwood, University of Winchester
Marcella Althaus-Reid, University of Edinburgh

Gender, Theology and Spirituality explores the notion that theology and spirituality are gendered activities. It offers the opportunity for analysis of that situation as well as provides space for alternative readings. In addition it questions the notion of gender itself and in so doing pushes the theological boundaries to more materialist and radical readings. The series opens the theological and spiritual floodgates through an honest engagement with embodied knowing and critical praxis.

Gender, Theology and Spirituality brings together international scholars from a range of theological areas who offer cutting edge insights and open up exciting and challenging possibilities and futures in theology.

Published:
Resurrecting Erotic Transgression
Subjecting Ambiguity in Theology
Anita Monro

Patriarchs, Prophets and Other Villains
Edited by Lisa Isherwood

Unconventional Wisdom
June Boyce-Tillman

Forthcoming in the series:

For What Sin Was She Slain? A Muslim Feminist Theology
Zayn R. Kassam

Our Cultic Foremothers
Sacred Sexuality and Sexual Hospitality in the Biblical
and Related Exegetic Texts
Thalia Gur Klein

Through Eros to Agape
The Radical Embodiment of Faith
Timothy R. Koch

Baby, You are my Religion: Theory, Praxis and Possible Theology of Mid-20th
Century Urban Butch Femme Community
Marie Cartier

Radical Otherness
A Socio/theological Investigation
Dave Harris and Lisa Isherwood

Women and Reiki
Energetic/Holistic Healing in Practice

Judith Ann Macpherson

equinox

LONDON   OAKVILLE

Published by Equinox Publishing Ltd.
Unit 6, The Village, 101 Amies St., London SW11 2JW, UK
DBBC, 28 Main Street, Oakville, CT 06779, USA

www.equinoxpub.com

First published 2008

British Library Cataloguing-in-Publication Data
A catalogue record for this book is available from the British Library.

ISBN-13   978 1 84553 153 9   (hardback)
          978 1 84553 154 6   (paperback)

Library of Congress Cataloging-in-Publication Data

Macpherson, Judith.
Women and reiki : energetic/holistic healing in practice/Judith Macpherson.
    p. cm.
Includes bibliographical references and index.
ISBN 1-84553-153-1 (hb) — ISBN 1-84553-154-X (pb)
1. Reiki (Healing system) 2. Women healers. I. Title. RZ403.R45M33 2007
615.8′51 — dc22
                        2006035587

Typeset by S.J.I. Services, New Delhi
Printed and bound in Great Britain by Lightning Source UK Ltd, Milton Keynes, and
Lightning Source Inc., La Vergne, TN

*This book is dedicated to
Calum Brand, born 7 September 1986 and Fraser Marr, born
29 March 1984, who died together on the 25th of April 2003.*

CONTENTS

ACKNOWLEDGEMENTS

This book has its roots in my PhD thesis and correspondingly my thanks go initially to my thesis supervisors in the Department of Religious Studies at The University of Stirling, Dr Malory Nye (now Professor at the Al-Maktoum Institute for Arabic and Islamic Studies) and in the latter stages of writing, Dr Timothy Fitzgerald. Both of these scholars critically engaged with my work and taught me much about how to turn my ideas into a book.

I am also grateful for the constructive comments and suggestions I have received over the years from other members of the academic staff. Their particular perspectives have broadened my fields of enquiry, as has the three years I have spent teaching for the Open University on the course, *Religion in the Modern World.* Insights from my students over these years has been inspiring. I would also very much like to thank my editor, Dr Lisa Isherwood, for her support, questions and critiques. She enabled me to remain relatively sane throughout the writing process.

I would like to thank The Carnegie Trust for providing me with a Personal Research Grant which, in combination with funding from The University of Stirling Graduate Research Fund allowed me to carry out extensive fieldwork in Scotland. Similarly, bursary support from The Salisbury Centre in Edinburgh and The Findhorn Foundation in Forres enabled me to attend many workshops and residential events.

I am deeply grateful to all those I have met in Scottish healing circles, for it is their stories that make up the body of this work. I have worked hard to represent these narratives fairly and hope that I have achieved this aim.

I would like to thank in particular Dr Mary Keller for inspiring me to pursue a PhD in the first place. Her friendship and unwavering commitment to academic excellence will not be forgotten. Her trust in my ability to have this work published has been both a comfort and a drive throughout the long, and at times tortuous, writing process.

I thank too Hugh Macpherson, for without his technical support I would have been in considerable difficulty. To my son, Michael, I offer heartfelt thanks for his love and awareness that endless hours would have to be spent on the computer in the completion of the writing process. I am immensely proud of him and his developing willingness to engage in feminist debates. I thank also all of my friends who have stoically endured hours of academic rambling. In particular I would like to express my deepest gratitude to Mandy McKerl and Rosie Crawford, for without them, life would be a much duller place. They are both very special women whose friendship I value immensely.

Finally, I would like to honour my parents Alan and Marjorie Taylor for their love and unwavering faith in my abilities, which has enabled me to move forward through all of life's challenges.

To all of the above, and to those I have inadvertently forgotten, many thanks for your support, advice and friendship.

INTRODUCTION

This book is born out of my experiences of journeying in the healing community. Within these circles I have had the opportunity to listen to women's voices, voices that spoke of the sense of empowerment to be found through revaluing their own experiences and finding 'new' connections with the sacred and with others. As I spent time with these women I also became more aware that these dialogues were constructed as rhetorics of feeling, with the hands being the locus for 'energetic touch'. At the same time, new frameworks of meaning were constructed where 'suffering' was regarded not as a passive experience but rather as 'a stage in life' which may be actively worked through with the support of a healer, initially at least.

What women healers vocalize about themselves also depends on their historical background (in this case predominantly white, middle-class) and micropolitical circumstances (the particular setting they are currently in and who they are with). This means that, for example, as women carried out the majority of their healing work in the private sphere they were able to devise rituals and utilize symbols which had their roots not only in mainstream Christian, Buddhist and Sanskrit traditions but they could also draw from those that were 'of the Goddess' or utilize other forms of female symbolism. This, I shall argue, may be one aspect of healing practice that enables women to work as active agents even if, as we shall later see, while women predominated at the 'grass roots level' of 'doing' healing work with family and friends, it was men who appeared to take on the predominant role in writing up healing practice and theology – as in the case of Reiki, a spiritual healing practice 'rediscovered' in Japan in the 1920s.

Hence it was with a 'pre-academic' background of being among healers in place, that I commenced my research into scholarly representations of contemporary spiritual practice; this following four years of undergraduate study within the field of religious studies at the University of Stirling. In particular my interests lay in the field defined as 'New Age', for it was here that many academics appeared to locate healers in the contemporary European and American cultural contexts. And here I discovered an initial problem, for the term 'New Age' is itself contested in that there is no clear agreement with regard to its delineation. I would propose however, based on my experiences within healing circles, that core themes within this field of thought and practice are:

1. Turning to the 'self as authoritative' in regard to health and spirituality (with corresponding critiques of institutionalized religion as being dogmatic, and biomedical approaches to health as flawed due to the exclusion of 'the spiritual'.
2. Regard for the earth as a living, spiritual entity and not just a material resource.
3. Emphasis on the holistic nature of all life and the possibility of transformation to higher levels of reality when this is realized through healing work on self and others.

Once I began to read the multiple writings on all aspects of this field I was also immediately struck by the androcentric positioning of the majority of writers. Women were made invisible by their collapse into the generic male, with male experience and male points of reference being taken as normative. This, since most academic writers acknowledged the at least numerical significance of women in 'New Age' thought and practice, I found to be highly problematic.

So as I took my first tentative steps as an ethnographer (a writer up of culture) and returned to healing circles with the aim of writing women back into their own healing stories (how arrogantly noble that sounds), I was aware even at this early stage of the tensions to be found in this 'project.' For as a scholar of religion re-entering a field where I had previously been a participant I had become 'both [the] subject and agent of scholarly analysis' (King 1995: 2). Hence I was to find, as McGuire succinctly states, that 'the highly personal role of the ethnographic researcher impels us to grapple with issues of bias and representation, relationships and 'objectivity', and it problematizes the very ground of our knowledge and understanding' (1992: 197).

Of particular significance to this work is the fact that I, like the 'subjects under study' experience life through a gendered body. So how may we begin to define 'gender', this being a signifier of particular interest to feminist scholars across academic disciplines?

Gender

As in things academic, this is also an area of considerable debate. For 'there is no clear consensus among scholars (feminist or not) on what is meant by the concepts of 'gender', 'female/male', or even 'women/men' (Nye 2003: 76). Perhaps one way to engage with this debate is to start with 'the body'. For the body may be understood as being both as 'a surface of social inscription and as the locus of lived experience' (Grosz 1993: 188). As Grosz further elaborates in relation to theoretical approaches to the body as being a site for knowledge production,

> The body may be regarded as a *hinge* or threshold: it is placed between a psychic or lived interiority and a more socio-political exteriority that produces interiority through the *inscription* of the body's outer surface. Where psychoanalysis and phenomenology focus on the body as it is experienced and rendered meaningful, the inscriptive model is more concerned with the processes by which the body is marked, scarred, transformed and written upon or constructed by the various regimes of institutional, discursive and nondiscursive power as a particular kind of body (1993: 196-97).

Put simply, who I am as an embodied being is a personal lived experienced in that it is 'I who sees, hears, smells, touches, feels and investigates and lives life', this being mediated to some considerable extent, by 'external' often institutional, forces. For example, though I may choose to have body piercings or tattoos in order to display aspects of 'how I perceive myself', these same may have to be covered, when in public, by dress appropriate to the situation, if I want to be accepted.

Yet my body is not just a surface which I can dress and upon which life plays, and here I find Grosz's analogy of the body as moebius strip useful, for she describes the moebius strip as 'a two dimensional flat plane, which, when rotated in space, creates both – and in a sense neither – an inside and an outside. Tracing the outside of the moebius strip leads one directly to its inside without at any point leaving its surface' (1993: 198). Looked at in this way, it becomes clear that 'events inscribed' on the body surface and life experience will also have an internal effect with regard to a person's moods and psyche. In turn, bodily appearance and behaviour will be regarded and judged by others. Hence 'The body becomes a text, a system of signs to be deciphered, 'read' and read into...by others as *expressive* of a subject's psychic interior' (1993: 198) [italics original].

For example, the body is increasingly subject to medicalisation. A person should be of an appropriate weight, shape (this, in the West, being slim) and level of fitness and if not, be prepared to partake in diet and exercise regimes and even surgery to achieve these ends. Hence,

> Food, dieting, exercise and movement provide meanings, values, norms and ideals that the subject actively ingests, incorporating social categories into the psychic interior. Bodies *speak,* without necessarily talking, because they become coded with and as signs. They speak social codes. They become *intextuated*, narrativised: simultaneously, social codes, laws, norms, and ideals become *incarnate* (Grosz 1993: 199) [italics original].

So how does gender relate to all of this? Well quite simply, and without wishing to essentialize, 'bodies are different'. Let us return to Nye's *Religion, the Basics* again. Nye states that 'a distinction is often made between two particular elements of difference: between *sex* and *gender*' (1993: 76), with 'sex' being seen as biologically 'based' while 'gender' is of cultural derivation. Correspondingly our 'sexing' begins at birth with, in the Western context, a biomedical doctor defining us according to, primarily, our genitalia. We are located as being different to each other - as being male, with penis, or female with uterus and vagina (or with no penis). Our bodies are hence 'used' as authoritative indicators of who/what we are. However, an initial problem arises with this sexing. Biomedical doctors are products of culture. They have been taught how to define our bodies utilizing science as a category of analysis (though few human beings would think they had a problem also knowing what it is to be a man or a woman). Therefore we are defined by our biology – this being culturally constructed and once sexed, are expected to display appropriate behaviour and conduct with social order being seen as dependent on most of us keeping to these 'patterns'. It is this latter that is our gendering. Therefore how we "as man or woman" are expected to act and look, depends on our social, cultural and historical contexts and how our differences – our sex, as men and women - are defined.

However, it would be an incomplete picture if we simply stated that sex refers to 'the biologically given differences between men and women whereas gender refers to the social and cultural meanings ascribed to these differences' (King 1995: 6). One writer who has made a significant contribution to the rethinking of the gender/sex distinction is Judith Butler. Butler argues that since biology is a cultural construct which is discursively written onto a person's body, then normative heterosexual 'givens' of 'what it is to be a man or a woman' can be disrupted.[1] This may leave space for a multiplicity of forms of sex and sexuality to be practiced including 'other-than-hetero-sexualities' (Lemert in Seidman 1996: vii).

> It would make no sense, then, to define gender as the cultural interpretation of sex if sex itself is a gendered category. Gender ought not to be conceived merely as the cultural inscription on a pregiven sex (a juridical conception): gender must also designate the very apparatus of production whereby the sexes themselves are established. As a result, gender is not to culture as sex is to nature, gender is also a discursive/cultural means by which 'sexed nature' or a 'natural sex' is established as 'prediscursive' prior to culture, a politically neutral surface *on which* culture acts (Butler 1990: 7) [italics original].

So our categorization as man or woman – and our gendering – does not exist in a vacuum. We all 'live in the world' and our discursively constructed identities (and possibilities to resist or transform the same) depend on our historical contexts, our race, ethnicity and our class. 'As a result it is impossible to separate out 'gender' from the political and cultural intersections in which it is culturally produced and maintained' (Butler 1990: 3).

And this is why gender can also be used as an analytical category so that feminists in academic and non-academic settings may examine how gender constructions 'create uneven and unjust power structures' (King 1995: 2) and bring these to light so that these may be challenged. For as Graham states ' "Gender" denotes the nature of our experiences as women and men, female and male, feminine and masculine: the origins and attributions of these categories, and their implications for all aspects of individual and corporate life' (Graham in Isherwood and McEwan 1996: 78). Correspondingly theories of gender engage with:

a. How individual gender identities are conferred and maintained and how these relate to a sense of self;
b. The relationship of gendered relational patterns to power, delineation of roles, labour, customs etc.; and

1. Though the reality of this positioning may be open to debate.

c. Deeper cultural structures where gender ideologies (often of patriarchal privilege) organize ideas of being a man or a woman. 'For the fundamental metaphors of our very cultural life and social order are imbued with representations of gender' (Graham in Isherwood and McEwan 1996: 78).

For as Davis argues, drawing from Young (1990), it is very often privileged groups such as 'white, Western, bourgeois, professional men – [who] are able to take on a god's eye view as disembodied subjects' (1997: 10) and judge both men and women, according to their gendered standards of healthiness, beauty, purity and deviance; these being standards which one can 'never hope to meet'. This means that 'Subordinate groups are defined by their bodies and according to norms which diminish and degrade them as 'drab, ugly, loathsome, impure, sick or deviant' (Young 1990: 123). They become 'other'. "This 'aesthetic scaling of bodies' as [Young] calls it, is not only central to the construction of difference, it is the mainstay of processes of domination as well' (Davis 1997: 10).

For women, this means that they are typically located according to male derived standards of femininity. They should be of the 'appropriate' body shape, caring, nurturing and supportive and sexually available to their male partner. In turn, 'women's corporeal specificity is used to explain and justify the different (read: unequal) social positions and cognitive abilities of the two sexes. By implication, women's bodies are presumed to be incapable of men's achievements, being weaker, more prone to (hormonal) irregularities, intrusions and unpredictabilities' (Grosz 1993: 14).

> The coding of femininity with corporeality in effect leaves men free to inhabit what they (falsely) believe is a purely conceptual order while at the same time enabling them to satisfy their (sometimes disavowed) need for corporeal contact through their access to women's bodies and services (Grosz 1993: 14).

I would argue, however, that it is maybe precisely women's corporeality that provides the ground for a transformatory politics. For, in relation to this work, healers regard their bodies as 'holistic wholes', where mind, body and spirit are seen as being indivisibly related. Correspondingly the gendered body is sacralized and regarded as the powerful medium, in and through which, healing work may be done.

Hence although this book is not concerned with the theorisation of body and gender *per se*, what I am interested in is how we may begin to examine gender's relationship to agency 'as healer'. For as McNay argues, we need 'to distinguish more precisely between practices of the self that are imposed on the individual though cultural sanctions and those that are more freely adopted...' (2000: 9). Are such practices of the self, where the individual engages in the formation (reformulation) of their own identity, empowering, inhibitive and regulatory in nature? Might we do better, as McNay suggests, to move forward from determinist (material feminist) accounts of economic, political and social dimensions of gender inequality which may lack 'an understanding of how these structures are worked through at the level of subject formation and agency' (McNay 2000: 16). For although inequalities clearly remain within social and private spheres, once one understands the formation of subjectivity,

> not in one-sided terms as an exogenously imposed effect but as a result of a lived relation between embodied potentiality and material relations, then an active concept of agency emerges. Understanding agency partly as the capacity to manage actively the often discontinuous, overlapping and conflicting relations of power provides a point from which to examine the connection between the symbolic and material relations that are constitutive of a differentiated social order (McNay 2000: 16).

Therefore within this book, where I provide the first academic study of energetic healing and Reiki in central Scotland, with the focus of my research being on the teaching of energetic healing in workshops and related textual material, I place emphasis on exploring how gendered spiritualities may be actively constructed. For as Dominic Corrywright has stated 'the web of New Age spiritualities is crucially sustained by the individual and collective weavings of women and this is particularly evident in healing and therapies' (2003: 131).

I argue that women's predominance in healing circles has a lot to do with personal projects of redefinition and self-transformation. This sort of 'work on the self' does not occur under, as radical feminist Daly (1991) and Sjoo (1994) would state, overarching patriarchal paradigms. Rather 'healing of the self' is located within 'fluid fields of force' (Foucault 1980). Therefore throughout this book I build up a decentralized narrative of power and locate women as active healing agents. In order to construct this narrative I draw from research in the fields of Goddess and women's spiritualities, for here we find useful evaluations of how women re-inscribe their bodies as sacred and empowered through, in the former, imminent ties to the Goddess. I relate my research to Meredith McGuire's empirical study of healing in the American context, where she argues that 'if the creation, maintenance and transformation of individuals' gender identities are indeed among the foremost identity work to be accomplished, then extensive empirical study of the many contemporary instances of gendered spirituality is very worthwhile' (McGuire 1994: 254).

Hence, in the first two and last chapters of this book I engage with feminist and ethnographic theory in general. I argue that discourses of power are multivalent operating within academic, religious, bio-medical and holistic healing circles and at the individual level. For debates abound in relation to, for example, the prioritization of text over experiential practice—the latter being central to New Age healing in Scotland. I introduce my position as a *bothsider*, an academic researcher and a practicing healer, as this positioning has raised its own set of theoretical and personal questions. And I draw from the aforementioned research in the parallel fields of Goddess and women's spiritualities.

In chapter three I introduce healing and curing models of health. I adopt Meredith McGuire's analytical framework of healing types. In this way I can locate my narrative of women's power and consciousness of healing into the debates between male dominated biomedical approaches to health and the apparently egalitarian holistic (mind, body and spirit) approaches to the same.

Chapter four engages with representations of 'the body as energetic' at the micro 'in the field' level and is primarily descriptive. Within these pages I provide a picture of how the energetic body is discursively constructed hence providing some necessary background for later ethnographic material.

> Speak not only of healing as a method, but also of those being healed: who they are, what processes of illness and recovery they pass through. Healing narratives subtly reinforce specific notions of personhood, of the character and development of illness, and provide a structuring script through which relevant parts of the [person's] life history can be interpreted (Hammer 2001: 356).

Chapters five and six focus specifically on the healing practices and discourses of Reiki, this healing modality growing significantly in popularity in a worldwide context. I propose that Reiki provides the practitioner with contrasting notions of 'the healthy body' to bio-medical and mainstream religious significations of the same and enables the development of empowered models of subjectivity 'as healer'.

In the final chapter I pull the book together as a whole and return to some of the questions asked in my opening material, noting my distinctive contributions as a *bothsider*. Throughout I acknowledge that my location as researcher/healer is just as materially and politically located, as are healers in the field. Overall, I place emphasis on evaluating distributions of power and the development of new liberating models of subjectivity in healing epistemologies. For I do not regard women healers as some homogenized, disempowered other, about whom I, the feminist academic, write. Therefore I would argue that when one begins to interpret 'what it is to be a healer' and underpin this with gender as a category of analysis, we need to think also of a person's agency 'anthropologically in terms of [their] practical engagement with the world in which they live, including the discourse by which they routinely explain, defend, and excuse that engagement, and therefore the traditions of arguments on which they draw *effectively* (or as J.L. Austin would put it, *happily*) for such purposes' (Asad 2003: 33) [italics original]. For, as Gedalof argues, if we see 'Women' only as passive ground, we fail to capture the dynamic complexity of the multiple networks of power and women's place in them, and the possibilities for discordance between those multiple networks' (1999: 185).

Chapter One

SETTING THE SCENE

This book is the first ethnographic study of Reiki and energetic healing in the British context. Overall the book argues that if we are to build up an accurate and comprehensive picture of healing thought and practice we must locate gender, representation and power as central elements throughout. For to date, even though women healers predominate at the grassroots level in both local and international contexts, this key issue has been largely ignored in most academic studies of 'New Age' and alternative spiritualities.

I propose that the narrative of women's power and consciousness of healing can be located into the debates between largely male dominated biomedical approaches to health and the apparently more egalitarian holistic discourses and practices (e.g. mind, body and spirit). And I argue that the women in the study operate within fluid fields of force, engaging in personal projects of redefinition, transformation and self-empowerment. By using the work of writers such as Michel Foucault and Meredith McGuire, I aim to show how healers are using Reiki and other healing spiritualities to engage in a politics of reclamation.

In order to begin this evaluation of the development of new constructions of identity within the New Age[1] scene in central Scotland, I have chosen to follow feminist historian Joan Scott's positioning that 'gender is a primary field within which or by which means of power are articulated' (Scott 1986: 1069) For while, as earlier observed, much academic material has been produced on the historical location, modes of participation and beliefs within

1. As I will discuss in Chapter Two, the term 'New Age' is problematic as Sutcliffe states, it would be misleading to accept the hegemonic (academic) view that the 'New Age' is a 'homogeneous entity' or that it should be assigned 'to a homogeneous cultural epoch or astrological era' (2003: 9). Therefore I employ the term New Age while remaining sceptical 'as to the reality it denotes' and locate it within implicit quotation marks throughout (cf, Levi-Strauss 1962: 15).

New Age networks, the at best cursory, inclusion of gender is highly problematic. For it is precisely within these fields of contemporary spirituality that we may find new ideals and alternatives to traditional gender roles. Hence there is space within these fields for women and men to reinscribe, redefine and reimagine their own bodies and their constructions of masculinity and femininity so that possibilities occur for the reclamation of power.

It is worthy of note, however, that while I do, in the later stages of this work, bring in some sociologists' usage of Foucaudian thought, I am also in accord with McNay when she argues that 'recent theoretical work on identity offers only a partial account of agency because it remains within essentially negative understanding of subject formation...[with] the idea that the individual emerges from constraint' (2000: 2-3). It would be better, therefore, to acknowledge that as individuals mutually construct hegemonic and subordinate discourses, space remains for independent thought, action and active negotiation of positioning.

I would argue, therefore, that the evaluation of the formation of gendered identities is crucial work for the scholar of religion. I have placed emphasis on examining how participants are taught to heal in workshops (the Salisbury Centre in Edinburgh being an important location for this) and in evaluating how participants respond to learning new ways of being 'as healer'. In order to support my ethnographic material I have drawn from various New Age textual literature, both historical and contemporary. Hence sources include, for example, workshop teaching manuals and texts recommended by healers. In this way I also hope to construct an understanding of the issues underlying healing practice.

The basic questions of my research on healing in Scotland are framed well by Meredith McGuire, for she has examined healing in suburban America. McGuire argues that,

> If the creation, maintenance and transformation of individuals' gender identities are indeed among the foremost identity work to be accomplished, then extensive empirical study of the many contemporary instances of gendered spirituality is very worthwhile (McGuire 1994: 254).

I shall relate my empirically researched fieldwork material on Reiki and energetic healing to writers such as McGuire, while also drawing from feminist research in the parallel fields of Wiccan and Goddess spirituality. For in the latter we find writers such as Helen

Berger (1999), Wendy Griffin (2000) and Carol Christ (1980) who have provided us with comprehensive evaluations of how women may form new and empowered, 'healed', identities.

Overall I will hence examine how 'the subjective and collective meanings of women and men as categories of identity have been constructed' (Scott 1988: 6) within healing circles and the relationship of these constructions to significations of power. This shall be located alongside an examination of feminist critiques of patriarchal structures and the relevance of these dialogues to 'contemporary spiritualities' and 'holistic health'.

I will argue that discourses of power and authority are multivalent operating within academic, religious, bio-medical and holistic healing circles and at the individual level. For example, debates abound in relation to the prioritization of text and the benefits of quantitative or qualitative approaches to academic research, while in healing circles, some aspects of experiential practice also appear to be in tension with male textual reformulations of healing theology.

In general, I shall regard 'healing' as being an aspect of popular religiosity – popular in that healers 'adopt practices which may be at odds with the religious [and bio-medical] specialists' views' (Thomas 1995: 37). For if one locates 'healing' as such, then this should enable an examination of counter hegemonic discourses of identity and power. And I shall utilize the term 'healing circles' for two reasons. First, it is a motif that is commonly used in the Scottish context. Second, I am following Meredith McGuire in her usage of the term. For she proposes that healing circles tend to be held in members' homes and that they are commonly composed of people who believe that they 'can gain power and control over their lives' (1998: 26) through learning forms of metaphysical and psychic healing. She also observes that within such circles emphasis is placed on providing social and emotional support for members, with social interaction on a day-to-day level. This is very similar to practitioner behaviour in the Scottish situation where women predominate, hence my adoption of the term.

My personal position throughout this work will be that of a *bothsider*, an academic writer and practicing healer. Being a *bothsider* has, as we shall see, raised its own particular set of theoretical and indeed personal questions. For I have been changed by my experiences within healing circles as here we find Western science, rationality and objectivity being critiqued with regard to their appropriateness as interpretative frameworks. Yet this book is written for academic evaluation where, in part, '"the empirical and logical rationality that defines knowledge as knowledge of fact" is a rationality that is not hospitable to "the insights of art, religion, fantasy or dream"' (Goulet citing Burridge 1960: 251 in Young and Goulet 1994: 18). This means that tensions have arisen with regard to my own subjective positioning 'as healer' and as academic researcher. However, we would also do well to remember that academics do not sit in isolation cut off from the rest of the world. For as Paul Heelas has proposed, some academics show distinct signs of being influenced by spiritual assumptions and experiences in the same way that some 'New Agers …write in ways which are hard to differentiate from the academic' (1996:10).

My experiences of this 'fluidity of identity boundaries' began primarily with my initiation as a Reiki practitioner. In learning to heal I entered a new world of meaning, a world where emphasis was placed on 'sensing energy through the hands' and 'trusting intuitive guidance' rather than 'seeing' solely within academic and scientific paradigms. I was taught to feel 'the energy flow' within the physical body and to acknowledge that there are 'aspects of being' that reason cannot grasp.

This has been an enlightening and challenging experience. For it is hard to write about 'the feel' of doing healing work. Similarly, while a practical demonstration of Reiki would be readily acknowledged—and indeed expected—by a New Age audience, no such space is made within academic circles. One should, therefore, keep firmly in mind the highly complex nature of sometimes competing, sometimes overlapping 'senses of self' and 'plurality of roles' and the relationship of the same to 'authoritative' discourse and practice. Therefore, throughout this work, my engagement with these sorts of tensions will be reflected in my choice of academic writers. Later in this book, for example, I introduce questions about the artificially constructed nature of academic text and the political positioning of the researcher.

Before I outline further the discourses running through this book, and on a methodological note, it is important to appreciate from the start that within New Age networks (and on occasion within academic writing on this field of contemporary practice), there is a tendency to use terminology somewhat loosely. Correspondingly when I review populist discourse within New Age textual material throughout this book, such as books, healing workshop manuals and New Age web sites that promote holistic healing as part of various energetic cosmologies, we shall find that 'religiosity', 'religious-like', 'religious/spiritual philosophies', 'spirituality' and 'spiritual' are regularly intermingled by writers and practitioners alike.

The most significant point when we come to Scottish healing at least, is that 'the spiritual' is generally regarded as being 'personally experienced'. 'Religion', in turn, is generally regarded as being problematic in its institutionalized form as the location for dogma, patriarchal hierarchies and mediated access to 'the spiritual'. And although this work focuses on healing in central Scotland, it might sit just as well in the North American or European contexts. For here too, Reiki and other forms of healing practice are carried out on a daily basis with similar aims and ambitions.

Throughout my fieldwork I have subscribed, as Paul Stoller has proposed, to the fundamental rule that even though I am going to research from the position of the 'intellectualist gaze', I also need to appreciate that 'one cannot separate thought from feeling and action – [for] they are inextricably linked' (1989: 5). I therefore ground my theoretical research in descriptive ethnography for how people come to knowledge of 'what it is to be a healer' is intimately tied to one's embodied state and perceived connections with 'all that is'.

It is also my intention throughout this research to apply a feminist hermeneutics of suspicion so that I may ask, utilizing gender as an analytical category, questions such as:

- If New Age healers promote the balancing of 'masculine' and 'feminine' elements within the individual, then who promotes this sort of standpoint and why? How does this relate to representations of the body 'as energetic'?
- If healers promote new forms of gender identity, how does this relate to 'assertions of power, authority and privilege' (McGuire 1994: 284)?
- How do healees/healers form new conceptions of health and disease? How does this relate to reinscriptions of the body and discourses of power?
- Are New Age women engaged in a politics of reclamation with regard to healing practice and theologies of the same? How

does this relate to the corresponding development of new and empowered identities 'as healer'?

As mentioned earlier, when I ask questions such as these I shall keep firmly in mind the centrality of embodied experience within New Age discourses. For as the New Age body is socially constructed and trained through a diversity of practices from yoga to fire walking, an examination of its sensual responses and strategies for empowerment is essential.

Fieldwork Context: Scotland

Fieldwork has been carried out primarily in 2000 and 2001. I was initiated as a Reiki practitioner at two weekend workshops in Dunfermline, the first in August 2000, the second in November of that same year. I continued to take part in monthly Reiki gatherings over the next eighteen months until these stopped with the 'retirement' of our Reiki Master. I met up with other practitioners until 2002 and still 'do' Reiki for friends and family.

In May of 2001 I also took part in a three day 'Reiki Techniques' workshop at The Salisbury Centre in Edinburgh. And although this material will form the basis for another book, in this work, I draw selectively from questionnaire material as completed by 33 of the 40 participants (see Appendix B) and follow-up phone interviews as carried out in May and early June of this same year with the ten respondents who had agreed to be contacted.

The Salisbury Centre was also the location for a 'Healing Circle' taught by Maureen Lockhart. I travelled to this one night a week for six weeks in the spring of 2001. It was also at this location that I participated in a 'Healing Through Consciousness' two-day workshop in the summer of 2001. Both of these events are discussed in Chapter Four.

I also visited numerous health fairs in Edinburgh, Glasgow, Stirling and Dunfermline and have continued to keep in contact with healers in Tayside and Fife. During this period of fieldwork I always informed participants of the general direction of my book — namely that I was researching healing from a gender perspective — though I did not explicitly voice my particular interest in multivalent discourses of power and representation.

Having personally engaged with and travelled along a 'seekers' path' before commencing this research, I knew the location of many New Age bookshops and I had spent considerable time perusing the Mind Body and Spirit sections of mainstream bookstores. I was aware of the popularity of the 'spiritual shopping' perspective where one could purchase crystals and incense, Buddhas and Ganeshas and place these in the home where they might be used in 'spiritual practice'. However, at this point I had not taken part in New Age workshops where one could actually learn to heal or where one could listen to emotional, narrated life stories of 'what worked for me in my spiritual journey home'. It is to my experiences of these sorts of workshops that I turn in later ethnographic chapters. However, the initial appeal of locations such as The Salisbury Centre in Edinburgh is perhaps the emphasis on learning particular types of healing in a weekend or evening workshop so that these can later be utilized at home for practical, transformative effect. Their brochure puts it in the following manner,

> We believe [that this Centre] provides a valuable resource to anyone
> who would like to improve the quality of their life by becoming more
> internally conscious and aware (SC2: 2003 Brochure).

Hence learnt skills are taken back into the local community where circles of healing practice become located – frequented primarily by women. It was primarily for this reason that I chose to focus on the above centre. This location appears to be the starting point for many women in central Scotland on their way to 'improving their life' in a holistic manner and in the forming of circles of 'like minded' acquaintances. The Salisbury Centre also appears to be so well regarded in central Scotland that they do not need to advertise at health fairs. Rather, past attendees spread news of their experiences to other men and women in a generally 'why not go and try this…it worked for me' kind of format. And it was precisely this 'word of mouth' transmission of experiences of healing practice, which led me to one of the primary focuses of this book. For in nearly all of the locations I had visited, I kept hearing the same question. 'Have you tried Reiki yet?'

Reiki is described by practitioners as being a healing practice that was rediscovered in Japan in the early years of the nineteenth century. It is highly popular within British and across American settings, with further groups practising in Japan, Europe and Asia. Therefore this seemed to me to be an ideal practice to focus on rather more extensively. My initial aims were to find out more about shared constructions of 'how the world works' and look at how these ideas related to people's experiences of the actualities of healing practice, while also looking at the formation of gendered identities and power. In order to facilitate this research I have spent over four years within Reiki circles in central Scotland and have stepped sideways in New Age fields to learn more about auras, chakras and perceptions of the relationships between energetic pathways and the body as holistic.

Hence I am in accord with James Clifford (1986) for example, when he argues that it is necessary to study people in fluid social and political cultural contexts where they engage in continual dialogues of power and representation. This positioning is of considerable relevance to this study of healing. For healers do live in a world where identity boundaries are blurred (as with, for example, my location as a *bothsider*). And healers do learn to represent their practices and beliefs in particular ways for particular audiences in decentralised relationships of power.

However, before I begin to present ethnographic and literary material as found over these last four years, it will be useful to briefly locate this particular study of New Age healing and gender alongside feminist critiques of contemporary methodological debates - as found in social and cultural anthropology. These will be drawn from the work of Henrietta Moore (1988) and Marjorie Woolf (1992). Specific feminist ethnography relating to healing in the parallel fields of Wicca and Goddess spirituality will be introduced in the next chapter. I will close this chapter by introducing feminist historian Joan Scott's (1986) 'gender as an analytical category' framework, for this framework will be conceptually underlaid throughout this book as it fits well with Meredith McGuire's proposal that 'analysis of gendered spirituality may shed light on new patterns of individual-to-society relationships, the changing nature of identity and autonomy in modern contexts, and how religion (in both traditional and new forms) shapes and reflects these changes' (1994: 274).

Feminist Ethnography

A common theme as introduced in this chapter has been the acknowledgement that issues of power and authority must remain central to anthropological research. This research for example, is a first step in addressing the academic under-representation and

silencing of women engaged in New Age practice in Scotland –
particularly as women make up around seventy percent of
participants. For power operates at all levels of 'received knowledge'
and is a particular concern for feminist writers. Marjorie Woolf, for
example, proposes that,

> The feminist's sensitivity to power as a factor in all our research, and
> our enhanced understanding (through political struggle) of both the
> ubiquity of gender asymmetry and the deep roots of male privilege,
> should make us even more cautious about postmodernist 'reforms'
> than other social sciences (1992: 135).

For Woolf, the fact that the male dominated sciences and
humanities 'accepted reservoirs of knowledge (and the source of
power for centuries)' now considers itself ready to 'modestly
reconsider the partialness of their truths and the ambiguities in the
construction of their knowing' (1992: 135) misses a rather
fundamental point. While these postmodernist writers engage in
the 'new' field of self-reflexive critique with its central issues of
power and representation they overlook the fact that this 'new'
position has come directly out of feminist critiques (1992: 135). Yet,
she proposes, although feminist work engages critically with similar
issues to postmodernists, 'Feminists who have only recently gained
some academic security might think carefully about whether intense
reflexivity in their research and writing will be evaluated as being
in the new post-modernist mode or simply tentative and self-
doubting' (Woolf 1992: 135).

Mascia-Lees, Sharpe and Cohen propose, in their critique of
postmodern anthropology, that while both feminism and
postmodernist anthropology 'assume a self-consciously reflexive
stance toward their subjects, there are significant differences
between the two' (1989: 23). For feminist anthropologists would
address themselves to women's experiences and examine the
interrelationship of these experiences to questions of power and
struggle, this in turn defining their research goals. This stance would
lead 'the feminist scholar to design projects that women want and
need' (Harding cited in Mascia-Lees, Sharpe and Cohen 1989: 23).
However, Mascia-Lees, Sharpe and Cohen state that although the
potential of postmodernist anthropologists 'with their mandate for
self-reflection...is the capacity to decenter experience' (Harding cited
in Mascia-Lees, Sharpe and Cohen 1989: 23), these anthropologists

with their literary emphasis aim to expose power relations in ethnographic text—and then leave these imbalances as static facts. They argue that,

> Ultimately the postmodern focus on style and form, regardless of its sophistication directs our attention away from the fact that ethnography is more than "writing it up"...[therefore] politically sensitive anthropologists should not be satisfied with exposing power relations in the ethnographic text, if that indeed is what the new ethnography accomplishes, but rather should work to overcome these relations (1989: 33).

If we return to Woolf we find that she also questions the postmodern concern with representation, responsibility and the improvement of research methods. Does this concern, she asks, really extend to the field, or is it solely engaged with 'different (better?) ways of writing ethnographies' (1992: 136). Do postmodern ethnographic authors, with their 'new' concern for responsibility still miss the fundamental point that the end result of their research should be communicable? For, she suggests 'Experimental ethnography so obscure that native speakers of English with a Ph.D. in anthropology find it difficult to understand, is written for a small elite made up primarily of first world academics with literary inclinations' (1992: 138). Hence some of these postmodernist writers, with their exclusive/excluding written material 'contradict the ostensible purpose of experimental ethnography, to find better ways of conveying some aspect of the experiences of another community' (1992: 138). If she is right in this assumption, then what does a feminist position have to offer to the field of ethnographic research and in particular this study of New Age healing?

For Henrietta Moore, feminist critiques in social anthropology and ethnographic accounts are not so much about the absence of women in texts, but rather how these women have been historically represented. So once again issues of representation are brought to the fore. Moore states that from the 1970s, with the arrival of the new 'anthropology of women', a three-tiered male bias was identified. First, researchers import their own biases into fields of research in relation to 'expectations about the relationship between women and men' (1988: 2), hence men are seen (or are expected to be) controllers of cultural information and also as more accessible for research. Second, many societies have an inherently held view/ bias in that 'women are considered to be subordinate to men' (1988:

2), this then being reported to the anthropologist. And third, when researchers observe this sort of asymmetry they assume this to 'be analogous to their own cultural experience of the unequal and hierarchical nature of gender relations in Western society' (1988: 2).

Moore argues that once the feminist anthropologist has deconstructed and corrected these layers of bias, the next problem to arise was that all anthropologists were also heirs to this sort of sociological tradition and that ' "adding" women to traditional anthropology would not resolve the problem of women's analytical "invisibility": it would not make the issue of male bias go away' (1988: 3). Hence problems lay at the analytical and theoretical levels, which must be reworked and redefined. 'Feminist anthropology [is about] confronting the conceptual and analytical inadequacies of disciplinary theory' (Moore 1988: 4).

> Feminist anthropology is more than the study of women. It is the study of gender, of the interrelationships between women and men and of the role of gender in structuring human societies, their histories, ideologies, economic systems and political structures (Moore 1988: 6).

However, Moore also argues that it is necessary to distinguish between the anthropology of gender and feminist anthropology. For while the former relates to 'the study of gender and its cultural construction' (1988: 188), the latter standpoint studies 'gender as a principle of human social life' (1988: 188). Hence feminist anthropology must be distinguished 'from those frameworks of enquiry which study gender or women from a non-feminist viewpoint' (1988: 188). And yet, she argues, this feminist anthropology is much more than women studying women. For as there is no such thing as a universal category, 'woman', neither is there a 'monolithic patriarchy'[2]. Correspondingly, the feminist anthropologist must not assume that patriarchal structures are the same 'the world over' but rather examine the specifics and nature of such structures in specific contexts (1988: 189). This is precisely why I am, in this book, going to develop a decentralized narrative of power in relation to healing in Scotland. I intend to build up throughout, based on specific empirical evidence, a picture of how constructions of 'gendered spiritual identity' are developed and represented and the relationships of these to experiential practice.

2. A point I shall come back to in relation to radical feminist Mary Daly. For Daly does argue that patriarchy is monolithic underlying all 'systems' of the world.

For all of these 'identities' are intimately tied to power and perceptions of authority. And I shall keep firmly in mind the 'political and theoretical complexities of trying to speak *about* women, while avoiding any tendency to speak *for* them' (Moore 1988: 191 [italics original]).

For Henrietta Moore then, feminist anthropology has played a crucial role in the development of theories that examine the cultural construction of gender and gender identity (1988: 187) and have promoted the importance of deconstructing the categories of 'woman' and 'patriarchy'. Similarly, feminist anthropologists emphasize that women experience their lives in different forms according to historical and sociocultural setting, race and class. 'Lives are shaped by a multiplicity of differences, differences that may be perceived categorically but are lived relationally' (Moore 1994: 20).

> In the final analysis, the contribution of feminist anthropology to contemporary feminism is simply to point to the value of comparison and to the importance of acknowledging difference...The justification for doing feminist anthropology has very little to do with the fact that "women are women the world over" and everything to do with the fact that we need to be able to theorise gender relations in a way which ultimately makes a difference (Moore 1988: 198).

Moore's ideas, above, bear similarities to feminists in other fields of research. Feminist historian Joan Scott, in her *Gender: A Useful Category for Historical Analysis* (1986) states that concern for gender as an analytic category only arose in the late twentieth century 'at a moment of great epistemological turmoil' (1986: 1066), where there has been some shift from scientific to literary paradigms in the social sciences encompassing (at times), the blurring of genres of enquiry. For Scott, this is also the time when feminists find allies in scholarly and political circles and where feminist theory and the development of the same are of great importance.

Scott also cites Michelle Rosaldo, who states, 'It now appears to me that woman's place in human social life is not in any direct sense a product of the things she does, but of the meaning her activities acquire through concrete social interaction' (1986: 1067). This is an interesting point and one worth reflecting upon as we progress through this ethnography of healing. For, I will argue, "doing" healing work and "being healed" *does* have a direct effect on "women's place in human social life"' (1986: 1067).

Scott further proposes that, following on from Rosaldo, in order to provide a meaningful explanation of women's place, we must look at the nature of interrelationships between individuals and social organizations and appreciate that these relationships are often unequal and 'discursively constituted in social "fields of force"' (1986: 1067). For,

> Within these processes and structures, there is room for a concept of human agency as the attempt (at least partly rational) to construct an identity, a life, a set of relationships, a society with certain limits and with language—conceptual language— that at once sets boundaries and contains the possibility of negation, resistance, reinterpretation, the play of metaphoric invention and imagination (1986: 1067).

This statement is also of considerable relevance to this study of healing. For as we shall see, women healers do develop new identities, become part of new social circles and 'work' as active healing agents even if at times they appear to be constrained within male theological superstructures. And women healers do resist some theological representations and reinterpret these to suit their own particular 'ways of being' — this, for example, being related to Goddess spirituality.

Scott, like Moore, emphasizes that feminist historians should now be willing to theorize their practice and that gender should hold a central part in this theorization. Her position when defining gender as an analytical category is that gender is, as it has been historically, a way of signifying relationships of power. Therefore any change in social relations will lead to corresponding changes in representations of power (Scott 1996: 1068). This she suggests can be seen in:

a. Culturally available symbols and representations of women; both embodied and in mythology.

b. Normative concepts that interpret and constrain symbolic representations of women.

c. Gendered relations in kinship circles; which encompass political and economic issues.

d. Subjective identity.

I would argue then, that the use of feminist methodology as introduced above—where emphasis is placed on the culturally and historically constructed nature of gender difference —will allow us to examine how gender difference relates to other forms of perceived difference within New Age healing circles. For as we shall see, New Age healing ontologies are also drawn from many cultural and religious traditions. Each of these has its own historical 'baggage' in the form of, for example, dogmatic positioning and hierarchical forms. Hence, when healing practitioners draw from particular authoritative New Age textual frameworks my etic (academic) voice comes to the fore in this book and evaluates how practitioners are using and representing these in healing practice. For, I would propose, all discourses within New Age healing circles are ultimately to do with power, be this the power that heals, the power to heal, or being healed.

Chapter Two

The 'New Age'

Introduction

In the previous chapter I proposed that if we are to build up an accurate and comprehensive picture of healing thought and practice in Scotland we must locate gender, representation and power as central elements of this project throughout. For as we shall see, healers are taught 'the truths' of particular ways of being which incorporates not just their healing practice, but also 'the socializing of emotions and bodies' (McGuire 1994: 273). And I have noted my initial observations of the tensions that may arise from holding a *bothsider* perspective in relation to the blurring of emic and etic boundaries and the representation of healers' voices in text. For within New Age circles, as much value is placed on personal awareness and bodily practice as on textual exegesis. So although bookstores in Scotland do carry a considerable amount of written material, when the practitioner goes home to read the same, in all likelihood, incense will be burned and 'mood music' played to enable the learning of healing material, which will then be tested empirically 'in the field'. New Age healing is an eminently embodied experience.

In this second chapter I will open with a review of academic literature relating to the fields of New Age thought and practice keeping the issues raised in Chapter One firmly in mind. For I am particularly concerned to identify here, how various writers have interpreted the historical sources for the constructions of 'new' identities in New Age networks. With this background in place, we may move forward to examine how this specifically relates to healing practice in Scotland and multivalent discourses of power. For as we shall see, healers draw from textual material in ways that both mirror (in the writing up of theology/theology and history) and diverge from academic investigation. However, before we go further it is useful to note a point made by Steven Sutcliffe, that

'Searching for a fixed canon in this popular marketplace of ideas only perpetuates an implicit model of Christian biblical exegesis' (2003: 20).

Correspondingly, when I have gathered material from, in this chapter, several key academic theorists, all of whom seek ways of defining the New Age I am aware of the tensions to be found in this project. So when I have chosen to draw more from the writing of Paul Heelas rather than, say, that of Wouter Hanegraaff,[1] the latter making 'a philosophico-literary case for considering New Age to be a modernistic restatement of a neglected current of Western religiosity, namely "esotericism"' (Sutcliffe 1998: 19), I do so because while Hanegraaf's emphasis is on textual exegesis, Heelas has been 'out in the field'. Second, I utilize Heelas's evaluation of New Age's roots which he sees as lying in assorted historical traditions, because I too have, as a primary concern, a wish '…to explore the New Age as a cultural and practical resource employed in everyday life' (1996: 5). For most certainly underneath this 'umbrella term' we do find individual teachers and groups providing a plurality of options for redefinition of the self and new (and supported) transformed identities.

Similarly, when I incorporate Stuart Rose's gender related findings from his dedicated survey of New Age participation, I do so because Rose has provided us with one of the few quantitative surveys in this field. As such his material provides a useful starting point for my own evaluative research as does Steven Sutcliffe's motif of the New Age *seeker* and his historical evaluations. For even though this term is not explicitly used by practitioners in the Scottish context, implicitly it is the way that individuals appear to engage in self-transformation.

An introduction to research in the fields of Wiccan and Goddess spirituality is also located here for as noted earlier, within these arenas, emphasis is placed on 'transforming the self' and becoming healed and whole. Overall then, I will continue to build up a decentralized model of gendered power relations in New Age

---

1. Hanegraaff's *New Age Religion and Western Culture* 1998 is a useful read on underlying themes as found in the scholarly delineated field of 'New Age'. However, as Sutcliffe correctly observes, even though 'he asserts rather than demonstrates his bold claim that a considerable part of the literature [not entitled New Age] is little more than the written reflection of New Age practices'…Hanegraaff's model of 'New Age religion' remains curiously decontextualized (2003: 34).

circles with the intention that this material will also assist in the project of rewriting women back into the diverse fields of contemporary spirituality.

All in a Name

Within the New Age one finds an enormous diversity of beliefs and practices. Seekers in this field may pick and choose from a wide diversity of 'spiritual options'. They may participate in classes in meditation or sacred dance, try out fire walking as a transformational technique related to self development and learn healing practices where crystal dowsing or 'angel guidance' might be promoted as 'additional tools' to spiritual growth. The seeker may go on retreats or workshops with titles such as 'Soil, Soul and Society', 'Universal Healing Dimensions' or 'Voice, Spirit, Roots'[2] to learn how to 'connect with sources of energy deep in the body' or explore '…a new trinity which integrates the personal, the social and the natural'.[3]

However, initially one should also be aware that the term 'New Age' itself is primarily of academic construction and 'it exemplifies an enduring mystification in category formation in Religious Studies' (Sutcliffe 2003: 10). Sutcliffe engages most usefully with this issue and questions in whose interest is it, to locate an enormously diverse range of beliefs and practices under such an 'umbrella term'? For 'what debate there has been among practitioners on the meaning of "New Age" has most often amounted simply to a nexus of conversations, occasionally arguments, within a decentred and theoretically unbounded matrix of viewpoints and pressure groups, here locally-focused, there widely dispersed, but almost always mutually tolerant and hence diffusive rather than regulative' (2003: 11). Sutcliffe goes further, however, and he is worthy of quoting at length here.

> Through taxonomic sleight of hand the phenomena have been accorded a homogeneity and concrete presence that the historical record simply does not permit. But this does allow the "New Age" to be set up like a stooge to be knocked down by a variety of vested interests. For example, it has been demonised by conservative evangelical

2. These particular workshops were all run at The Salisbury Centre in Edinburgh in the autumn of 2000.

3. As found in (SC2: 2003).

Christians...[while] in other constituencies, "New Age" is sniggered at as "touchy-feely" spiritual consumerism. Parties with axes to grind here include rationalistic sceptics (Basil 1988) and paternalist social scientists (Bruce 1998), for whom "New Age" is a codeword for shallow, self-indulgent, even – one senses *plebeian* and *vulgar* spirituality that should not be given scholarly oxygen. This unlikely confluence of critics shows that "New Age" has triggered curiously exaggerated and intemperate reactions in very different social power bases [and to this we may add bio-medical approaches to health] (2003: 10) [italics original].

It is therefore important to remember then, that as one begins to look at academic categorisations of 'what is New Age', that there is no such thing as a neutral position – my own included – and that debates abound with regard to the appropriateness of various disciplinary standpoints in relation to investigations of the same.[4] Hence although it is outwith the remit of this book to engage with debates about the strengths and weaknesses of various approaches, it is still worthy of note that reactions in the West, academic or not, to New Age phenomena may have a lot to do with the prevailing emphasis on 'our advanced nature', this being based on rationalistic and scientific frameworks, and that this may flow through into academic disciplines. Correspondingly, any return to 'irrational' ways of being (such as healing) may then be seen as a threat to the dominance of 'proven' interpretative frameworks. However, what we should not lose sight of, is the fact that it is *real people* that academics place in the pages of a book and that these people have a right to be represented as fairly as possible – a real methodological challenge. For as McCutcheon asserts, drawing from Lincoln (1999) initially, '*scholarship is myth with footnotes*' (italics mine).

Because scholars in the study of religion are methodological reductionists, their explanations are purely a function of their interests and the theories they propose and apply ("Given my theory of social formation, rituals function to...," etc). This means that scholars of religion must own up to their own curiosities, instead of mis-portraying them as eternally interesting and obviously relevant questions (McCutcheon 2003: 153).

4. See, for eg., Russell T. McCutcheon's *The Discipline of Religion* (London: Routledge, 2003) where he examines how the Academy of Religion's 'classification of the world supports the creation of specific senses of freedom and conduct, thereby managing and curtailing specific types of speech and dissent'.

So let us begin looking at some academic evaluations of New Age.

Wouter Hanegraaff

Hanegraaff proposes in *New Age Religion and Western Culture* that although the term New Age is a poorly defined label meaning different things to different people, it is the defining of its boundaries rather than its core that is problematic (1998: 9). In order to do this he utilizes Colin Campbell's concept of the 'cultic mileu' (1972: 122), 'suggesting that the latter became at some point self-consciously aligned to "the New Age Movement". But he advances little evidence for how, why, where, and by whom this transformation comes about' (Sutcliffe 2003: 24). Yet Campbell's proposition that the cultic milieu is a constant feature of society and that groups within this environment all share a position as 'heterodox or deviant items in relation to dominant cultural orthodoxies' (1972: 121) might be of some use—although I doubt that healers in Scotland would appreciate being called 'deviant' (and critiques abound with regard to the appropriateness of calling the New Age a 'movement'). For Campbell also argues that these groups also draw 'stimulus from the presence of the mystical tradition' (1972: 121) and emphasize that unity with the divine can be achieved through a variety of paths, which 'tends to be ecumenical, super-ecclesiastic and tolerant in outlook' (1972: 122-23). Hence, fluidity of boundaries is the norm. These points are of relevance as within Scotland, it is precisely this fluidity of boundaries that allows for the development of new 'senses of self', with the significance for women being that they are not constrained in totality under patriarchal organizational structures or by normative doctrines. This means that they can actively engage in 'finding or constructing an alternative to institutional religion: something *other*, something *more*, something *better*' (Sutcliffe 2003: 216) [italics original]. In general then, and here I use Sutcliffe's concise evaluation, 'Hanegraaff depicts "New Age" as a commodification of Western esoteric thought for a secular culture' (2003: 24) and goes to considerable length to elaborate on this, drawing from over one hundred texts as obtained from New Age bookstores in Holland. This is useful work but lacking I would argue, time spent 'in the field'.

Paul Heelas

Heelas is in accord with Hanegraaff when he asserts that some New Age roots lie within 'older' religious traditions such as Buddhism, Taoism or Sufism, or in pagan or American Indian cosmologies. This does appear to be the case. However, one might well ask questions here with regard to such reifications. Are Heelas, Hanegraaff (and, as we shall see, some key male Reiki writers) engaged in a continuing project of androcentrically constructing knowledge? Where are the women healers and other significant women in these accounts? For as Steven Sutcliffe has observed, women do not appear to not leave much in the way of 'historical footprints' in New Age circles, often appearing to be subsumed in both practice and theology by men. As he succinctly puts it, 'while George Trevelyan has been called the "father of the New Age", I know of no claims for a "mother"' (2003: 221).

Heelas also proposes that within all of these diverse beliefs and practices 'one encounters the same (or very similar) *lingua franca* to do with the human (and planetary) condition and how it can be transformed' (1996: 2). However, Heelas also suggests that considerable rivalry exists between various practices and traditions as 'adherents of particular paths not infrequently think of themselves as better than those engaging in other (possibly very similar) activities' (1996: 17). In this he is correct.

Heelas also categorizes New Agers as perennialists, this viewpoint enabling them to search experientially for the hidden esoteric core of a particular traditional belief system while by-passing any dogmas and doctrines as ego driven. This perspective also allows the New Age adherent to maintain self-authority as 'the truths within the traditions and the New Ager are the same...[and that] the same wisdom can be found at the heart of all religious traditions' (1996: 28-29).[5] This point is of relevance to the Scottish context and particularly relates to my argument for a decentralized narrative of power. For as we shall see in Chapters Five and Six, tensions do arise within Reikian healing circles in relation to the perceived authority of specific male theological superstructures and their relationship to grassroots practitioners who eclectically and democratically pick and mix practical techniques.

5. This viewpoint is very similar to that held by the nineteenth century Theosophical Society, this being a major influencing factor on the contemporary New Age.

As Heelas (1996) is primarily concerned with the contemporary New Age movement, he begins his examination of its development within the nineteenth century. At this time the Theosophical Society was highly influential, as was its later offshoot the Anthroposophical Society founded by Rudolf Steiner (1996: 45). Heelas informs us that three key figures arose from this era: Helena Blavastsky (1831-91), Jung (1885-1961) and Gurdjieff (1866-1949). Blavatsky founded the Theosophical society. Jung has had enormous influence on the New Age with regard to his expositions on the psyche, 'the inner child, dream therapy, and counselling from a holistic framework, while Gurdjieff was 'the person who has done the most to introduce and emphasise transformational techniques' (Heelas 1996: 47) with a corresponding shift from 'writing and reading to practicing spiritual disciplines (Heelas 1996: 47). Hence, Heelas proposes that by the 1920s much of the repertoire of the current New Age was in evidence.

He proposes that the 1950s' interest in self-spirituality formed the basis for the 1960s counter-cultural Age of Aquarius, communities such as Findhorn and the Human Potential Movement (the latter focusing on psychological methods of stripping away the outer layers of experience to find the authentic self within). As during the 1960s, there was also great interest in a wide variety of 'traditional' spiritual teachings, at this time spirituality and psychology became intertwined into the basis for many current New Age therapies. This intermingling appears to be very common in Scottish healing circles and we shall come across specific examples of this in Chapter Four.

Heelas proposes that after the 1960s, there was less of an emphasis on dropping out by joining communes, in favour of incorporating personal spiritual development into everyday life. However, this did not bring about the demise of counter-cultural perspectives. Instead of joining communes on a full-time basis, those seeking spiritual awareness continued to work in mainstream society, while taking part in activities that were counter-cultural, in that they promised experiences which were not nurtured by capitalist modernity. These experiences emphasized the importance of detachment from the ego in order to reveal the spiritual realm (1996: 54).

For Heelas, those involved in the 'quest' for new relationships with the earth/others outside of a materialistic perspective can be regarded as part of 'new social movements who, while being of a broadly secular (humanistic, naturalistic) variety, have a New Age wing: spiritual environmentalism, ecofeminism, and healing, for example' (1996: 56). These movements outlived the counter-cultural era of the 1960s by stressing the importance of fulfilling one's true potential through personal experience of the 'inner self as spiritual'. To this end, numerous courses, events and activities could/can be participated in which 'enable participants to experience alternatives to what the mainstream is able to provide, most teaching the importance of going beyond the ego' (1996: 57).[6]

However, Heelas informs us that one of the most noticeable developments of the New Age over the last twenty-five years has been the proliferance of groups that offer courses and seminar training where 'detachment enables participants to experience their spirituality, the depths of their nature as human beings. And this serves to unleash potential, including the ability "magically" to obtain results' (1996: 60). Put alternatively, these groups offer training in harmonial spirituality 'where the unconscious has the function of restoring harmony between the individual and an immanent spiritual power' (Fuller cited in Hanegraaff 1998: 483).[7] These are common themes in Scottish healing circles.

I will return to Heelas' work shortly, for his interpretation of the New Age foundational 'self-ethic' is of considerable relevance to this work on the development of new gendered identities and relations of power. However, in order to complete this initial appraisal of the historical location of the New Age I shall move on to introduce Steven Sutcliffe's work in which he promotes the role of the New Age seeker. This may also provide us with a rather useful alternative model to Campbell's 'cultic milieu'.

Steven Sutcliffe

Sutcliffe argues that the role of the seeker is central to New Age phenomena, that 'seeking' is not exclusive to the New Age but has been constitutive of 'alternative' religiosity since the mid-nineteenth

---

6. For a listing of some of these 'spiritually informed ways of becoming an authentic person' see Heelas, *The New Age Movement*, (1996: 57). I will be noting throughout fieldwork whether/how gendered constructions of 'authentic' models of subjectivity are promoted.

7. For a fuller examination of the American types of spiritual psychology and the role of the unconscious see Hanegraaff, *New Age Religion and Western Culture* (pp. 483-96) and Robert Fuller, *Americans and the Unconscious*, 1986.

century and that 'the largely post-war career of New Age is but a comparatively recent development in what amounts to an alternative network of seekers and experimental religiosity. Thus New Age can neither be understood outwith the historical context of modernist alternative religiosity, nor in isolation from the seekers who advocate it' (1997: 97).

In his later work *Children of the New Age* (2003), Sutcliffe provides us with a most useful analysis of the usage and development of the term New Age itself. As I noted at the beginning of this chapter, this motif is primarily of academic construction. Sutcliffe argues that '"New Age" represents at its narrowest a specific millennialistic emblem, and at its most diffuse — at its most symbolically overdetermined — a loose idiom of humanistic potential and psychotherapeutic change that could be, and has been, called anything from "human potential" to "mind, body and spirit", from "holistic" to "spiritual growth"' (2003: 10). It is within this arena that the New Age seeker carries on a behavioural tradition of individual personal religiosity. Therefore rather than seeing the New Age as a movement, it is better understood as 'a populist collectivity: a cluster of seekers affiliated by choice — if at all — to a particular term in a wider synchronous and diachronous network of religious alternativism' (1997: 98). This New Age collectivity, he continues, has its roots in apocalyptic and millennialist expectations where since the 1930s, adherents have subscribed to the ideological viewpoint that 'humanity is on the threshold of a New Age, an immense cultural shift analogous to the Renaissance which will dramatically augment human power in the context no longer ethnic or national, but global — even cosmic — in scale' (1997: 98). However, he also correctly informs the reader that from an emic perspective, few would see themselves as New Age. Rather 'individual choice dictates usage of, or affiliation to, the term, as one might indeed expect from a phenomenon popularly received as a prime example of contemporary religious individualism' (1997: 101).

Sutcliffe also argues that there is no totalitarian rejection of mainstream religiosity within New Age circles, for 'strong strain[s] of neo Christian piety and mysticism have flavoured the arena...[rather]...the stance is less one of being "at odds" with Christianity than with the hegemony of "institutional religion"' (2003: 12). This leads Sutcliffe to provide an alternative working definition of 'popular religion' as other than solely criticism of high culture.

Popular religion is the quest for (a) more simple, (b) more direct, and (c) more profitable relationships with the divine (Moldonado 1986: 6, cited in Sutcliffe 2003: 12, [emphasis original].

Sutcliffe's positioning above and usage of Moldonado is succinct. For emphasis is placed within Scottish healing circles on simple direct relationships to 'the divine' and if this involves appropriating practical elements of mainstream religiosity from Christianity or Buddhism then this is seen to be for the 'better good', not just of the individual, but of society as a whole. Hence we find, in the Scottish context at least, eclectic mixing of elements of mainstream religiosity such as meditation and the laying on of hands 'as Jesus did', in combination with a critique of the 'high cultures' of institutionalized religion and bio-medical approaches to health.

Sutcliffe also provides us with a useful framework from which to examine the network of alternative beliefs and practices in Scotland. He argues that the typical form of the amorphous network of alternative beliefs and practices extends,

> ...both synchronically (cf. York 1995) and historically. Their webs of activity and material residue span the shortfalls and disputed lands between traditional religions, cultic and cultural enclaves, and religious and secular spheres in general. In other words, the alternative network is a largely extra-ecclesial countercultural web that both generates and supports variant religious cultures. As such it has persisted in the shadows of mainstream religion and penetrated its margins for the last one hundred years or so (Sutcliffe 1997: 102).

I would propose that examining the alternative network as 'an extra-ecclesial counter-cultural web' may be beneficial, because regarding the beliefs and practices in this field as 'alternative' rather than Campbell's 'deviant' should enable an evaluation to be developed of what the 'alternative' is decrying. It is anticipated that this alternative perspective will be interrelated with issues of gender, identity and power. As to whether practitioners of healing regard themselves to be 'alternative' or prefer the term 'complementary' is a matter of personal debate. For the usage of one or other of these terms suggests to me that there is a power dynamic working in healing contexts between conventional biomedicine and 'spiritual' approaches to health. This, I would suggest, is actively being played out on the gendered body. For as

Sutcliffe states, the role of seeker is popular among those individuals who are 'virtuosi willing to select, synthesise and exchange amongst an increasing diversity of religious and secular options and perspectives' (1997: 105).

It is important to note, however, that the role of 'seeker' in the Scottish context is very much dependent on being financially able to choose such a role. For within the Edinburgh alternative 'scene', there appears to be a predominance of white, middle-class participants who are economically able to choose to develop their inner spirituality. This applies equally to teachers of healing practice but with a shift towards male dominance at higher teaching and publishing levels. Therefore, while Sutcliffe is correct in stating that there has been a shift away from seekers being located within the social group of theologians etc., it would appear initially that the New Age, and alternative health, may in fact be 'riddled' with hegemonic and counter-hegemonic discourse. It is important then, when we see the following sort of statement, to cast a critical eye over it and apply a feminist hermeneutic of suspicion. For Sutcliffe states that 'in the alternative networks, and in connection with New Age in particular, the notion of a "spiritual quest" has moved away from its particular prerogative of a typical social group—typically theologians, contemplatives or mystics—to become a popular egalitarian norm' (1997: 106). This point will be reflected upon later.

Let us return to Paul Heelas' interpretation of the New Age's essential *lingua franca*, Self-spirituality, showing how gender should be regarded as an essential component of this.

Heelas and 'New Age' Self-spirituality

Heelas proposes that New Age teaching has three essential elements:
(1) Your lives do not work.
(2) You are Gods and Goddesses in exile.
(3) Let go/drop it. This teaching 'explains why life—as conventionally experienced—is not what it should be; it provides an account of what it is to find perfection; and it provides the means for obtaining salvation' (1996: 18).

(1) Your lives do not work

Heelas proposes that,

> The great refrain running throughout the New Age, is that we malfunction because we have been '*brainwashed*' by mainstream society

and culture. The mores of the established order—its materialism, its competitiveness, together with the importance it attaches to playing roles—are held to disrupt what it is to be authentically human. To live in terms of such mores, *inculculated by parents, the educational system and other institutions*, is to remain the victim of unnatural, deterministic and misguided routines: to be *enslaved by unfillable desires and deep seated insecurities*; to be *dominated* by anxiety-generating imperatives such as creating a good impression; to be locked into the conflictual demands of the ideal relationship (1996: 18), [italics mine].

I have italicized several points in the above where 'lack', 'desire' and 'power' appear to be central motifs. If, as Heelas proposes, the New Ager subscribes to the viewpoint that it is societal brainwashing which causes human malfunction through the institutions of the school and the workplace—where historically emphasis has been placed on the adoption of competitive and materialistic roles—then surely one must evaluate the promotion and development of these subjectivities acknowledging their gendered nature. For although many parents will promote 'competitiveness' in their sons and daughters as a desirable trait, one wonders whether this will always be towards the same ends? Will not, for example, these roles differ greatly in relation to the family's cultural heritage and location in class systems? Hence I am in agreement with feminist historian Joan Scott when she asserts that we need to analyse constructions of meaning and relationships of power while calling into question unitary, universal categories and historicised concepts otherwise treated as natural - such as man/woman or absolute such as equality or justice (1992: 253).

I would argue that once we do this we can examine where women's experiences of 'brainwashing' differ from men's and how these experiences may lead men and women to seek within New Age self-developmental practices. We can ask questions such as if, from a New Age perspective, men and women are seen as 'victims...enslaved by unfulfillable desires and insecurities' (Heelas 1996: 18), then who locates the male or female 'as victim'? Do women and men perceive their 'victimised bodies' in the same way? We can examine what it is within New Age ideology that appears to provide women and men with personal empowerment. And we can examine Sutcliffe's theme of 'alternative practices spanning the shortfalls of religious and secular spheres in general...' in much greater depth once we approach this with a feminist hermeneutics of suspicion.

(2) You are Gods and Goddesses in Exile

Heelas states that for the New Ager, experiences of the 'Higher Self' and inner spirituality stand in sharp contrast to those afforded by the ego or lower self. For 'the inner realm alone is held to serve as the source of authentic vitality, creativity, love, wisdom, power [and] authority' (1996: 19). For 'Perfection, it is maintained, cannot be found by tinkering with what we are by virtue of socialisation. Neither can it be found by conventional (political etc.,) attempts at social engineering' (1996: 19).

Heelas argues in the above that people who subscribe to a New Age worldview believe that it is to the inner or 'Higher Self' that one must experientially turn in order to live authentically. For the 'lower' ego driven self is corrupted and has by inference become detached or withdrawn, focusing on secular rather than spiritual 'ways of being'. But what, one wonders, is this 'authentic' self? Who promotes this model of subjectivity and why? What is the New Ager being authentic to? Does this differ for men and women? And, if as Heelas suggests, New Agers maintain that we cannot reach 'perfection' by 'tinkering with what we are by socialisation...or by conventional political attempts at social engineering' then I would propose that there is serious potential within this theme for maintaining the patriarchal status quo. For to suggest that to engage in any political 'tinkering' is both ego driven and invalid may promote the ideology that 'women must accept their lot' and look for 'power within' rather than 'power in society'. This, of course, also relates to the last New Age motif as proposed by Heelas, that of 'let go/drop it'. Once again as this teaching relates to the ego and the socialized mode of being then any engagement with this motif must also examine how this relates to men and women's perception both of themselves and of their 'opposite sex' other.

(3) Let Go/Drop It.

Heelas argues that within this third New Age motif lies the experiential framework for actually moving 'out of exile into authentic experience' (1996: 20). For from a 'Self as spiritual' perspective one needs to learn how to re-connect with one's inner self in order to see that authority comes from within and not from the ego 'that internalised mode of the traditions, parenting routines and all those other inputs which have constructed it' (1996: 20). This is why there are numerous workshops and courses covering the 'spiritual disciplines…variously known as "processes", "rituals" or "psychotechnologies" for example' (Heelas 1996: 20). These various practices hence 'provide paths within' (Heelas 1996: 47) so that each person realizes that the socialized mode of being, experiences of the past (in this or past lives) no longer have a hold. 'A new future will be enabled where the Self is liberated' (Heelas 1996: 47).

Once again we can see in the above exposition that power is of central significance. For if a person is to detach from external societal 'pressures', be these in the home or the workplace, and instead focus on their 'inner journey' through perhaps meditation, yoga, dance or shamanic drumming, then this new 'cleansed ego-free' person will also incorporate new taught ways of being so that s/he may follow this path. And while Heelas is absolutely correct to assert that for those who engage with Self-spirituality one of the most fundamental of assumptions is that 'authority lies with the self' (1996: 21), I would argue that this 'self' still apparently 'feels that it has to be taught' what it is to be authentic and empowered. Correspondingly, should we not ask questions about the normalizing, political role of such teaching discourses and how they are brought to fruition? For as we shall see in the ethnography to follow, workshops that focus on, for example, teaching the person how to get back in touch with their intuition or inner voice are highly popular. And if a person is taught to stop blaming society and work on themselves through spiritual disciplines and practices, there is potential for people to get locked into a perpetual spiral of 'seeing the guru' in order to advance along the path so that one can authentically relate to 'all that is' and the 'natural order of things'? As one New Age newsletter puts it—this coming from a 'spiritual teacher who speaks from his direct experience of self-realisation' and through living in 'complete surrender',

> Surrender to life as it is and not how you want it to be. You've got to surrender to it and shed that, that's not real in your life – and underneath that you'll find yourself, your true nature: joy. It's there. It's shedding, not adding, that sets you free (BP: Bernie Prior 2002: 3).

Within Heelas's three 'essential elements' then, we have a wide diversity of themes that must, I would argue, be examined from a gender perspective. For failure to do this will provide only a partial picture of the development of New Age models of subjectivity. I shall return to some of the points raised here in the final chapter of this book, where I shall apply a gender centered critique utilizing writers such as Meredith McGuire, Joan Scott, Helen Berger and Wendy Griffin.

New Age Women

Throughout this chapter I have begun to examine how when writers such as Heelas and Hanegraaff examine the New Age predominantly from a gender blind perspective, they fail to tease out how gender affects individual epistemologies and practices.[8] This is significant, for when, for example, we come to examine the specifics of New Age healing in relation to Reiki initiation rituals or 'learning to dowse the aura', the inclusion of gender as an analytical category will allow us to begin to examine whether women have constructed these for particular 'gendered ends'. Do women's rituals have different focuses than men's? How does this relate to gendered representations of the body, emotions and power? What relationship does socio/historical context have to current representations of the role of the gendered healer? Do frameworks of meaning have gendered elements? If so, what are these?

I would also suggest that a predominantly androcentric approach to the interpretation and representation of New Age healing allows for, at best, a study where women are not included or acknowledged, and at worst, the potential for women healers/ healed to be doubly subsumed; being seen as either gullible due to their non-scientific 'belief' in the efficiency of such practices, or as charlatans, due to their promotion of such practices to fee paying clients. This relates intimately to constructions of knowledge as truth—science being a key example here.

For example, James McClenon has argued in *Wondrous Healing* (2002) that human therapeutic rituals (healing) have been based on evolutionary processes and natural selection. Humans with genes which 'enabled' hypnotisability would have been favoured, these

8. For example Hanegraaff, in his *New Age Religion and Western Culture,* dedicates only a few pages to an appraisal of gender. This he relates in particular to the New Age theory of polarity and complementarity with its two poles of masculine and feminine.

humans developing healing rituals and forms of religion, which would be connected with medical practice. 'Unlike the prevalent theories explaining the origins of religion, these arguments are amenable to scientific evaluation' (2002: 45). Hence it appears that healers and 'those adhering to New Age spiritualities' are located under the 'over-arching paradigm of knowledge and experience...[of] scientific empiricism' (Corrywright 2003: 61), even if at times science is drawn from and developed into 'new science' in populist works such as David Bohm's *Wholeness and the Implicit Order* (1980) or Fritjof Capra's *The Tao of Physics* (1996). It is also worthy of note that writers of 'new science' appear to be predominately male, though in the fields of energetic healing, Barbara Brennan's psychological approach is highly rated. We shall look more specifically at Brennan later in this book.

However I shall further elaborate on the importance of utilizing a feminist hermeneutic of suspicion at this point, with an appraisal of Stuart Rose's survey of New Age participation in 1994-95 and his later 2001 paper entitled *New Age Women: Spearheading the Movement?* This I shall initially relate to one particular New Age writer, Marilyn Ferguson.

Rose's examination of the New Age movement encompassing primary beliefs and practices is based on a material sample of 908 individuals—these having completed his questionnaire in 1994-95. The aim of this questionnaire was to 'establish the socio-demographic characteristics of participants [while] bringing to light how they describe their spirituality' (1998: 5). Rose states that, while a 1993 monthly Gallup survey (aimed at reflecting the population at large) showed that only 3 percent of the British population reported 'spiritual well being' as being of primary importance to their lives, and only 25 percent of respondents reported that spirituality was of major importance, this was not in accord with his survey findings within New Age circles.[9] Here Rose found that 56 percent of participants indicated, 'that spiritual affairs are always

9. Rose's survey appears initially to be fairly representative of the New Age as a whole, for he drew his survey material from questionnaires inserted into *Kindred Spirit* which, he states, is the widest selling New Age magazine in the UK. However, it may also be the case that those who bought and answered this questionnaire are more committed to a 'spiritual lifestyle' than those who partake in alternative health for its physical benefits. It is also necessary to appreciate that 'being spiritual' may mean different things to different people.

involved in their activities' and 'more than 90% report that they are actively pursuing a spiritual path' (1998: 12).

These findings are of considerable importance to the study of complementary health in Scotland. For if, as Rose proposes, spirituality is of such central concern to New Age participants, then I can examine how this relates to popular religion as more simple, direct and profitable relationships with the divine and the relationship of gendered identities to the same.

Rose bases three claims on the responses in his questionnaires. Initially, he proposes that the New Age tends to be amorphous in nature, as participants are drawn from all age groups, socio-economic backgrounds and genders. His first significant gender related finding is that 'as New Age ideology emphasizes a shift from male dominated society to one in which the female content is much greater, there is a much higher level of women participants than men' (1998:6).[10] Second, Rose states that as there are large numbers of women participating in the New Age, 'there is likely to exist a significant number of ideas and activities which have a heightened or even specific female content and appeal' (1998: 6).[11] When he relates this to specific practices, he finds that women tend to favour activities that have a high healing and bodywork content (offering practical physical benefits) such as aromatherapy, homeopathy and massage and healing workshops (that engage with spiritual belief), or that women practise the divinatory arts such as astrology and Tarot reading, which from the New Age perspective are for personal holistic guidance (1998: 7).

Rose's third point is that while women predominate in New Age activities, 'in the mid 1990s among important teachers, women are still outnumbered two to one by their male counterparts' (1998: 7). This finding bears marked similarities to the make-up of highly regarded male teachers in Reikian circles. For as we shall see, four of the key writers within this field are indeed men; these same men being engaged in an ongoing project of rewriting 'authoritative' Reikian theology.

10. In Rose's sample of 908 New Age participants, 70 percent were women, 30 percent men.

11. It is very important to note that many 'mainstream' churches also have a predominance of women participants, even though they do not emphasize the importance of a specific female content.

But let us return to Rose's contention that 'female content' within New Age frameworks is significant.

> There is a much higher female participation[12] in the 'New Age' than male, as 'New Age' ideology promotes the relevance of a higher female 'content'.

Rose argues 'participants themselves are fully aware of the increasing female content of the New Age movement' (2001: 331). He cites several questionnaire responses from women in relation to this. These persons attributed women's predominance in New Age circles to 'a resurgence of the female principles of caring/nurturing', 'a better balance between the male and female principles in the human race' and that as 'male is no longer so dominant... female energies, gifts, visions, etc., [are] now more free and influential in hopefully leading to correct [the] balance between male and female' (2001: 331).

This sort of positioning above relates rather well to influential New Age writer Marilyn Ferguson's evaluation of models of masculinity and femininity. Her book *The Aquarian Conspiracy* (1980) is viewed by many New Age practitioners as being transformational in its own right. And although this text is not as popular in Scottish healing circles as it once might have been, her particular standpoint regarding models of masculinity, femininity and transformation still appears to underpin much New Age thought in Scotland. This book is also frequently cited by academics writing on the New Age. For example, Heelas sees it as 'authoritative' (1996), for Hanegraaff it is 'the most characteristic manifesto of the New Age *sensu lato*' (1998), while for Albanese, it is 'the now classic description of the harmonic model' (Albanese in Lewis & Melton 1992).

Within this text then, Ferguson promotes 'alternative thought' as a transformative tool, effective both at individual and societal levels. For, she argues, when one begins the transformative process towards autonomy and 'connectedness' then the self will be re-born, enabling the individual to 'transcend cultural roles and decry custom as authority' (1980: 389).[13]

---

12. It would appear from Rose's paper that 'participation' for women involves hands on healing practice of the body which incorporates 'spirituality'. This claim has been examined in the field and has been confirmed.

13. One wonders whether Ferguson's transformative model of subjectivity where she encompasses both 'autonomy' and 'connectedness' is either simply paradoxical or if it is iconoclastic?

Ferguson proposes that cultural roles are often underpinned by ideas of what it is to be a man or a woman. This leads her to state that for many men, 'the women's movement was important in their own change - not only because it focused on the trampled potentials of half of the human race but also because it questioned the supremacy of those masculine characteristics valued in society: competition, manipulation, aggression, objectivity'[14] (1980: 389). For on an individual level, 'As women in transformation are discovering their sense of self and vocation, men are discovering their sense of relationship. During these equalising shifts, the basis for male-female interaction is being redefined. Men are becoming more feeling and intuitive, women more autonomous and purposeful' (1980: 389).

Both Rose and Ferguson acknowledge the centrality of 'balancing male and female elements' within New Age cosmologies. This is most certainly the case within Scottish circles, as we shall see. However, Ferguson also proposes that 'According to very old wisdom, self discovery inevitably involves the awakening of the traits usually associated with the opposite sex' (1980: 389). Now while she is correct in her assertion of this to some considerable extent, I would argue that in the Scottish context at least, much greater emphasis is still being placed on the 'feminine' attributes of 'caring and nurturing' than on developing, for example, the 'masculine' trait of competitiveness. And while Ferguson sees women as now recovering from centuries of male domination by 'reintegrating' themselves into society now that 'the basis for male-female interaction is being redefined' (1980: 389), I would still suggest that this redefinition needs to be looked at most carefully. For when Ferguson makes statements such as 'Women are neurologically more flexible than men, and they have had cultural permission to be more intuitive, sensitive, feeling' (1980: 226), then who exactly 'in culture' is giving women this permission? And surely her sweeping generalization that women are neurologically more flexible requires further unpicking. For 'neurology' relates to the scientific study of nerve systems and genetic traits etc., as much as it does to matters of 'free choice'.

If we move on to examine the specifics of Rose's survey in relation to actual participation, we find a significant emphasis on practices

14. Hanegraaff makes the valid point that as *The Aquarian Conspiracy* was written in 1980, it should be viewed as representing 'the earlier cultic milieu as becoming conscious of itself as a movement and not authoritative (as many academics view it) on later New Age developments' (1998: 106).

with a high healing and bodywork content, which offer practical physical benefits. As we shall see in later chapters, this most certainly appears to be the case in Scotland. However, Rose informs us that his findings show '...that men appear less interested in the majority of New Age ideas and activities—and participate less in them— in relation to women' (1998: 8). That 'women's healing activities involve high levels of physical touching and movement while men's healing activities appear to be more cerebral' (2001: 340) and that, with regard to 'differences between men and women in general ...women [are] much more aware and in tune with their bodies than men' (2001: 342).

What we appear to have in place in the above is the promotion of New Age men as being more cerebral, with New Age women being more bodily orientated. This requires further thought. For are we seeing here the continued reinforcement of the same men/mind, women/body dualism that many New Age women find so abhorrent? Or is it the case that women are consciously choosing practices with a bodily emphasis as a counter hegemonic discourse to location of the female body 'as less'?

Rose also points out that 'even though women appear more populous than men in the movement, the most mentioned teachers are still outnumbered two to one by their male counterparts' (2001: 330). So are we beginning to see the patriarchal re-acquisition of bodily healing practice from women by 'cerebrally orientated' male teachers in the same way that the Christian church, bio-medical and therapeutic perspectives have done so historically? For, in this case, women may be being taught that it is wise to continually return to a male New Age teacher to learn how to become even more ego-less—while purchasing one of his self-help books to aid her in this process. Further, Sutcliffe makes a rather interesting point when he argues that there is a tendency within New Age circles to segregate women to the private domain while men remain in the public sphere. He relates this to, for example, the 'domesticated habit' as found in the Findhorn Community (2003: 20). Having been there myself on Experience Week, I would agree with him that the ethic of 'work is love in action'—this relating to cooking, cleaning, housekeeping, DIY, gardening *et al*,[15] may well to some extent at least, account for the popularity of this centre for women, in that it might be seen as

---

15. It goes without saying that not all women are enthusiastic when it comes to such activities!

'safe', familiar domestic space. Therefore for Sutcliffe, women are still located by 'the dominant prevailing gendered discourse' (2003: 220).

However, Shoshaner Feher suggests there are two theoretical themes that explain women's high levels of involvement with the New Age. First she argues, women are drawn to this field of practice for here they are allowed to move out of their traditionally defined religious roles and 'have a voice' (1992: 183). This 'finding a voice' is a common theme in feminist critiques of patriarchal traditional religious structures and society in general. For example, Ursula King suggests that finding a voice 'has much to do with a newly discovered and newly developed sense of self. It is the expression of a new identity among contemporary women' (1992: 2). However, she also makes the point that there is an underlying theme in women's voices. This theme engages with issues of power, responsibility and concern, for...

> Some people consider the [women's] voices as truly prophetic as they express a vision which links together the personal, social, spiritual and political dimensions of human life...In other words feminism seeks a change in consciousness and a change of the organisation, power structures and fundamental values in our society — a new culture and a new civilisation (King 1992: 3).

Second, Feher proposes that women find something appealing within New Age structures that they cannot find in other religions (1992: 183). So let me once again relate these points to Rose's survey of New Age adherents.

Rose states that the majority of women engaged in the New Age are white, over thirty, and from the middle-classes (1998: 11). This is of some relevance in that these women are more likely to be economically comfortable and reasonably well educated. Further, the majority of these white middle-class women will have either directly or indirectly been brought up within, or have knowledge of, Christian frameworks of reference. Within this Christian framework, God is espoused as a male deity who is 'other', being not of this world but 'omnipotent, omniscient, omnipresent, static, unchanging in his perfection' (Bednarowski 1992: 169).

As within Christianity, it is predominantly male clergy who are perceived to have access to the sacred, it also becomes necessary for women to utilize this clergy as intermediaries; they having been authorized by the Church to provide 'divine salvation' to those that repent. This also requires the sinful women to be saved from an 'embodied' state, for 'To be saved means salvation from the world, from the body...from one's very humanness. Saving power can only come from without' (Bednarowski cited in Lewis and Melton 1992: 69).

Bednarowski also proposes that established religions maintain control over women by portraying them as 'even more fallen than men, more fleshly, more trapped in matter. Thus women are not only more susceptible than men to sin; they are objects of temptation as well, for they pull men down into matter—into the non-sacred' (1992: 169). At the same time, established religions find ways to maintain control over access to the sacred, as they are 'fearful, particularly, of ongoing revelation and of mystical experiences that cannot be controlled' (1992: 169).[16] Hence women are located by established religious traditions as sinful, fleshy, corrupting and trapped in the body, while men may gain access to the sacred through intellectual training and practice as provided by male clergy 'in ways that are hierarchical and excluding' (1992: 169).

Yet many women that I have met in the Scottish New Age scene no longer accept traditional religion's emphasis on male supremacy in 'all things spiritual'; this applying equally to 'Christian New Agers' or those of differing religiosities. For rather than only allowing women access to the sacred through male derived and male focused ritual, the New Age appears to emphasize the God within and the self as sacred; hence the self is perceived as capable of discerning its own unmediated spiritual truth for it becomes 'the way, the truth and the life' (Partridge 1999).

Now Rose proposes that,

> the means of spiritual empowerment employed by New Age women appears to stem from contact with, or synthesis of, a number of teachings or influences. The resulting spirituality appears not to be rigid or inflexible but fluid and malleable and developed according to the progression of each person's spiritual quest, In fact...it would be rare indeed to find one teacher or teaching that could completely encompass this path (2001: 338).

---

16. This 'control of the mystical experience' is examined by Grace Jantzen, who, in examining Christian mysticism's historical roots, notes how 'the delimiting of mysticism through the centuries was crucial to maintaining male hierarchical control in church and society' (1995: 3).

What we see in this quote above, once more, is that women may choose for themselves to visit a variety of teachers in order to progress spiritually. This may well be a good thing and certainly allows the individual to pick out elements that personally suit. But equally there might be the danger of getting on to a kind of treadmill of 'spiritual therapy'. And although for the New Ager, the 'self', as we have seen, is not to be regarded as being an isolated entity for most often, spirituality in the New Age is seen as some form of connection with an all pervading 'Force' or 'Energy'.[17] How this Energy is described and 'to be connected with' is once again the stuff of numerous workshops and publications. All of these to be purchased — the New Age is big business.

Ultimately then, although New Age teachers eclectically pick from a variety of traditions which they then mould into new forms according to their own empirical testing of their efficiency, the 'spiritual visitor' to any particular teacher must at least initially put their trust or faith in that person as an expert of sorts, until they test the 'truth' of that path for themselves. And as within the New Age there are competing theories about how one should think or act, with the corresponding development of written cosmologies, which very often relate to older religious traditions. I would propose that one should also look carefully at how these 'new' forms of spiritual practice are being developed and promoted. Particularly as it is men who are, in the majority, the authoritatively regarded teachers.

Before I draw this chapter to a close I am going to introduce feminist anthropology in the fields of Goddess spirituality and Wiccan circles. For within these fields women have turned from mainstream religions which are deemed to be patriarchal and have developed personal rituals that have led to healing, self empowerment, new senses of identity, revaluing of the female body and renaming reality. Correspondingly there are marked similarities with women's spiritualities and practices within New Age healing circles, even if within Reiki and similar spiritual healing practices 'the Goddess' is not the central 'motif' for empowerment.

17. This issue of power is central throughout the New Age and will be engaged with continually throughout this research.

Goddess Spirituality

Wendy Griffin argues that even at the time of editing her *Daughters of the Goddess* in 2000, there was still a decided lack of research into the practices of Goddess spirituality and that academic funding for this was very difficult to obtain. She further posits that funding for research into religious groups seen as being 'dangerous cults [which threaten] to kidnap children or kill themselves or others' (2000: 14) is more readily available.

> This may be particularly ironic, as most practitioners of Goddess spirituality believe it *is* a serious threat to traditional religion and customs, not in the way that most people expect, but in its insistence on using very different frameworks of meaning and its reconstruction of gender and identity (2000: 14) [italics original].

If Griffin is correct in her assertion regarding the availability of academic funding for research into Goddess spirituality, then this suggests that the field of religious studies as a whole has a tendency to locate popular contemporary spiritual practices at the 'lower end' of the academically important continuum. For as Sutcliffe has observed, 'popular spirituality' in the Anglo-American domain 'has traditionally (and unaccountably) received little scrutiny from academics' (2003: 217). So is there a political academic agenda going on here, with 'Religion' being deemed worthy of academic investigation leaving 'popular spirituality' out in the cold? Think back here also to Sutcliffe's perception that for sociologist Steve Bruce's, self-spirituality was both plebian and vulgar.

And surely, if it is predominantly women who write about Goddess/women's spirituality, then might one not regard this as potentially another example of women being silenced — with regard to the availability of funding — both academically and in 'contemporary spiritualities' where as we have seen, they predominate. Yet further questions should also be asked with regard to the lack of male writers in this area, for all of these issues are indicative of an ongoing discourse of power. This is why, as was observed in Chapter One, feminist writers are so concerned with the continuance of patriarchal paradigms within academic research and publication and actively engage in locating women back into text. However for the moment, let us return to Griffin.

Griffin states that while Goddess spirituality does not have an authoritative text, this, in itself, is a positive boon enabling a fluidity of practice. For this 'lack' enables women to worship singly, communally in covens, at home or at the garden altar and devise rituals that suit personal, particular needs (2000: 14). This sort of 'individualized' practice is also rather similar to that of Scottish healing circles. For here too one need not be affiliated to any particular organization or fixed practice even if, as with the case of Reiki, a male theological superstructure is in place (and in the process of ongoing revision) with men being in the process of re-writing 'authoritative text'. Hence questions will be asked later in this book in relation to Reiki regarding whether women are, for example, being reconstrained when emphasis is placed on 'woman as caring and nurturing'. For this emphasis is rather different from representations of women in Wiccan covens. Here, the 'Mother [is regarded as being] sexual, powerful, loving and demanding...a whole, integrated adult' (Griffin 2000: 18). And although this last quote relates particularly to the High Priestess's role, it is still the case that these same Priestesses promote a radically transformed image of mothering for all women—this at odds with traditional patriarchal constructions of the same.

Furthermore,

> Wicca, while questioning moral issues, is part of the process in late modernity of reembedding moral issues through lifestyle choices. Ritual practices, community activities, and spiritual quests help to define lifestyle choices and are part and parcel of the re-creation of the self within Wicca (Berger 1999: 6).

This Wiccan positioning is also akin to the emphasis in New Age cosmologies of developing and transforming the self to fulfil its 'divine potential' so that one may, in turn, have a morally (and practically) beneficial effect on the world as a whole. This we shall see is particularly relevant in healing practices such as Reiki where the trained practitioner may communally 'beam healing energy' to places where conflict and disaster has occurred. This recreated self as active healing agent stands, according to influential New Age writer Caroline Myss, radically apart from Protestant notions of predestination as preached by John Calvin in the sixteenth century. For according to this framework,

> ...our purpose in life is to fulfil the duties and responsibilities that God has assigned us, but because human nature is essentially corrupt, we cannot achieve salvation (the reward of Heaven) except by the

grace of God. Moreover, to the Calvinists, God has predestined certain people to receive that grace and not others, leaving us dependent on a kind of luck controlled by the Divine, which has already decided our fate. Acting morally is all but reduced to a form of hoping that one is already among the elect (Myss 2002: 40).

Myss however, argues that each person when consciously acting out of right intention, makes life choices based on motivations that are 'compassionate and sincere' (2002: 41) for these 'reflect our intimate connection with the Divine' (2002: 41). We shall see in the ethnographic chapters to follow, the significance of 'right intention' when healing self and others and the popularity of ontological standpoints like Myss's in Scottish healing circles.

Marylyn Gottschall makes a further point, which very much relates to this ethnography of New Age healing. For Gottschall, 'those who denominationalize Goddess worship make a case too strongly' (2000: 61). She argues that while there is a general continuity within Goddess worship of a 'gynocentric symbol system and a canon of popular feminist spirituality writings, its inherent vitality and inherent instability make it difficult to contain' (2000: 61). The Goddess movement is a '...highly syncretic, dynamic and increasingly diverse form of popular religiosity' (2000: 61). Gottschall's positioning above, mirrors Sutcliffe's thoughts on New Age seekers. For here too fluidity of boundaries and syncretic dynamism are the norm. Correspondingly, once again I would argue that the development of a decentralized narrative of power relations in healing circles is a more fruitful way of evaluating this vibrant and diverse form of popular religiosity.

I would however like to raise a couple of key points here. When we enter the fields of healing in Scotland, what we find is a general emphasis on *women's spirituality* rather than Goddess spirituality. This appears to be a lot to do with the fact that some women do not support the anthropomorphisation of deity or 'All that is', often regarding the same as 'love' or 'energy' rather than as God or the Goddess.

Second, as succinctly stated by Emily Culpepper and on a theoretical note, the term 'spiritual' itself is highly problematic (as I have observed in relation to Hanegraaff earlier in this chapter). For it also carries 'a heavy load of dualistic, anti-body associations behind it which feminists recognize as ultimately being a key component of the androcentric oppressive dichotomy between female and male' (cited in Puttick 1997: 200). This positioning may be found historically within religions such as Christianity, where transcendence (out of the body) and immortality (the body may die but the well trained soul will live) are goals. And yet it is the body through which we experience life. We identify ourselves with our bodies. 'Our *agency* as active personae in society is accomplished through our bodies' (McGuire 1990: 284). Hence our '"engendered" body is...both the instrument of power and the site of struggles over power' (McGuire 1990: 293).

As we shall see, this statement is also of relevance when women learn self-developmental 'techniques' that actively engage with the *energetic* body — the chakra and auric 'systems' as described in Chapter Four of this book. For here emphasis may be placed by workshop participants on 'developing their higher spiritual chakras' rather than their root 'sexual' chakras.

Having noted these two points, let us return to some specific examples of how women's bodies are portrayed as empowered within feminist, Wiccan and Goddess spirituality circles — remembering that some New Agers are also Goddess worshippers. For all of these adherents locate their spiritual practice within social and political realms and see the Goddess as a liberating force from patriarchal mainstream religion.

Women 'involved' within Goddess spirituality form new narratives of 'what it is to be a woman' and how to relate to, and understand, people and the world in general. Emphasis is placed on 'the personal as political', a theme common in feminist thought, and on becoming liberated from dualistic patriarchal paradigms where the sexual body is seen as 'less' or sinful. This is a major shift of positioning from traditional Christian representations of deity as male and transcendental. Rather, the Goddess is acknowledged as being imminent, 'the flow of energy linking all things and making the whole biosphere sacred' (Griffin 2000: 77). As human beings are also part of nature, then the female body becomes sacralized. This sort of thinking breaks down traditional patriarchal understandings of the gendered body and respective moral codes and 'guidelines' for behaviour.

The Goddess may also be identified with as a symbol of self-healing and planetary healing. In the latter (though the two are intertwined) she is often referred to as Gaia. 'She is also an important symbol of female empowerment, legitimating women's own power and independence, and inspiring them to formulate and realise their own potential and goals' (Griffin 2000: 77).[18]

Therefore, within Goddess spirituality there is a breaking down of male dominated paradigms relating to the female body and, for example, its age related reproductive processes; menstruation, gestation, lactation and menopause etc. All of these life events are reconfigured positively. The menstruating woman should still worship and work in the world. The post-menopausal woman is honoured. She does not have to hide 'distasteful…age spotted flesh and sagging skin' (Griffin 2000: 79).

> In writing the body, whether this is done through verbal or nonverbal messages, women in Goddess spirituality are deconstructing patriarchal religious metanarrative. They transform gender identity by subverting traditional meaning and representation of what it means to be female, simultaneously creating new definitions of appropriate gendered behaviour for women. This process redefines the boundaries of what is acceptable.
>
> Done in a spiritual context, this writing of the body provides 'truth messages' (Ellwood 1993) that encode the world-view of Goddess spirituality. The body thus represented tells a new cultural narrative, one where Divinity is immanent, the female body is sacred, women are strong and authentically beautiful, mind and body are part of an integrated whole, sexuality is celebrated and not always linked to reproduction, and patriarchy is a temporary aberration rather than a natural condition (Griffin 2000: 84-85).

The key characteristic that links Goddess spirituality, Wicca and New Age spiritualities is an emphasis on healing. By learning techniques to heal self and others, women are transformed and develop new ideas of what is to be a 'whole woman' and may begin to break out of patriarchal patterning. For although there is diversity of thought about bringing politics into practice—some Wiccans for example seeing Wicca as non-political while feminist Witchcraft 'by its very nature is a challenge to the political system of patriarchy' (Greenwood 2000: 144). There appears to be fairly general consent that for the woman to become empowered and healed she must look within for her connection to the Goddess. She must regard her body as the locus of power because of this connection and see it

---

18. The Goddess is also inspirational for some men and may be 'communicated with' or 'called forth' in some New Age locations, where 'the boundaries' between healing and Paganism may be blurred.

as 'the source of self affirmation and identity' (Greenwood 2000: 139), rather than being possessed by '...alienations of patriarchal culture. Healing involves coming to understand the way that domination has become internalised' (Greenwood 2000: 145).

For as I shall discuss in Chapters Five and Six where we look at Reiki, 'the Goddess' has been *utilized* by writers such as Diane Stein. I have chosen the word 'utilized' for a reason, primarily because we might do well to situate her writing within realist and non-realist positionings. Put simply, does Stein regard the Goddess as a symbolic resource, a mind set or is she an objective reality? Much has been written on this academically but initially one example will suffice. For the purpose of clarity I am going to draw from Melissa Raphael in relation to her evaluation of Carol Christ's shift from 'being' non-realist to realist.

Raphael argues that the 'gradual evolution of the Goddess from woman-self to Goddess-self to Goddess-in-herself' (1999: 145) is exemplified in Carol Christ's spiritual biography. In 1978, Christ gave a keynote paper 'The Great Goddess Re-emerging' at the University of California at Santa Cruz. 'In this paper, "Why Women Need the Goddess: Phenomenological, Psychological and Political Reflections", Christ claims that the Goddess is, essentially, a symbolic "affirmation of the legitimacy and beneficence of female power"; "a symbol of the new found beauty, strength and power of women"' (Raphael 1999:146).[19]

> Yet by the time of publication of her 1987 book, *Laughter of Aphrodite*, Christ has begun to refer to the goddess Aphrodite as speaking *to* [italics mine] her 'clear as a bell', bestowing wisdom upon her, speaking through 'golden laughter' – a revelatory experience that confirmed and initiated her as a priestess of Aphrodite.[20] Nearly two decades after her presentation of a non-realist theology, Christ's moving autobiographical narrative theology, Odyssey to the Goddess: A Spiritual Quest in Crete has become quite evidently realist. Here, Aphrodite is a divinity with whom Christ has a complex, intimate relationship that she herself perceives as a relationship with a divinity outside and beyond herself (Raphael 1999: 146).

19. Christ, 'Why Women Need the Goddess: Phenomenological, Psychological and Political Reflections', Carol Christ, *Womanspirit Rising*, (San Francisco, CA: Harper Collins, 1992), pp. 273-87 (276), 286. See also, p. 287.

20. Christ, *Laughter of Aphrodite* (New York, Harper and Row, 1978).

It will be interesting to observe where 'women of the Goddess' fit into realist, and non-realist debates in relation to healing and the removal of internalised 'ways of being'. Let us return to Greenwood for the moment, as her engagement with Feminist Witchcraft's critique of the internalization of patriarchal culture, does seem to resonate with Paul Heelas's 'self ethics'. For even though Heelas appears to ignore the patriarchal dimensions of these self-ethics, both writers do engage with notions of the role of the ego in illness and health.[21] We shall also find this concern running throughout ethnographic chapters where New Age practitioners stipulate that internalized 'ego-driven mores' cause blockages in the energetic body and dis-ease.

And although within New Age circles healing may appear to be de-politicised initially, I would argue that it is impossible to separate 'the healing body' from its sociopolitical context and with the issues of power and gender. For if one of the primary drawing features for women in Scotland who become involved within New Age networks is 'healing', then why exactly is this the case? Are New Age practitioners equally concerned with patriarchal structures as causes of dis-ease? If, as Rose found in his 2001 appraisal of New Age women, thirty two practices showed a strong bodywork content with twenty two of these having a female participation bias (2001: 230), what is this saying about women's development of new 'senses of self' and empowerment? Why did Rose find that 'almost four out of five practising therapists' (2001: 230) or 78 percent were women aged between thirty-five and fifty-four? (These findings being in accord with Scottish healing contexts). But it is with the following statement that, for the moment, I will close this chapter. Rose proposes that, in relation to his survey findings indicating multiple usages of New Age therapies,

> Many practices are used regularly rather than on a short term or ad-hoc basis – that is, at times they are used habitually as part of everyday life. This leads to the speculation that such New Age practices are thought of as a healing requirement for the maintenance and nurture (likely to be in tandem with their spiritual paths) rather than as a 'distress' or shorter-term requirement to relieve temporary illness or disease (2001: 339).

21. Greenwood states that within feminist witchcraft there is an emphasis on shaministic healing where internalized patriarchal structures are broken down in the ego and new senses of identity are developed (Griffin 2000: 145).

Certainly in the Scottish context healing practices are adhered to in the long, rather than the short term even if many women do appear to become involved initially with the same due to chronic dis-ease and corresponding distress, which they feel has not been treated successfully by bio-medical approaches to health. In order to look at these questions more fully I shall, in the next chapter, introduce how evaluations of 'states of being' relate to medical anthropology and specific writings on healing, energy work and the New Age in general.

Chapter Three

HEALING IN THE 'NEW AGE'

Over the last two chapters I have begun to paint a picture of the New Age scene, with an emphasis on textual enquiry. As we have seen, one of the most visible aspects of New Age thought and practice is the widespread concern with health. In this chapter I shall begin to relate to the healing typology of Meredith McGuire. For she has provided us with a methodologically sound qualitative study of ritual healing in suburban America. In this she examines the role of the healer, transformations of the self and help-seeking beyond bio-medical models of health. Her work is significant in that she evaluates the widespread use of alternative medical systems by middle-class persons and their notions of health and wellness, sources of healing power and associated healing practices. Correspondingly her writing forms a useful basis for this examination of healing in the Scottish context and the construction of a decentralized narrative of power. This will be followed with the inclusion of some relevant points as made by Hedges & Beckford in *Holism, Healing and the New Age* (2001). I shall also introduce here medical sociological evaluations of the body, healing and society, placing emphasis on these writers' usages of Foucault to unravel the power dynamics of these fields. However initially, it will be useful to examine how the term 'healing' itself has been used. For in the Scottish context, 'healing' is often defined against biomedical 'curing' models of health and hence intimately relates to identity and power.

Healing

Wouter Hanegraaff proposes in *New Age Religion and Western Culture* that his etic evaluation of the meaning of the term 'healing' is more precise than emic interpretations of the same. He adopts the medical anthropological terminology of Arthur Kleinman in relation to 'disease' and 'illness' in support of his position. For Kleinman,

> DISEASE refers to abnormalities in the structure and/or function of organs and organ systems; pathological states whether or not they are culturally recognized; the arena of the biomedical model.
> ILLNESS refers to a person's perceptions and experiences of certain socially devalued states including, but not limited to, disease (cited in Hanegraaff 1998: 43).

Hence for Hanegraaff, while diseases are biophysical conditions which medical practitioners aim to cure, the state of illness is more than just a physical malfunction but involves the 'social, psychological, and spiritual condition of the sick person...and constitutes the proper domain of healing' (1998: 43). He is correct to assert that in traditional cultures the healing of illness is of considerable significance, while probably, in the West, it is on specific diseased conditions that the bio-medical practitioner concentrates — the latter approach being critiqued by some due to its loss of emphasis on healing the whole person. This most certainly is a common criticism in Scottish healing circles. For within this field of practice healers will try to restore health to the whole person — she/he being seen as having spiritual, emotional and physical aspects, which are intimately related to surrounding environmental factors and influences. As Hanegraaff states, 'The scope of factors relevant to healing, illness and health is therefore extended far beyond the reaches of conventional Western medicine' (1998: 43).

I would like to raise a couple of points in relation to Hanegraaff's above proposals. First, many healers would dispute that his etic interpretation was more precise than their own, for he is applying a medical anthropological interpretation of 'healing' that does not fit well to New Age representations. Healers in the Scottish context often refer to the 'dis-eased' body. This dis-eased body is not at ease with its self and with its way of life. It is not in harmony with its spiritual path. It is constrained and limited by its ego-driven needs and materialist tendencies. It is fragmented. It is not whole. Dis-ease is not solely a pathological state. It is a de-valued state. For the dis-eased person will often express feelings of suffering and loss in relation to 'how I am perceived and how I perceive myself'.

A brief example. In the summer of 2001 I took part in a weekend workshop at the Salisbury Centre in Edinburgh entitled 'Healing Through Consciousness' and run by a facilitator who had trained in Barbara Ann Brennan's School in America where teaching is based on the human body as being energetic.[1] One of the participants at this workshop was a woman called Alison, who expressed guilt at being 'not happy' as a working, married, mother. For although she was secure in a material sense, she stated that she was experiencing feelings of suffering due to lack of connection with her spiritual side. Because of this, she wanted to develop a new sense of herself in relation to the world 'as holistic'. Therefore, as we shall investigate further in the following chapter, dis-ease and suffering are intimately related to embodied senses of self and the need to feel valued and 'whole', and the corresponding development of supportive frameworks of meaning.

Hence my research findings tie in well with Hanegraaff's proposition that 'traditional and New Age approaches to healing share a concern with meaning...illness is typically given symbolic form by being interpreted in the context of general cultural beliefs' (1998: 43). For within Scottish healing circles a person's physical health is seen to be intimately related to its holistic state and the connections between self and others. This, of course, relates to the social constraints and roles that each person 'plays'. However mind, body and spirit 'states' are given further depth within Scottish New Age healing circles in that they are regarded as 'energetic'. Therefore if a person visits a healer for help with a dis-eased condition, this will be attributed to imbalances or blockages in that person's energetic pathways in the esoteric body. Consequently, there are numerous courses within the Scottish New Age scene, which cater for the healer who wishes to learn to see and interpret auric and energetic states. This is the central interpretative framework for New Age healing work in Scotland and is, I would argue, intimately related to the engendered body as both instrument and site of power.

For when a person is advised that they are an energetic holistic entity, and that in order to be healthy this must be 'worked on', then this leads the individual to seek courses that practically teach this way of being. Hence they draw from a wide diversity of

---

1. I shall provide more material on this in the next chapter.

interpretative frameworks, eclectically picking and mixing, and what
has most relevance personally. But once on this course of personal
redefinition, they also find that they have (or at least ought) to
become disciplined in their holistic practice. This positioning may
be clearly seen in, for example, the Salisbury Centre in Edinburgh
where the Deed of Trust outlines as one of its key objectives, the
wish to 'help and educate young people to develop their physical,
mental and spiritual capacities and their self discipline and loyalty
to mankind'. In order to fulfil these objectives teachers help the
New Age student to learn appropriate thought, behaviour and
practice until they themselves can self regulate their emotions,
attitudes and spiritual practice. Hence 'appropriate' bodies are
produced in healing circles as they are in other areas of society.

Having begun to set the scene, let us now return to the
representation of healing in Scotland. I shall relate this initially to
Meredith McGuire's taxonomy of 'healing types', bearing in mind
however that there is considerable blurring of boundaries between
these in the Scottish context. I would suggest therefore, that these
'types' might be more usefully regarded as being constitutive
elements of healing practice, which relate to the formation of various
models of subjectivity — of energetic being in the world.

Meredith McGuire

In *Ritual Healing in Suburban America* (1998) McGuire presents her
investigative, interview-based research, among some one hundred
and thirty healers and healing groups in suburban Essex County
and New Jersey. She proposes that that there are five main types of
alternative healing thought and practice:

- Healing as practised by Christian groups, in accord with the
  teachings of Jesus 'as healer', emphasizing the importance of
  healing to the early church.
- Healing as afforded through harmony within, this found
  through practices such as meditation, which focus on inner
  spirituality and contacting the 'true self'.
- Those healers who acknowledge the role of the ego in generating
  illness, as to be found within Eastern spirituality and human
  potential groups.
- Practices concerned with healing through the use of 'external
  powers', such as spirit guides, psychic groups or crystal usage.

- Practitioner techniques where the patient is treated through a specific practice such as shiatsu, chiropractic or acupuncture (1998: 18-31).

Christian Healing Groups

McGuire proposes that healing for Christian groups (fundamentalist, Pentecostal, neo-pentecostal, healing cults and non-denominational groups) is primarily based on 'New Testament descriptions of Jesus' ministry and the place of healing in the early church' (1998: 19). For according to Hanegraaff, in spite of the New Age's common critique of mainstream Christianity, its interest in Eastern religion and its religious inclusivity of thinking, 'it is still Christ who dominates New Age speculation wherever the need is felt to explain the relation between God and humanity by some mediating principle' (1998: 189). This, I have found, leads important international healing figures such as Bruce MacManaway, Richard Gerber, Caroline Myss *et. al.* to acknowledge the importance of Jesus as healer par excellence while also incorporating Theosophical and 'Oriental' elements in their healing practice.

New Age literature on 'Jesus as healer' is also commonplace. For example, New Age author David Harvey states in *The Power to Heal* (1983), that while references to spiritual healing are to be found in the pre-Christian era and within the Old Testament, as far as the West is concerned the best-known healer is still Jesus. He proposes that Jesus' life and teachings established a new phase in the history of healing while providing at the same time a link with older traditions. For 'Jesus was the apotheosis of the healer-priest who had played such a central role in Egyptian, Greek and other religions. He cured the sick through the laying on of hands, by command, by anointing them with his saliva and, as in the case of the centurion's servant, by the power of his mind at a distance…In the most dramatic way he showed that the physical body could be healed by spiritual means' (1983: 38).

These sorts of positioning in relation to 'Jesus as healer' are highly characteristic of the eclectic tendencies of New Age 'historiography' (Hanegraaff 1998: 318). For as Hanegraaff proposes, 'It seems that New Agers are not interested in incompatibilities between fine (and even less fine) points of historical detail; what matters to them is only the very general belief that Jesus was an Essene…[and that] the rise of Christianity has been one big mistake, based on regrettable misinterpretations of Jesus' message and intentions' (1998: 318-20).

As we continue to review of Meredith McGuire's 'healing types', noting how her ideas will inform the design of my fieldwork, we would do well to keep Hanagraaff's statement in mind. For while he is generally correct in this assertion, he has also based this positioning solely on textual enquiry in Holland between 1990 and 1992. Accordingly, he has, while providing an excellent account of New Age thought, not brought out in entirety the nuances of experiential 'fluid' practice in the field. For these 'nuances' to be brought into the study of religions we must, I would argue, promote empirical research so that we can find out more precisely what New Agers actually *do* in their, in this case, healing practice, and then relate this to gender, reformulations of identity and agency. Hence I would be in agreement with Dominick Corrywright when he states, 'The history of religions is an object lesson against over-reliance on texts as expressions of religiosity' (2003: 26-27), a point I raised in the previous chapters.

To return to McGuire and her research among Christian healing groups; McGuire found that membership is primarily white female with 'men [being] conspicuously predominant in number and influence among the leadership of all groups (1998: 19). This applies even if membership is entirely female as, for example, in Women's Aglow International. Here 'the international organization requires that each chapter's advisors be men (since they believe that Scripture teaches that women should be submissive to men's authority' (1998: 19).[2] Healing activities in groups such as Women's Aglow usually involve the 'laying on of hands' and prayer and are often related to marital or family problems with a mutual network of support developing.

A key difference with this form of religiosity and the New Ager in Scotland appears to lie in the former's interpretations of health. For while the New Ager usually goes to a healer because of disease, the recruit to the Christian group (as above) typically does not have a pre-existing condition; 'rather through the experience of the prayer group, members come to realize their needs for healing and to believe in dramatic healing power' (McGuire 1998: 38). The

2. Women's Aglow fellowships have developed worldwide with over thirteen hundred groups. It takes its name from scripture, namely Romans 12:1, where Christians are admonished and told to 'Be aglow and burning with the Spirit' (McGuire 1998: 19).

concept of health is in turn centred on the group's beliefs that even if the physical body is healthy, the 'person' might not be. For 'health refers to attitudes that are ultimately linked with spiritual sources' (McGuire 1998: 38), to be healthy is to have a good relationship with God…and Jesus is 'the embodiment of their ideal of health' (McGuire 1998: 39).

In the above (Christian healing groups) we can clearly see that women are located 'as less than men' — their location as such being based on doctrinal 'truths'. They have two 'male' figures as role models of health, Jesus and God, and are told that it is not possible to reach 'their' perfect state in this lifetime. Correspondingly, the group member must regularly attend healing meetings to enable a progression along the path to health 'until the final "healing" — death' (McGuire 1998: 39). This does not initially appear to be an empowering situation for women. And yet emphasis is placed within these sorts of Christian groups on healing emotional, spiritual and relational problems with a mutual network of support being built up. Healing is done for family members and friends and for others in the healing group. Society as a whole is seen to be in need of healing 'in the sense that it [is] not in the right relationship with God' (McGuire 1998: 41), leading to violent crime, 'alcoholism, adultery and abortion' (McGuire 1998: 41). This form of healing then, appears to be bounded by patriarchal structures and moral codes and a 'literal' interpretation of the Bible 'as truth', with the foremost cause of illness being sin (McGuire 1998: 46).

> 'It's because of [personal] sin that we derive all the illness in the world'
> (Woman respondent, McGuire 1998: 47).

While it has been outwith the scope of this book to examine Christian healing groups in Scotland,[3] McGuire's material above is useful to note in relation to notions of the causes of health and disease in Christian groups and the location of 'healing power'. For these appear to differ from the ideas I have encountered in Scottish healing circles. Here emphasis is placed on negating the 'principle' that sin causes dis-ease, while Jesus becomes 'healer par excellence' and a role model, rather than the unattainable embodiment of perfect

---

3. I have not spent time with Christian groups primarily because, as Heelas has argued, they place emphasis on external healing agencies with a corresponding shift of authority from the Self, this taking 'us away from New Age Self-spirituality' (Heelas 1996: 81-82).

health. This shift in positioning appears to allow women more space to heal self and others on a 'more level playing field' in that they appear not to be locked into traditional hierarchical, patriarchal leadership structures. However, for the moment let us return to McGuire's second motif, that of 'harmony within'.

Harmony Within

McGuire states that within this motif considerable emphasis is placed on inner spirituality where one works to 'get in touch with one's true self' (McGuire 1998: 24) through practices such as meditation. This kind of 'thought' she locates within 'Metaphysical Groups' such as Christian Science, Religious Science and Unity, (Unity School of Science). Membership of these sorts of groups is more diverse than Christian groups with black, white, young and elderly members. In Unity, a prime example of this sort of group, middle-class white women predominate in membership and leadership roles. 'Members [are] not particularly sectarian about their beliefs, compared with Christian healing groups, but they [are] not as eclectic as adherents of meditation, human potential, or occult beliefs' (McGuire 1998: 24). Unity differs from the aforementioned Christian groups because of its emphasis on the self as transcendent. Life's events are not chance affairs but intuitively known to the 'inner spirit' as activities of God. If one is true to the moment and learns the lesson from life's experiences, then one opens the way for divine experiences. Hence emphasis is placed on the 'here and now' and individual responsibility, while power is seen as being located within the self (McGuire 1998: 22-24).

Most importantly, illness, for metaphysical Groups, is not regarded as being 'a result of sin', while Divinity is imminent rather than transcendent. Hence, health is attainable. As members told McGuire, 'We're made perfect; it's what we do—it's our wrong thinking that brings about the imperfections' (McGuire 1998: 81). For a healthy mind equates to a healthy body, health is not solely spiritual and one should regard oneself as being inherently moral, kind, thoughtful and caring because 'we're a likeness of God' (McGuire 1998: 81).

These types of groups hold 'philosophies' rather similar to those we find in Scottish healing circles. Here, too, we find emphasis on meditation as a tool to clear the mind from 'the obstructions of negative thinking' in favour of positive thought and speech. Similarly, metaphysical groups' emphasis on experiential individualized practices such as 'positive visualizations' is also commonplace in Scotland. McGuire notes that members when suffering from severe arthritic pain, may visualize themselves in active roles such as dancing—now pain free—to support their positive affirmations for the same. Or they may visualize themselves in a stream of healing white light, which may be seen as representing Christ (1998: 224) this in turn 'removing' pain and increasing flexibility.

McGuire also tells us that group members may visualize a carefully self-constructed room or garden, which one may 'visually alter' according to need. The member may go to such 'imaginary space' as a retreat 'and these visualizations are clearly part of a believer's prevention and healing of illness'. However 'they [are] not typically images of action. Most visualizations used in Christian, meditation and psychic occult groups involved imagining action or interaction which produced change' (McGuire 1998: 225). This is an interesting point and shows the blurring of boundaries between 'healing types' of practices and beliefs in both America and Scotland. For I have found in similarity to Tanice Foltz, who researched healing with a Hawaiian Kahuna in California in the 1980s, that visualizations of quiet spaces such as gardens may 'be active'. For *actual* healing of self or 'a client' may be visualized and effected within this 'imaginary space'. This occurs as a result of focusing on one's vibrational rate to, as Brennan advised, align it with the patient's energy so that energy from the Universal Energy field may be entrained. The key points here are that visualization and 'mental channelling of energy or vibrations' (McGuire 1998: 226) have enormous 'appeal in contemporary society…Especially important is the extent to which these uses of imagery are creative, individualistic and active' (McGuire 1998: 226).

And we would do well to reflect that in the Scottish context, the emphasis on 'restoration of order, harmony and perfect peace to mind and heart' has multiple representations with healthiness being regarded as the natural state of life, while dis-ease may occur due to a lack of connection and faulty thinking. For in order to 'realize one's place in the universe, and to accept this position "as where one is destined to be now"' (McGuire 1998: 136), one must also discover (and have a balanced perception of) the particular reasons and meaning of 'why I am here'.

This is why I feel that, as mentioned earlier, McGuire's 'types' would be better seen as constitutive elements of healing practice. For once one enters the province of 'quieting the noisy mind' then one may also find a multiplicity of opinions regarding the role of the ego in dis-ease generation.

Ego-generated Illness

McGuire's third category of healing type, where adherents regard illness as being in some way 'of the mind' and ego-generated is not uncommon in Scottish healing circles, though again multitudinous representations abound. For as we shall see in the following chapters, this sort of positioning is common in groups inspired by Eastern spiritualities and human potential philosophies. McGuire also found 'fuzzy boundaries' within these sorts of groups and indeed on the individual level. 'Typically…respondents wove together complex, and continually changing strands from several approaches for their personal belief and practice' (McGuire 1998: 95). Emphasis was also placed on the relationship between illness and karma, with negative thoughts and actions reaping negative results at both individual and social levels. Hence as with all the other healing types, 'there is a strong emphasis on personal responsibility for health and illness, especially the responsibility for one's self-awareness and lifestyle' (McGuire 1998: 108).

This finding is in accord with the Scottish context where eclecticism reigns supreme in healing circles, as is an emphasis on the social and individual causes of illness. For New Agers would have little difficulty in subscribing to the view that 'ego-involvement and its concomitant attachment to illusionary sources of happiness misdirect the individual's energies and produce illness' (McGuire 1998: 106). As a respondent informed McGuire,

> I keep in my mind a lot of affirmations to help me live in the world, but don't be of it, because it's only a transient experience. We're here to accomplish certain things and certain purposes on this earth…But people shouldn't get tied up in the physical things of living, the mundane things like greed, with money (McGuire 1998: 106-107).

This emphasis on the individual having 'a certain purpose on earth' may also be found in New Age writing and teaching. We will see this with Helen Stott when she states that when all the chakras are aligned and supported in the body then one can 'move into the fullness of our individual essence—which is of course our life work' (WMH 2001: 6). While for New Age author Caroline Myss, this 'life's work' is a 'sacred contract', that each of us in on the earth to fulfil, this relating to our 'archetypal inheritance'. I feel Myss is worth quoting at this point, as her work is rather popular within Scottish healing circles as 'transformatory tool kits' for the Self.

> Our archetypal inheritance is prehistoric, primal. It comes from our own energy origins in the Divine, which is also the source of our Sacred Contract—the guided plan for our life. We co-create our Contract with divine guidance, and it includes many individual agreements— or subcontracts—to meet and work with certain people, in certain places, at certain times (Myss 2002: 35-36).

It is this focus on having a purpose in life, which is spiritually guided, that underpins a lot of New Age thought. We need, so the narrative goes, to let go of ego-driven mores and selfish, self-serving behaviour and get back in touch with our higher spiritual purpose. And while yes, this may lead some New Agers to emphasize 'working on the self' and withdrawing to 'retreats' such as The Findhorn Community, in general, emphasis is placed on taking responsibility for one's Self and actively healing the social factors that are causing distress and corresponding dis–ease, such as problems at home or in the work- place. The individual is regarded as an empowered being that intuitively knows the right choices to be made in this life and realizes that negative thoughts (whether internally or externally imposed) will lead to ill health. Correspondingly, there is also often a sense that one should actively engage politically and 'through the raising of world spiritual consciousness' effect changes on a global level. In turn, this will lead to less materialism, violence, corruption, exploitation and pollution. In general, as a healer in Edinburgh informed me, it is felt that once one gets back in touch with the inner or higher self, one 'becomes aware that in order to truly be, it is necessary to let go of limiting ego-driven "I" issues...for these will prevent you from coming home'. [4]

This type of statement also requires, of course, some unpicking in relation to gender, power and representation. As I mentioned

4. This perspective was given to me by Rob, a male healer practising in Edinburgh.

earlier in Chapter Two, in relation to Paul Heelas' New Age self-
ethics, how a person sees him or herself will have a lot to do with
the socially constructed nature of this journey through life
encompassing family history, educational opportunities, race, class
and gender. For as we shall continue to see in the Scottish context,
the majority of practitioners are white middle-class women, while
at the 'higher' levels of some published teaching on healing thought
and practice there is a tendency towards male domination. In the
latter, as with the 'aristocratic' Reiki Master Frank Petter, one finds
a predominance of people who have travelled extensively and whose
family backgrounds suggest a privileged lifestyle. One should also
note that, in relation to 'I' issues, the development of a 'sense of
self' is also implicitly related to gender. For in Fife healing circles
where women predominate, it is common to hear practitioners
locating themselves as wives and mothers – that is defining
themselves in particular domestic, relational roles – before they see
themselves as an individual 'in their own right'. Correspondingly,
if ill health issues arise, how these are related to by the healer and
healee is also intimately associated with the socially constructed
gendered nature of the persons involved.

External Powers

McGuire observes that psychic and occult healing is an enormously
diverse field of practice with extremely individualistic and eclectic
beliefs, where new meanings are attributed to older religious
cosmologies (McGuire 1998:130-31) For example, in the Scottish
context one might find the practitioner doing past life regressions
in order to heal damage from earlier incarnations, this being carried
into this life, and tying this in to 'karmic debt'. However, McGuire
correctly notes that an underlying emphasis within Psychic or Occult
groups is 'on a notion of a transcendent healing power – something
outside and greater than the individual' (McGuire 1998: 130).

   She locates within this category Spiritualist groups who have a
long historical tradition of 'asking' for 'individual guidance via
mediums and spirits' (1998: 131); where the 'spirits' may be turned
to for personal assistance and assurance in life choices (and, often,
in the Scottish context, as 'healing guides'). For as we shall see in
Chapter Four, practitioners do call on their 'guardian angels' when
doing healing work, or ask their spirit guides for assistance in

decision making regarding where the hands should be placed to maximise the efficiency of 'healing energy'.

How these 'external forces' are perceived and are represented again appears to relate to the socially constructed nature of the person involved. For example, at the Salisbury Centre's 'Healing Circle', angels are often described as being white and with Christian names such as Metatron and Michael, while spirit guides were depicted as being Native American, shamans, Tibetan monks or as acquaintances from past lives.

Ideals of health and wellness for Psychic and Occult groups relate to ideas of 'the ability to be in control of one's daily life and to handle crisis situations' (McGuire 1998: 135). Emphasis is also placed on realizing one's connections with the universe in general and being open to the realization that one is placed in the universe for very particular reasons and that 'the goal is not to change the current situation, but to discover the meaning of it' (McGuire 1998: 136).[5]

McGuire also found that psychic adherents regard the healthy, alive individual as energetically connected to the cosmos or universe with a healthy energy field or aura. These ontologies are also central to Scottish New Age thought as is the emphasis on 'love', as a 'necessary quality for healthiness' (McGuire 1998: 136), alongside a good mental outlook. Therefore, 'For most psychic adherents… health and wellness meant wholeness of body in conjunction with mind, emotion and spirit…Healthiness is not merely the absence of disease in body-mind-spirit, but real health requires a balance of all three' (McGuire 1998: 137).

Sources of healing power within psychic groups also appear to resonate with the Scottish context. For as I noted in Chapter Two, some practitioners object to the anthropomorphisation of deity instead favouring energetic notions of 'All That Is' and indeed, as McGuire has found, God being described as 'cosmic consciousness' or 'white light'; the latter being more identified with when doing healing work.

McGuire also locates crystals within her 'external powers' categorization. In the Scottish context, crystal dowsing is a popular medium/tool through which the practitioner may see visible 'evidence' of the aura and of chakra energetic states. For here

---

5. We appear to have a tension here in relation to how one should act in the world. For how does one actively bring about social change in self and others' life circumstances if, at the same time, one's place is predestined as a 'learning lesson'?

dowsing was used to enable the practitioner to see what is 'known intuitively'. Crystals are also not infrequently used in rooms where healing is carried out to enhance 'positive energy' or in the healing itself where they may be used to 'draw out negative energy' or 'clear energy blocks in the chakras'. So although crystals may be utilized in their own right, one often finds that they are part of 'practitioner techniques', McGuire's last healing category.

Practitioner Techniques

Within Scottish healing contexts practitioners utilize a multiplicity of techniques to enhance healing in self and others. Within Chapters Five and Six I shall look more closely at the Japanese derived practice of Reiki, for this form of healing is very popular in Scotland, as it is in Europe and America. But Reiki healers also commonly bring to this practice additional 'therapeutic' techniques. Hence the reflexologist may learn Reiki to enhance healing power, as may the aromatherapist or the person doing Indian Head massage. It is worthy of note however, that it is again predominantly women who learn bodywork techniques such as these above, that these practices are non-intrusive physically—the healee is not required to undress, for example—and they are perceived to be powerful yet gentle remedies for soothing out often stress related dis-ease and dis-comfort in people of all ages. This is why healing modalities such as Reiki are also often used on babies and children, and on plants and animals. Hence further research would, I feel, be valuably enhanced by looking more specifically at non-adult human healing in relation to issues of self in healing and, for example, the placebo effect.

It is impossible to describe fully all the variations of healing thought and practice here, or indeed in this book as a whole. What I have tried to bring out in the above introduction to McGuire's typologies, is the relevance of her material to the Scottish context, although noting considerable blurring of her boundaries. For her statement that 'all of these forms of healing...involve an alternative understanding of the nature and etiology of illness; healing power and the essence of health' (1998: 18) is of great significance. For new understandings of health are of major importance in the Scottish context and should be examined, I would argue, from a feminist positioning so that we may find out how and why women are drawn to these practices and how this relates to debates between biomedical approaches to health and holistic approaches to the same in relation to, for example, authority and power. I shall return to McGuire (and other theorists) in the final chapter of this book, where I also reflect on how the experience of fieldwork has affected my assessment of various standpoints—feminist or otherwise. Let us now consider Paul Heelas, James Beckford and Ellie Hedges and their academic interpretations of the significance of individuality and authority within New Age ontologies, which can be related to medical anthropological evaluations of the complementary medicine. For these writers have provided us with useful material that can be referred to the Scottish healing context.

Healing and Authority

Paul Heelas proposes that,

> The greater the importance accorded to inner spirituality, the more clearly healing is 'New Age'. When healing relies on external agencies, that is to say, power, authority and responsibility is taken away from the person and his or her Self: and this takes us away from New Age Self-spirituality. The authority shift—from without to within— associated with New Age epistemological 'Selfism' is what ultimately characterizes New Age healing (1996: 81-82).

This perspective appears to fit well with regard to Scottish New Age epistemologies—and, as we have seen, McGuire's American context—where emphasis is indeed placed on the 'Self-as-spiritual' with, Heelas usefully puts it, 'bodility-as-spirituality/energy' [sic] (1996: 82) being intrinsically healing. Now he also states that within New Age networks the emphasis on inner spirituality is allied to the premise that all human beings are inherently spiritual and as such that the human body has a 'natural' will and fundamental tendency towards health 'given the proper conditions'[6] (Coward in Heelas 1996: 82). Therefore a person visiting a healer with a diseased 'condition' will generally, in the Scottish context for example, spend some considerable time initially presenting their life history and personal health narrative before healing work is undertaken. Heelas further proposes that,

6. One should note here though that questions most certainly need to be asked with regard to exactly what are these 'proper conditions' and how they relate to the socially constructed gendered body.

In the detraditionalized and anti-authoritarian world of the New Age, the healer clearly cannot have the kind of authority exercised by the conventional science-informed doctor, the person who draws on an established body of knowledge— derived by logic-dominated ego-operations—to diagnose and prescribe (1996: 82-83).

Rather, he suggests it is the inner or Higher Self – this 'knowing' one's optimal health state – to which the healer tries to become aligned. We shall observe this positioning in Chapter Four in relation to Brennan's 'life tasks' and Myss's 'sacred contracts'. The healer will also, as Heelas has proposed, very often have personally experienced periods of dis-ease where 'listening to the true inner voice' (1996: 83) has enabled a return to health. Hence the healer will carry out spirit/ual works on others having empirically tested the efficiency of this for themselves as 'patients'. This empirical testing is, I would propose, a central theme in Scottish healing circles. For as Heelas has suggested, here healees do indeed generally perceive their healers to be spiritually authoritative and that 'spiritual connectedness' will manifest visibly in one's state of health; for even if at times there are health crises, the healer will relate his/her swift recovery to 'being energetically connected'. The body hence becomes the immediate visible representation of 'oneness with all that is'. And as we shall see in ethnographic material, although the healer may initially work to remove 'ego driven energy blocks', ultimately,

The authority of many healers rests on their claims to be spiritual...the entitlement logic running, "at heart we are all spiritual beings; I am in closer contact with my spirituality than you (I am healthy you are dis-eased); since we both belong to the same spiritual realm, I speak with your inner self when I suggest that you do this and that; instead of speaking as an external voice of judgement I speak as your guide" (Heelas 1996: 83).

Common critiques of New Age healing and spirituality often suggest that such practices are excessively individualistic. For by focusing on one's own health and self-spirituality there is a corresponding tendency towards 'self-absorption' (Schur 1974) and 'narcissism' (Lasch 1979: cited in Hedges and Beckford 2000: 174). This then leads to a corresponding disengagement from socio-political issues, so the argument goes. However in healing circles in Scotland, while there is considerable emphasis on the 'healed self as spiritual', when it comes to 'doing' healing work this is usually expressed in terms of the healer being 'a balanced, grounded and open channel' through which healing energy — by whatever name — can flow to the healee. Now, while this may appear at first glance to be individualistic on the part of the healee receiving 'healing energy', and the healer 'working towards spiritual openness' in a sort of 'vertical hierarchy', I would argue that in the Scottish context, this is not the case in totality. For central to healing ontologies here, one finds continual emphasis on the spiritual and sacred connectedness of all animate and inanimate life. This fosters a sense of social responsibility and care for the same. Take, for example, the positioning of William Lee Rand at The International Center for Reiki Training based in America.

Rand suggests that a Reiki attunement[7] is often viewed as 'an initiation into a sacred metaphysical order that has been present on Earth for thousands of years.[8] By receiving an attunement you will become part of a group of people who are using Reiki to heal themselves and each other and who are working together to heal the Earth. By becoming part of this group you will also be receiving help from the Reiki guides and other spiritual beings who are working towards these goals' (Rand 1991, C-6).

One example of how Reiki practitioners network for social effect can be seen in the aftermath of the September 11th 2001 air attacks in New York and Washington. For following these tragic events Scottish Reiki practitioners linked up with their counterparts across the world to send Reiki healing to all those affected. The following e-mail was sent out to over 25,000 Reiki people worldwide from Rand's *Reiki.Org* website headed 'Helping You Accomplish Your Divine Purpose'. I draw selectively from this here due to its length.

> Please unite with us to send Reiki to the dead and injured and all those affected by the terrorist attacks on the World Trade Centre and the Pentagon. Also send Reiki for all related future events and to heal the planet.
>
> Let us unite at this time of great need to create a continuous wave of Reiki and prayer around the world. Please Reiki every hour on the hour wherever you are, as many times as you can or simply send it

7. These will be discussed in more depth in Chapters Five and Six.

8. Shuffrey also regards the Reiki attunements as a sacred ritual where the student 'remembers' his or her connection with The Reiki. For the attunement is a 'ritual of invocation' and 'direction of the Light, a holy act of purification' (1999:30).

continuously…As you send Reiki, you could meditate on all the others
worldwide who are sending Reiki and allow yourself to merge with
this great Reiki stream… (RICRT: 2001).

Therefore I am in accord with Hedges and Beckford, when they
state that holistic healing represents a 'fascinating re-mix of tradition,
expertise and modernity' (2000: 175) and that it is wrong to regard
holistic healing as excessively individualistic. For within New Age
ideologies 'The true self …is only one part of a much larger
whole…[which] involves commitment to values of benevolence and
justice' (2000: 172). They characterize the 'New Age representation
of the "true self" as naturally social, compassionate and attuned to
the rhythms of the natural world, working on self-actualization
through interaction with others and directed at the restoration of a
sense of wholeness' (2000: 178). Hence, for Hedges and Beckford
holistic healing would be better seen as a 'process' related to the
notions of 'flow' and 'tuning in' (2000: 169) which depends 'upon
forms of sociality and ideas that [are] collective and holistic'
(2000: 170).

They relate this to the experiences of eight female nurses who,
as part of their tuition in aromatherapy and holistic massage from a
Roman Catholic nun and nursing tutor, 'developed' as healers. The
study was initially conducted in 1982 by Ellie Hedges in relation to
the integration of complementary therapy to nursing practice (2000:
185). And as Scottish healing also appears to skirt the boundaries
of both conventional medicine and mainstream religiosity, then this
study is relevant to my ethnographic material. For here too (as we
shall see specifically in relation to Reiki practice), it is very common
to find women health care workers across all fields engaged in
healing both professionally and in the home. While with regard to,
for example, Christian ministry, there are many churches in Scotland
where healing services incorporating the 'laying on of hands' are
regular events.

Hedges and Beckford conclude, in relation to their above noted
study, that '"healing" activities…cut across the banal associations
characteristic of rationalized and bureaucratized healthcare and the
sensual solidarities evoked by the experience of healing' (2000: 184).
The process of holistic healing,

…provides opportunities for the expression of values such as love and
compassion, albeit within the ambit of professional nursing care.
Through a mutual tuning-in relationship between the healer and

patient and the source of healing energies, there is a blurring of the boundaries between selves which, as inter-subjective construction of transcendence, may bind people together. For some people this would also have sacred significance (2000: 184).

Within the above then, we have several core themes to be found in Scottish healing, themes similarly noted in McGuire's American healing research.

- An emphasis on 'love' in healing.
- The self as being 'naturally compassionate'.
- The predominance of women in healing.
- The importance of healing in/for community.
- The interconnectedness of all life raising issues of responsibility for the same.
- The centrality of tuning in to healing energies with corresponding sense of transformation of subjectivities.

For within Scottish healing circles, the primary critiques of society encompass expressions of dissatisfaction with mainstream religiosity and its negation of the body 'as less' and the predominantly male mediated nature of cognitively privileged theology. Similarly, with regard to conventional bio-medical approaches to health, many Scottish healers express deep dissatisfaction with this field of practice in relation to the body being symptomatically cured, with minimal attention being paid to the embodied and gendered nature of health and dis-ease. It is to the critique of bio-medical approaches by New Age circles that I turn next.

The Body and Medicine

According to Keith Bax in his (1991) discussion of the increasing popularity of contemporary folk medicine[9] in Western society, this has a lot to do with parallel transformations in the economy and cultural practice. He states that 'popular dissatisfaction with biomedicine has increased [and that] the cultural gap between biomedical practitioners has become much more visible in recent times' (1991:20). The two key connected elements of the term 'folk' in relation to medical practice are that of 'culture' and 'choice' (Bax 1991: 21) in that 'medical practices are intimately related to consumer preference patterns that operate within specific cultural milieux'

---

9. Bax uses the term folk medicine in relation to 'all of those practices which lie outside the "normal" sphere of orthodox medical practice' (1991: 20).

(Bax 1991: 21). He proposes that many members of Western societies assume that folk medicine has been eclipsed in Western countries by bio-medical approaches to health in similarity to the demise of 'community' and 'religion'. That is, the decline in folk medicine is seen as being 'inversely proportional to the index of urbanization or modernization, themselves "self evident" measures of the development of capitalism' (Bax 1991: 21). Bax critiques this standpoint. He argues that in the same way that secularization theorists have failed to see that a decline in mainstream church attendance does not necessarily mean a corresponding decline in religiosity, so too should sociologists of health appreciate that folk medicine is not dying out but may be just as vibrant having simply taken on new forms of expression '...far from being in its death throes, folk medicine is currently providing a viable alternative to biomedicine which is undergoing a major crisis' (1991: 22).

This statement is of relevance to healing in Scotland. For here holistic (mind, body and spirit) approaches to health do appear to be widespread with the emphasis on spiritual connectedness and apparently non-judgemental 'treatment' being primary drawing factors. Bax further argues that the continued popularity of folk medicine 'has a lot to do with the sense of alienation that biomedical approaches to health have induced among those consumers that use its services' (1991: 26). This sense of alienation is a commonly cited critique among those who venture into Scottish healing circles. For, while people entering this field of practice commonly acknowledge the usefulness and indeed the centrality of conventional medicine to acute operational and emergency situations, they also strongly feel that plurality of choice in relation to how one 'treats' one's own health is of considerable importance. They want to choose how they maintain their health and deal with disease in the same way that they can choose to consume other goods and services. And choice is made easy in that there are numerous varieties of healing practice to pick from; these may be found on health food and book shop notice boards, within libraries, colleges and coffee shops etc. Add to this the fact that it is possible to receive healing in as little as an hour or two, while one can learn the basics of some healing modalities in a weekend workshop and the individual's agency comes to the fore. For in 'the emic [practitioner] view, the individual, traditionally the passive object of hierarchical medical and ecclesiastical establishments alike, can metamorphose into a fully active subject…for whom self-realization and self-healing are two sides of the same coin' (Sutcliffe 2003: 180).

How then do bio-medical practitioners respond to these types of encroachment on their subject matter, the human body? Bax states that it is predominantly in urban areas that professionals (such as medical practitioners) mount their claims for legitimacy over more 'traditional' practices (and here one could potentially locate healing) seeing the latter as non-scientific and superstitious with little to prove that it actually works.[10] Certainly perspectives such as this do hold sway to some considerable extent and may be commonly heard in central Scotland. However, if one listens carefully to these dialogues one can also sense a feel of shifting power relations. For example, as Neerav, an Indian bio-medical general practitioner in my locality put it to me, 'we medical practitioners tend to regard alternative health practitioners as barefoot doctors'.[11] Yet he also added that as far as he was concerned, alternative practitioners should be regarded as useful additions to the health market. For 'many patients go to see their doctor with conditions that don't need treating medically. These people would be much better off going to alternative practitioners who can spend time with them…and just listen to what they have to say'. Therefore here Neerav appears to make a distinction between types of illness and dis-ease, with 'significant' pathological conditions requiring bio-medical treatment, social and psychological dis-ease, alternative therapies. Hence, there appears to be, in Fife and Kinross at least, some disharmony between bio-medical and holistic approaches to health with regard to the complementarity of the latter to the former.

10. This sort of positioning leads academic writer John Drane to propose in *What is the New Age Saying to the Church* (1991), that conventional, rationalistic, scientific medicine could be seen as being more at odds with the Christian viewpoint than New Age healing. For conventional medicine's rationalism 'consistently denies that there is anything that might be labelled a spiritual dimension to the human personality, and insists that the body is a totally self-contained and independent mechanical system. At least the New Age outlook affirms that people have a spiritual dimension, however muddled and mistaken the New Age concept of that spirit might be' (1991: 160). Therefore for Drane, New Age healing may appear to provide the Christian seeker with a spiritual dimension to bodily health, a dimension that is missing in conventional medicine.

11. The fact that this practitioner is Indian is of interest in that he also espoused the value of Ayurvedic medicine. Hence one wonders whether non-Western bio-medical practitioners hold the same positioning on folk medicine 'as less' as is common in the West.

And while consumers of 'medical care' do have options when it comes to the treatment of their bodies, it still appears to be the case that bio-medical approaches to health are often regarded as *the* authoritative discourse. For while, as Bax has suggested, Western consumers can, and indeed do, resist bio-medicine's monopoly on health it still appears to be the case that it is very common to turn to this first with a problematic health condition, while the complementary health practitioner will be 'the one to see' with chronic and unresolved conditions 'as a last resort'. I shall revisit some of these points later in relation to new ascriptions of meaning with regard to health. So let us, for the moment, return to a primary underlying theme in all discourses relating to health and the body — power.

I shall introduce initially Foucault's discourse on 'power'. My primary focus here however, will be on medical sociologists' use of this theorist in relation to health, medicine, power and knowledge. For as Brian Turner states, Foucault's analysis of power/knowledge has had a major impact on medical sociology, shifting this under theoretically directed discipline 'towards a sociology of health and illness, that is a critical epistemology of disease categories as elements of the moral control of individuals and populations. This movement was based on an implicit slogan, namely that the 'body is historical' (1997: ix).

The Body and Power

Foucault's Theory of Power

Foucault has critiqued historical conceptualizations of power 'as a macro structure such as the state which functioned to support industrial capitalism and which was displayed through the major public institutions such as the police, the law and the church' (Turner 1997: xi). For power, he argued, was not located in a central point from which 'secondary and descendant forms would emanate' (Foucault 1994: 163). Rather, power's 'condition of possibility' (Foucault 1994: 163) lies in fluid, unequal, unstable, local, force relations, where it is continually produced and exercised in innumerable day-to-day interactions. Hence there are multiple relations of power embedded in the workplace, in institutions, within families, and in sexual relations and knowledges — these causing divisions, inequalities and cleavages within society as a whole. For power is always exercised with a set of aims and objectives (Foucault 1994: 164).

Foucault further argues that within power relationships and networks one will also find multiple points of resistance. Such resistances are inscribed in relations of power as an 'irreducible opposite' (Foucault 1994: 165) and that they cause shifting societal cleavages and regroupings at local and individual levels.

> Just as the network of power relations ends by forming a dense web that passes through apparatuses and institutions, without being exactly localized to them, so too the swarm of points of resistance traverses social stratifications and individual unities. And it is doubtless the strategic codification of these points of resistance that makes a revolution possible...It is in this sphere of force relations that we must try to analyze the mechanisms of power (Foucault 1994: 166).

I would argue that we would do well to look within the 'umbrella' of 'healing practice' to see if there are codifications of healing points of resistance. For as I have shown, healing practitioners do resist dualistic notions of mind and body, inscriptions of the female body as less and the 'containment' and 'treatment' of the body and spirit by bio-medicine and mainstream religion respectively. Healers also promote 'new' ideas and definitions of what it is to be a 'whole' human being within multivalanced discourses of power. Hence we must also examine, with a feminist hermeneutics of suspicion, the production of such discourses within 'the field of multiple and mobile power relations' (Foucault 1994: 166).

One starting point would be to look at local centres of power and knowledge and to examine how specific discourses of healing have been constructed, by whom and why? For if healing/being healed, is 'constituted as an area of investigation this [is] only because relations of power [have] established it as a possible object; and conversely, if power was able to take it as a target, this was because techniques of knowledge and procedures of discourse were capable of investing it' (Foucault 1994: 167). Hence at the local level of healing one finds multiple discourses of power relating to 'self-examination, questionings, admissions, interpretations, interviews [which are] the vehicle of a kind of incessant back-and-forth movement of subjugations and schemas of knowledge' (Foucault 1994: 167). There are local resistances to bio-medical and religious constructions of 'the body' by holistic notions of the same. And there are incorporations and regroupings of holistic healing, bio-medicine and religious 'influences' on health—the incorporation of therapeutic touch into nursing practice or the incorporation of

Christian elements into healing practice being possible examples here. For 'Relations of power-knowledge are not static forms of distribution, they are "matrices of transformations"' (Foucault 1994: 167).

Foucault also proposed that 'power' is intimately connected to 'discipline', in that disciplinary practices produce individuals and institutions. His interests in power were also very much tied into an evaluation of how, historically, human subjects have 'been made'. For societies have always produced ideals of 'proper' bodies, minds and souls in order to define their own boundaries and identities. In *Discipline and Punish*, he describes discipline in the following manner,

> "Discipline" may be identified neither with an institution nor with an apparatus; it is a type of power, a modality for its exercise, comprising a whole set of instruments, techniques, procedures, levels of application, targets; it is a "physics" or an "anatomy" of power, a technology. And it may be taken over by "specialized institutions", (the penitentiaries or 'houses of correction' of the nineteenth century), or by preexisting authorities that find it a means of reinforcing or reorganizing their mechanisms of power" (Foucault 1984).

'Disciplinary modalities of power' (Foucault 1984) have continued to infiltrate all levels of society to the present day and may be found in, for example, schools, hospitals, psychiatric and psychological services at the micro level. No area of society is left untouched. 'On the whole, therefore, one can speak of the formation of a disciplinary society in this movement that stretches from the enclosed disciplines, a sort of social 'quarantine,' to an indefinitely generalizable mechanism of '"panopticism"' (Foucault 1984). where the principles of the same are 'institutionalized through everyday routines and mundane arrangements' (Turner 1997: xii).[12] Correspondingly,

12. The architectural principle of the Panopticon (prison) was that of a central observation tower from which the warder could see each inmate in his/her single cell (these in a semi-circle facing in towards the tower). However, the inmate could neither observe the warder, know when he was being observed, or see any other inmate. The principle underlying this construction was that of constant observation alongside a highly disciplined work regime with the aim of producing a remade 'ordered' individual who could, upon release, contribute to society as a whole. However, 'the major effect of the Panopticon: to induce to the inmate a state of conscious and permanent visibility that assures the automatic functioning of power' (Foucault 1977: 201) was also intimately related to 'self-discipline'. For in order to be released the prisoner had to internalize and act out 'normal', regimented behaviour at all times and be subjected to the anonymous gaze.

A real subjection is born mechanically from a fictitious relation. So it is not necessary to use force to constrain the convict to good behaviour, the madman to calm, the worker to work, the schoolboy to application, the patient to the observation of regulations. He who is subjected to the field of visibility, and who knows it, assumes responsibility for the constraints of power; he makes them play spontaneously upon himself; he inscribes in himself the power relation in which he simultaneously plays both roles; he becomes the principle of his own subjection (Foucault 1977: 201-202).

It is outwith the scope, and indeed the intention, of this book to provide a Foucauldian analysis of healing in Scotland. However, what I wish to bring out in the above is Foucault's concept of the 'all seeing gaze' and the corresponding 'subjection' of the observed; this occurring in bio-medical approaches to health and mainstream religious observance of the moral condition and disciplining of the soul. But it is not just in these fields that 'the gaze' may be observed. Within Scottish healing circles the healee is also submitted to 'the energetic gaze' in the form of auric reading. Hence, questions should be asked in relation to the multiple discourses and resistances to knowledge and power. I shall return to some of these issues in Chapter Seven. For the moment, let us examine some writers' use of Foucault in the fields of medical sociology, noting their relevance to this particular study.

Medical Sociology

Sarah Cant and Ursula Sharma propose 'it is possible to consider the general significance of complementary medical knowledges within the context of larger theoretical debates about the nature of knowledge in contemporary societies' (1996: 2). They are particularly interested in how and why some discourses of knowledge are publicly legitimized while others are discredited and how this relates to the perceived authority of experts. They also propose that 'complementary medical knowledge operates on a number of levels (formal and informal, local and general)' (1996: 3) and that it would be wrong to look at complementary knowledge solely in abstract and codified forms for 'knowledge is always "knowledge in practice"' (1996: 3).

As we shall see in later ethnographic material, there does, indeed in the Scottish context, appear to be many levels of healing 'practice as knowledge' as Cant and Sharma have proposed. Yet, healing knowledge in Scottish healing circles, while having common underlying themes such as 'the energetic body' and 'the connectedness of all life' does appear to differ in its application according to local/informal or urban/formal settings and in relation to written 'theological' accounts of 'divine energy as healing power'. Hence they are absolutely correct to argue the case for always locating knowledge in practice for, as I have mentioned earlier in this chapter, tension does exist in relation to hierarchies of power and the healthy or dis-eased body across not just between bio-medical and complementary perspectives but also within complementary fields in themselves.

Cant and Sharma state that since the nineteenth century, healing and folk medicine has been relegated to the realms of unscientific naivety or even quackery by orthodox fields of medical knowledge and practice. Being located as such has led complementary therapists to 'operate from a position of needing to establish their own credentials as "experts" and their own worthiness' (1996: 3). They draw from Foucault's (1975) *Birth of the Clinic* to elaborate on how bio-medical practitioners have promoted their status as experts while also progressively impersonalizing the human body. For Foucault, they state, medicine is a form of discursive practice where from the eighteenth century, medical practitioners have objectified the patient's body, gazing upon it to decide upon a course of treatment. In turn this form of medical observation considerably negated the value of the patient's own experiences of his or her bodily symptoms. For Foucault,

> The rise of a medical practice based on [the] objectifying "gaze" is related to the requirements of more precise modes of surveillance and control of populations (Foucault 1975: 1977). However, the exercise of the medical gaze is not simply "influenced by" or "a product of" the needs of the state or any other agency. Chez Foucault, the exercise of the medical gaze is the exercise of power itself, for power is dispersed and embedded in practices — the practices of the clinic as much as the practices of the state bureaucracy, the militia, the police, even the family (Cant and Sharma 1996: 11).

However, Cant and Sharma also argue that Foucault 'comes close to identifying medical knowledge as what Mauss called a "technique of the body", a socially learnt way of using the body, albeit experienced as entirely "natural" by those who practice' (Cant and

Sharma 1996: 11). This, they argue, may be seen in the way that medical students learn from their teachers in relation to 'cultivate[ing] a certain kind of moral subjectivity…for example, learning how to write up a case, to look for signs and symptoms, to "think anatomically" about people' (Good in Cant and Sharma 1996: 13). I would propose therefore, that as in this case, 'Biomedical knowledge in its abstract form is presented as the scientific and generalizable knowledge of every-day body and no-body which may obscure the fact that it is nonetheless socially produced and reproduced' (Cant and Sharma 1996: 13) one should also include gender as a category for analysis in any evaluation of health and the body.

For example, Margaret Shildrick states that women may complicitly support bio-medical and societal strategies of normalization 'over' their bodies with the acceptance and promotion of some forms of health care — these being seen by women as beneficial for women. From this perspective modern bio-medical 'surveillance', as found in the ultrasound of pregnancy or the triannual check-up for the elderly woman '…is characterized by the strategies of normalization which constantly measure, assess, record and project the limits of health' (Shildrick 1997: 57). However, Shildrick also proposes that once women recognize that 'strategies of normalization' are in place, then 'If it can be demonstrated that what has been naturalized as the truth of the female body is merely the discontinuous outcome of a complex series of normalizations, in which health care has been pre-eminently implicated, then it becomes possible to dissolve that devalued identity and theorize new constructions of female embodiment' (1997: 59).

The issues that Shildrick raises here are of considerable importance to this study of New Age healing. For the inclusion of this sort of analytical framework in relation to, for example, the 'naturalness' of the female body can usefully be transferred to the fields of complementary healing practice. The adoption of this perspective allows us to examine whether women develop new models of subjectivity within healing circles and if so, how these 'relate' to earlier 'incorporated' bio-medical interpretative frameworks.

I would further argue that once we continually employ a feminist hermeneutic of suspicion, we can ask questions regarding the formulation of 'alternative' models of health and see whether there are in situ in this field of practice, normalizing concepts and discourses relating to identity, power and the body. For in this field one finds that the complementary practitioner's knowledge of his or her clients is based on information taught and practice obtained in particular training schools, where the practitioner learns 'how sickness is caused and cured, and how bodies work with minds' (Heelas 1996: 13). And as very often that school is far from local being, for example, based on Eastern or Hindu philosophies, or in the case of Reiki coming from Japan, then it is important to appreciate there will be several layers of representation between 'source' material and end 'knowledge as practice'. Therefore while New Age healing may appear to provide a new holistic framework where the intellect, the body and the sacred may be interrelated with feelings, emotion and touch, we still should be aware of the underlying, often hidden discourses of power and their effect on the 'local' individual.

Brian Turner proposes that one of Foucault's key theoretical contributions was his examination of how early civilizations and the Christian church 'produced the self through practices of self-subjection' (Turner 1997: xii). This was related to the ethical systems underpinning Christianity and consisted of three processes. First, an ethical substance such as desire was identified, this to be 'shaped by moral activity' (Turner 1997: xii). Second, the individual had to feel morally obliged to subject him or herself to, for example, God. In turn ethical codes and discourses were constructed around such 'moral obligations'. 'These discourses of subjectivity then produce identities or roles...[and] become the object and focus of medicalization and normalization' (Turner 1997: xii).

> These practices of subjection and self-formation also involve the emergence of complex pedagogies of self-transformation and education...Finally, subjection requires the production of a moral order and an ethical ethos which becomes the organizing principle of practices of the self; a moral code evolves by which moral identities are shaped and guided. In contemporary society, these goals typically include not only the ideology of self-fulfilment through self-knowledge, but a range of preventative health policies and measures which can be seen as an extension of these self-regulatory activities (Turner 1997: xii-xiii).

I would like to pull out several threads here. I would suggest in relation to healing in Scotland that there are several 'ethical substances' which have been identified as 'in need of shaping'. The primary emphasis in this field relates to the mind and the ego and the subjection of these to 'allow through' the 'divinely inspired attribute' of 'love'. For this to occur the healee subjects herself/himself to God—or whatever name is used for the same —in that she 'allows herself to become a free channel through which healing energy may flow'. This sort of discourse of subjectivity then, produces roles and identities. In healing circles this is often 'the compassionate and nurturing healer'. For the healer is taught that in order to progress along the healing path s/he should continually work in a disciplined manner towards greater openness and receptivity so that s/he can be self-transformed and free from the desire-ridden drives of the ego. In order to assist the healer in this process and provide moral order and ethical guidelines there is a whole range of self-regulatory activities, these being provided by, at the higher levels of teaching and writing, predominantly men. And as Turner further proposes that for Foucault, 'power and knowledge [are] always inevitably and inextricably interconnected so that any increase in knowledge and every elaboration of knowledge involve[s] an increase of power' (1997: xiii) then one should, I would propose, bring to the evaluation of these discourses a feminist hermeneutics of suspicion.[13] This is why I shall be bringing in to the later evaluation of healing ontologies the writing of Daly, Joan Scott *et al.*

Feminism and New Age Spiritualities

Dominick Corrywright argues that 'feminist enquiry includes, ever increasingly, women's spirituality, an area which pertains especially to the field of New Age' (2003: 62). As we have seen, feminist enquiry is also central to Goddess spiritually, where traditional patriarchal religious representations of the woman's body and health are rejected in favour of an alternative worldview where the woman's body is resacralized due to the 'intimate, imminent, connection with the Goddess'. But feminism does more than this.

13. We shall also see in the chapters on Reiki how one writer, Diane Stein, has 'bust open' closed systems of 'knowledge only for the initiated' in her disclosure of the Reiki symbols, her aim being to enable all to learn Reiki.

Feminism as a field of study 'can be seen as a method of study which creates the object of its study. It uncovers a field of research, and unmasks reasons for the oversight of this field' (2003: 62). Think back here to Griffin's statement that it was very difficult to obtain academic research funding for Goddess spirituality and my comments on the general absence of women (apart from in quantitative surveys) in academic writing about New Age thought and practice.

Corrywright also observes that feminism is engaged in two projects, these projects closely resembling New Age spiritualities. Feminism negatively critiques existing patriarchal forms of societal structure while simultaneously creating a positive, harmonious vision of the future; this relating to postmodern concern, perceived decline in institutional authority and the 'relativisation of knowledge in conflict with juridical and scientific truth…[This involves for women] *active challenge*, whether or not that role is the final objective' (2003: 63-64 [italics mine]). Hence, practitioners of both feminist and New Age spiritualities:

- Develop a structured critique of past and present religious practices.
- Engage in the historical recovery and appropriation of belief, practice and human exemplars for a feminist spirituality.
- Develop and apply a methodology which reflects women's interests, knowledge and biological skills (and here Corrywright refers to mothering and menstruation).
- Elaborate a new 'mystical feminism' or 'feminist spirituality' (Corrywright 2003: 64).

These themes are observable in the Scottish context but with varying emphasis on particular themes. However, all women healees do regard themselves as active agents, in that they are reconstructing notions of gendered identity, not necessarily as 'of the Goddess', but there is emphasis in general on the female—and indeed male—body 'as sacralized' and in constant contact with 'all that is'.

Meredith McGuire has examined in the American context how religion and 'religious-like' beliefs, practices and rituals are being used in nonmedical healing groups and 'quasi-religious movements.[14] For here, too, emphasis is placed on gender identity

14. McGuire describes quasi religious movements as forms of non-official religious expression, historical examples being 'folk healing cults, witchcraft and spirit possession cults' (1994: 276).

transformations. This becomes a possibility with the creation of rituals and the construction of 'new images of what it means to be a man or woman' (1994: 274). She makes the point that 'gendered spirituality may be a prime example of ...new work for religion to accomplish' (1994: 274) as individuals reflect upon and develop new ideas of personal identity and autonomy. This may be of particular relevance as non-medical healing rituals often address 'gender-specific physical-emotional-spiritual needs of members' (1994: 274) and may be carried out for stillbirths, reproductive problems, hysterectomies and sexual or spousal abuse. These are obviously immensely traumatic events for the person concerned and surely flag up personal dissatisfaction with mainstream religious and bio-medical responses to the same. Correspondingly, issues of power must be central here and the re-empowerment of women. This is an area of research that women would want and need, and must be addressed with urgency so that practical assistance can enter the human arena (rather than stay on an academic shelf).

McGuire observes that while 'gendered spirituality movements' appear to be related to healing movements in that 'healing' is a prominent motif in both, she notes that they do differ in their emphasis on the possibility for *transformation* of 'gendered identities'. For some healing groups maintain traditional standpoints in relation to gender roles and moral constraints. This is relevant to the Scottish context in that within Reiki circles there does appear to be some fixity of gender role with women often locating themselves relationally as wives and mothers in the first instance. However, McGuire argues that 'Both responses [traditional healing and gendered spirituality] are necessarily active, because traditional gender roles and moral constraints can never be taken for granted' (1994: 275). Similarly, her observation that the 'core nature of gender identity and its expression has become open, fluid, even voluntary. Individuals have multiple options of what it is to be a man or a woman' (1994: 275) is also of relevance to this study. For healers do regard their bodies and emotions not 'as givens, but as reflexibly malleable parts of one's identity' (1994: 275).

> One's identity — including one's gender identity — thus becomes a continuing project to be accomplished. Rather than fading away in the sunset of secularization, religious and quasi-religious groups may become more important, in this situation, as the source of images of ideals and alternatives, as the social setting for self-transformation,

and as the mutual support for these identities. In the face of a relatively pluralistic and open set of possibilities, gender identities must be *accomplished*, rather than given. Religious and quasi-religious beliefs and practices appear to be important paths (among others) for doing identity work in modern societies (1994: 275).

In this chapter I have continued to construct a picture of how women 'as healer' or 'as healed' construct new seemingly empowered identities acting within fluid fields of force. I have also set some foundations for the next section of ethnographic material where I examine the specifics of healing practice in the Scottish context with particular focus on energetic healing, Reiki and the technique of dowsing. Here we shall find that new identities are constructed and that transformation 'to healer' is a life altering experience. For 'If the creation, maintenance, and transformation of individuals' gender identities are, among the foremost identity work to be accomplished, then extensive empirical study of the many contemporary instances of gendered spirituality is very worthwhile' (McGuire 1994: 284). This book is hence another step in the 'empirical direction'.

Chapter Four

ENERGETIC BODIES

Introduction

The body 'as energetic' is a central motif within New Age healing circles in Scotland. Therefore within this more descriptive chapter I shall begin to provide a picture of how this has been variously represented in relation to, for example, the agency of the gendered body. Overall I shall provide a conceptual framework for further ethnographic material (as found in Chapters Five and Six) where I shall 'mix and match' New Age textual material with experiential accounts of Reiki healing and practice. In turn these will be related to academic evaluations of healing, gender and power. For as McGuire has observed in relation to healing in the suburban American context,

> Power is a fundamental (if not the fundamental) category for interpreting healing...each type of healing group has distinct beliefs about the loci of the power to heal (or to cause illness) as well as different ideas about ways to channel and control that power. Etiologies of illness yield information about the group's ideas of illness causing power, and therapies embody ideas about how that illness causing power can be overcome by other sources/kinds of power. From this perspective, the treatment of illness is essentially the restoration of the balance of power—by weakening the antagonist's (disease-causing) power or by strengthening the victim's power (McGuire 1998: 226).

Central to all discussions of power in the Scottish healing context is 'the body as energetic'. My first experience of the body being described in this way was in 1995, when I visited a healer and chiropractor in Edinburgh following a period of poor health. This healer, over several months, not only enabled me to be dis-ease free but also introduced me to a whole new way of regarding my body, my self and my life. He provided a new framework of meaning which made sense to me and which felt empowering. This was based around the 'energetic whole' which encompassed 'the aura and chakras'. I was fascinated and wanted to know more. For here was a 'new' description of the world that seemed to present opportunities for health and wholeness of self and others that diverged from Western scientific and biomedical paradigms. So I began to peruse textual material and discuss this with interested friends. One of the texts that appeared to be highly recommended — and much utilized in healing circles — was Barbara Ann Brennan's 1988, *Hands of Light*. This training guide's focus is on 'how to see auras' and 'how to heal through the human energy field'. After much practice, guided by Brennan's book, I learnt the basics of how to see auras myself. Unsurprisingly this caused a major shift in my sense of 'how the world works' for here was a framework within which there appeared to be the potential to work on the self as an ongoing project and, in turn, learn to heal others.

When I heard of a healing workshop based on Brennan's work, it seemed a wonderful opportunity to do research in a field of personal interest. Hence I shall look initially at how Brennan's book provided the basis for this healing workshop at the Salisbury Centre in Edinburgh,[1] with a mix of her textual accounts of healing and descriptions of practice. Following on from this I will provide further ethnographic material relating to an evening 'Healing Circle', also held at the Salisbury Centre, for here too 'the energetic body' was the central interpretative medium for practical work and healing 'through the aura' as was an emphasis on 'connecting with our spirit guides'. Meredith McGuire shall be drawn from throughout to enable comparative evaluation of the British to American contexts. Some background then to the Salisbury Centre.

The Salisbury Centre

William Sawbridge, his wife Ludivina, Dr Winifred Rushforth, Mrs Anne Macauley and Revd Peter Lewis initially set up the Salisbury Trust in 1972. The Trust's aims were,

- The advancement of education in the unity of religious ideals in particular by the provision of courses in comparative religion and metaphysical and associated religious and spiritual subjects.

---

1. I shall also return to her writing in Chapter Seven where I argue that healers 'work' within dynamic, decentralized and fluid 'fields of force' (Foucault 1980).

- The help and education of young people to develop their physical, mental and spiritual capacities and their self-discipline and loyalty to mankind so that they may grow to full maturity as individuals and members of society and that their conditions of life may be improved in particular (inter alia) by the provision of courses and instruction in techniques of self discipline in the interests of social welfare.
- The provision of and research into spiritual healing to those in need and the relief and prevention of suffering caused by mental and physical ill-health or by social or economic circumstances.
- To co-operate fully with any other organization having similar objectives.
(Extract Registered, Deed of Trust, The Salisbury Trust, 1972).

In accord with the above objectives, The Salisbury Centre was set up in Edinburgh, this currently having a resident staff of three. It is now one of Edinburgh's most popular New Age locations. Their quarterly brochure[2] portrays this large house as a 'Holistic Education Centre for Body, Mind and Spirit' (SC1). It is a place where the visitor can take part in many types of evening or weekend workshops. There is a constantly changing range of these, some regularly presented options being pottery, sculpture, sacred dance, meditation, yoga and the 'traditional Chinese internal arts of Tai Ji Quan and Qi Gong' (SC1). Workshops are run every weekend of the year apart from during the Christmas period, when centre staff are on holiday. Each of these workshops has on average ten participants with many return 'seekers'. There are also weekday classes where one may learn, for example, baby massage, yoga for pregnancy, Pilates and relaxation techniques and regular evening classes in yoga, meditation, and self-developmental 'techniques'. There is also a resident Sufi group which meets bi-weekly, and a weekly healing group, The Salisbury Healers. Both of these groups are open to newcomers.

In accord with the Trust's objectives, emphasis is placed in all courses on a holistic approach to life and health, with visitors reflecting similar concerns. As one woman visitor in her thirties put it to me, 'I have come here to learn how to live life as it should be lived…fully…with love…and in the here and now'.

2. All pamphleture, brochure and workshop manuals are drawn from the researcher's personal files. These are referred to in the text by abbreviations and are detailed in 'Appendix A, Primary New Age Sources', this preceding the bibliography.

It was, then, to this centre that I travelled in the summer of 2001 to participate in a weekend workshop based on Barbara Ann Brennan's teachings. This was entitled 'Healing Through Consciousness' and the facilitator, Helen, had trained in Brennan's school in America for several years.

This was very much an experiential workshop with emphasis being placed on 'trying it out for yourself'. In practice this meant that participants would take part in an exploration of the human body where 'the dense physical aspects' were seen to be just the visible part of the 'energetic whole'. Most people present had heard of the aura and chakras, but knowledge of how to actually feel or sense these aspects appeared to be minimal. The ten participants, seven women and three men, were aged between thirty and sixty-five.

This workshop was held in the large and airy first floor teaching and practice room. The floor was of polished wood and piles of brightly coloured cushions lay stacked against the walls. A large bay window overlooked wooded gardens. This is a typical setting for healing 'work' and one gets the sense that emphasis is placed on providing a calming and soothing environment where participants should feel safe to disclose personal thoughts and feelings — to work on the self. The lack of formal seating arrangement, for example, fostered a sense of being part of a group in that attendees mainly sat in a circle on the floor, with shoes removed. Hence openness and receptivity appeared to be the attributes to be fostered.

The Manifestation of Illness

Helen opened the weekend by telling us that what we would learn at this workshop should be regarded as a good basis for any further practice of 'healing through the energy field'. We would learn how to restore health to the physical body by utilizing Barbara Ann Brennan's writing on energy work. For, Helen argued, although within a scientific viewpoint everything, including our physical body, is made up of energy — with the physical body appearing solid due to the density of this energy — there was much more to bodily interpretation than this. For, as stated in Helen's workshop manual,

> the physical energetic body actually grows on the matrix of the aura
> so that whatever is happening in your energy field you will develop
> in your physical self. This means that a healer will work on damaged

or blocked areas in the energy fields in order to heal corresponding dis-ease in the body...Healers across the world know this energy by many other names such as Chi, Prana and Yin-Yang complementarity (WMH 2001).

Further details were provided.

The aura shows all thoughts and emotions. Those who can see the aura describe it as a flowing field of colours and feelings.

When our thoughts and feelings are healthy and clear the physical body follows suit, but as this is the real world life has a tendency to get in the way.

If we are suffering in some way emotionally these feelings are then taken on and held by the physical body. Every cell in our body has a memory bank, as well as our brain, and all of our experiences are held somewhere in this cellular memory.

If enough so-called negative emotions are held the body can erupt and become ill – whether in an emotional or physical sense...

Bodywork, whether it be massage, healing, reflexology, or many other therapies help the body to clear the emotions it no longer needs to hold on to, and thus helps the body to return to a state of balance and health.

In most instances we are unconscious of what is happening, and healing is about us becoming conscious of what we are holding and doing in life. When we are conscious we have something to work on and the map of ourselves becomes a lot more readable (WMH 2001: 2).

Therefore within this initial framework there are considerable similarities with McGuire's findings in the American healing context. For she argues that non-scientific medical healing ontologies provide the individual with a therapeutic meaning system which ' "work" because they provide meaning and empirical proofs in support of their explanations...illness is named and given cultural form' (1998: 235). Hence 'ways of being' are promoted that should be implemented throughout daily life. The starting point in this instance was 'learning how to see auras'.

Sensing Auras

Helen advised us that if we wished to learn how to sense the aura for ourselves then Brennan's *Hands of Light* was an excellent book to learn from. For in this text Brennan describes the ability to see or sense the aura as High Sense Perception or HSP. With this sense one perceives things beyond the normal range of the human senses. Once a person has re-learnt HSP, they will see revealed 'the dynamic world of fluid interacting life energy fields around and through all things...this energy supports us, nourishes us, gives us life. We sense each other with it; we are of it; it is of us' (Brennan 1988: 5).

Brennan argues that the way to develop HSP is to 'enter into an expanded sense of consciousness' (1988: 6). This she states can be achieved through meditation or by simply 'silenc[ing] the noisy mind...[so that] a whole new world of sweet harmonious reality opens up to you' (1988: 6), a reality which previously was outside of perceptual range. In turn, once one learns to develop HSP then one's individuality will be enhanced (1988: 6) by being part of an interconnected energetic whole.

One might ask questions here, however, as to whether Brennan produces the energetic body as an object of study upon which healers (and the individual) can work. Is this possibly, *à la Foucault*, a technology of power where the individual is taught how to conduct her/himself and thus maximise potential (as healed/healer) by further application of a technology of the self? For as Foucault has argued, individuals may 'effect by their own means or with the help of others a certain number of operations on their own bodies and souls, thought, conduct and ways of being so as to transform themselves' (Foucault 1988: 18), which in this case would be towards the 'whole' and healed human being. I shall return to these points in Chapter Seven.

It was therefore, to an exercise in 'sensing energy' that Helen first turned in the early stages of her 'Healing Through Consciousness' workshop. For this participants were to use a dowsing crystal to provide a visible representation of the energetic states of the chakras in the human body. The chakra system was presented in the following manner:

> The chakras play a role very similar to the organs of the physical body. In fact they are the organs of the energy body...The word Chakra means Wheel, and the chakras do in fact have movement, which is very important to understanding how the chakras work and their importance to our health (WMH 2001: 2).

Helen described the seven major chakras as running up the front and middle of the body from the 'tailbone' ending at the crown of the head. Each chakra was said to resemble 'an ice cream cone' with the base of each being located in the spinal column. It was from here 'in the vertical power current of the spine' that the wheel-like motion of the chakra would draw energy into the body. This energy would in turn dissipate through the spinal column to the rest of the body. I have summarised some of the further characteristics of the chakras as given.

1. Each governs a physical region of the body and an emotional state.
2. Each chakra is also 'governed by a colour, and the colours follow that of the rainbow', with the root chakra at the base of the spine being 'seen' as red.
3. Hence, this red root chakra 'helps keep us close to the earth [while] as we move further away from the earth the colours become softer and lighter'.
4. There are partner chakras at the back of the body as 'all areas of the body should be in balance if a person is healthy'. Therefore 'much can be discovered by examining the balance between the front, and back of the body'.
5. Each chakra has a 'screen on the wide part furthest away from the physical body. This screen literally does screen information, and often times can become torn or disfigured in some way. When this happens the protective element of the screen is removed, and information that is in some way harmful can be absorbed' (WMH 2001: 1-2).

Helen also advised us that these 'screens' vary at different times in a human being's life. For example, newborn infants do not have protective screens on the surface of their chakras, it being for this reason that 'babies and young children need the protection of an adult's aura to keep them safe'. However, she added that adults will also have daily changes in the state of their auras according to what is happening in their lives. 'For generally you will find that there are certain patterns which remain [in the energetic body] until our process has evolved and cleared' (WMH 2001: 3).

This last statement again ties well into the commonly held New Age perspective that illness is first reflected in damage in the energetic body and that trained healers can pick up signs of this before actual physical illness manifests. It ought to be noted however that, in the Scottish context at least, the majority of people visit a healer when their body is 'displaying' some sort of physical disease. I have not heard personal narratives from people who have visited a healer with 'auric trauma' before this manifested at a physical level. Rather, once a person has incorporated 'new' energetic epistemologies into their 'way of life' then they are more likely to describe a period of personal dis-ease as being attributable to 'blockages in the chakras'. I would argue, in similarity to the American context, that epistemologies such as Brennan's foster a sense of order enabling the individual to understand the causes of dis-ease and manage their own health. Therefore as McGuire has found, healing 'is linked with personal empowerment; issues of meaning, moral order and responsibility; and alternative [non-medical] understanding of the self in relationship to society' (McGuire 1998: 202).

The Meaning of Illness

It is with statements such as Brennan's, 'It is essential that we deal with the deeper meaning of our illnesses. We need to ask, what does this illness mean to me? What can I learn from this illness?' (1987: 7) that a framework is set up wherein the nature of 'being dis-eased' is further signified. For writers such as Brennan also state that illness is simply a message from the physical body that some life situation is being ignored. Therefore the way to resolve this situation–which does not necessarily mean the negation or removal of physical/emotional 'symptoms' but may also mean the acceptance of the same–is couched very much in an evolutionary sense. From this perspective then, a person evolves as a 'true' individual when s/he returns to 'walk a spiritual path'. Note Brennan's following positioning.

> A return to health requires much more personal work and change than simply taking pills prescribed by a doctor. Without personal change you will simply create another problem to lead you back to that source that caused the disease in the first place. I have found that the source is the key. To deal with the source usually requires a life change that ultimately leads to a personal life more connected to the core of one's being. It leads to a deeper part of ourselves that is sometimes called the high self or the spark of divinity within (1987: 7).

I would propose that this sort of thinking needs to be examined in relation to the agency of the gendered body. For on a very simple level, while it promotes the idea that an individual must look at life circumstances and change them, this I would suggest might not always be possible. For while certainly an individual may make beneficial changes in relation to their diet or exercise regimes, when it comes to 'bigger picture' issues, such as marital disharmony or financial difficulties, then these kinds of dis-ease inducing actualities may be seen to be more 'fixed'. For I have found in Scottish healing contexts that there appear to be many layers of perception relating to one's potentiality to return to a state of health. Those women that I have met who have chosen to change their life circumstances have, in the majority, been economically able to do so. They have come from white, predominantly middle-class, financially comfortable lifestyles with good educational qualifications. They have been able to afford to visit a New Age healer in the first place so that they can enable their, to use Helen's words, 'process to evolve'.

Writers such as Brennan also often incorporate into their healing practice emphasis on the scientific location of the same. For there is a tendency to interpret the spiritual body and the sacred psychologically. Hence, in Brennan's case, 'enabling one's process to evolve' would be rooted in an awareness of our 'character structure' or psychological type. This she bases on Wilhelm Reich's research to which she adds an energetic overlay of aura and chakra patterns. Brennan states that Reich found that the people he treated could be fitted into five major character types. For Reich,

> people with similar childhood experiences and child/parent relations had similar bodies…people with similar bodies had similar basic psychological dynamics. These dynamics were dependent not only on the types of child/parent relations, but also on the age at which the child first experiences life so traumatically that it begins to block its feelings and therefore the flow of energy and to develop the defence system that will become habitual (Brennan 1988: 109).

I do feel that it becomes problematic, however, when Brennan uses a framework that categorizes people into Schizoid, Oral, Psychopathic, Masochistic or Rigid character structures (1988: 110-28). It is not clear why she is choosing a psychological framework to underpin her potentiality to heal the energetic body by seeing auras. What are the hidden socio-political discourses that cause her to choose to frame her arguments within such a scientific perspective? Why is she representing 'the person to be healed' within this sort of typology? For as Carrette states, 'psychological facts' arise out of and are part of particular historical conditions (2001: 116). 'In this sense psychological theory as much creates its objects and subjects as discovers them. Psychology sets up certain disciplinary conditions through which a particular body or subject can be defined' (2001: 116) and through which it will later be represented.

Hence, once more I would propose that it is necessary to acknowledge the interrelationship of the socially constructed gendered body with power, agency and knowledge, in relation to both the healer and healee. By doing so we can examine how 'the naturalness' of the human condition may be set up in the healing context and, if necessary, 'disturb the taken-for-grantedness and self-evidence' (Tyler in Peterson and Bunton 1997: 78) of the same. For in the healing context, and more specifically in the writing of Brennan, the healee is located within a 'psychologically typed' body through which they must complete their 'life process'. This will involve the individual in 'getting back in touch with their true nature' through following a spiritual path which will enable a deep reconnection with the 'high self' or 'divine spark' (Brennan, 1988: 7) within.

We will see how these points raised above relate to Helen's interpretation of 'defences and masks' later in this chapter. So let us return to the Salisbury Centre and take a further look at the chakra system and its relationship to emotional states.

The Chakras and Emotions

The presentation of the chakra system in Helen's workshop saw them being tied into two initial sets of groupings, these offering 'insights into our individual makeup' (WMH 2001: 4). The first grouping encompassed 'Reason, Will and Emotion'. For 'by looking at our chakras we can understand whether a person works from a position of reason, will or emotion (WMH 2001: 4). Therefore front chakras 2, 3, 4, 5, are *emotion* chakras, 1, 2, 3, 4, 5, back chakras are *will* chakras and chakras 6 and 7—both front and back—are *reason* chakras. The chakras are described as the 1st being at the root of the spine while the 7th is at the crown of the head.

The second grouping was, Helen stated, whether these chakras were of the earth or of the spirit. 'Our first three chakras are very much about our dealings and issue with earth based realities, whereas the top three chakras are a reflection of our spiritual abilities'. Hence, the earth based chakras 'give us the support to move into the higher worlds, and the spiritual chakras the insights to help us deal with life on earth'. In commonality with most

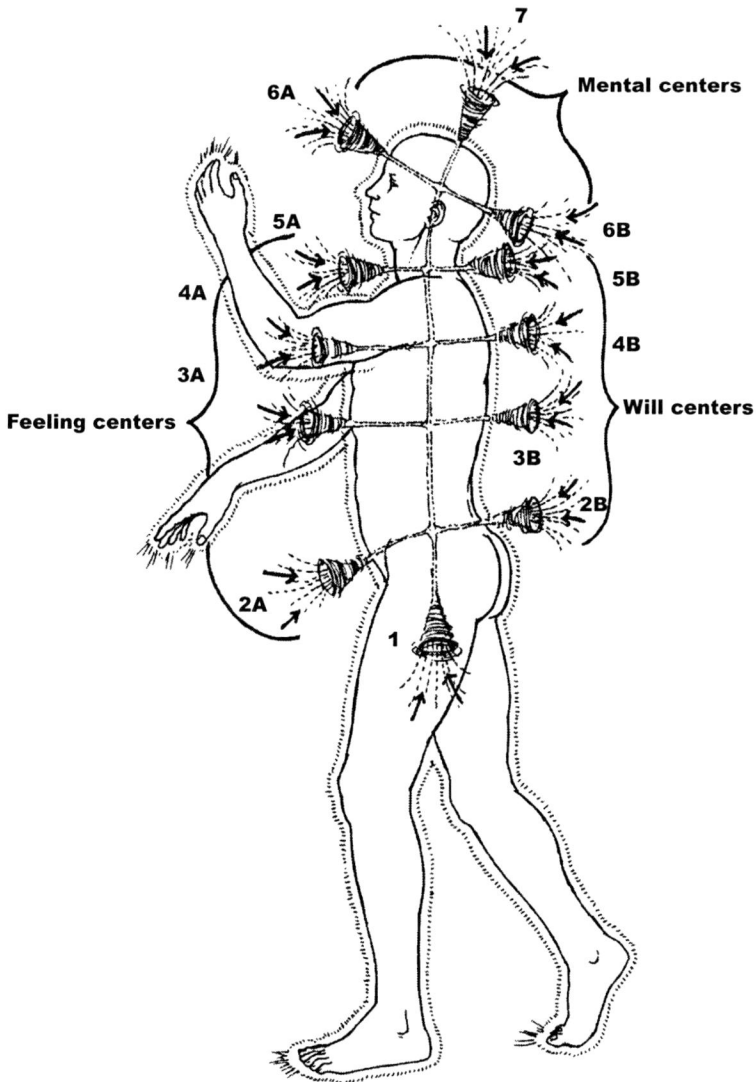

The Seven Major Chakras, Front and Back Views [Diagnostic View] (Brennan 1986: 46).

'energetic frameworks', Helen proposed that the heart chakra 'was the transforming centre for earth and spiritual energies to meet and express' (WMH 2001: 6). This I have heard as being commonly described as the need to 'open the heart to give and receive unconditional love'. Helen also proposed that for a person to be healthy, all the chakras, both front and back, must be 'in balance and support one another'. For 'when all the chakras are aligned we can move into the fullness of our individual essence–which is of course our life work' (WMH 2002: 6). Now Barbara Ann Brennan also states that 'the process of healing is really a process of remembering—remembering who you are' (1987: 147), where,

> No matter how miraculous the result, the healer really induces the patient to heal himself through natural processes, even though they are beyond what is considered to be natural for those who are not familiar with healing...When all the energies in each body are balanced, health occurs. The soul has learned its particular lesson and, therefore, has more cosmic truth (1987: 147).

We have in the above statements three clearly articulated standpoints. First, although the 'patient' is induced to heal him or herself this possibly 'miraculous' event still relies heavily, initially at least, on the expertise of the healer and the acknowledgement of what are 'natural processes' by all involved. As Helen put it 'along this journey of ours we often need helpers to assist in translating this map of ours, so it is important to find therapists with whom you resonate and feel safe' (WMH 2001: 2). Second, health is seen to be intimately related to the soul and its level of 'cosmic truth' (Brennan 1987: 147) in relation to each person's 'life work'. Now Brennan's elaboration on this is that the 'life task' has two forms.

> First, on a personal level, there is a personal task, which has the purpose of learning to express a new part of one's identity. The parts of the soul that are not one with God help form the specific incarnation in order to learn how to be one with the creator and still be individuated. The world task is a gift that each soul comes into this physical world to give to the world (1988: 109).

This whole set of suppositions rests on the premise that 'the energy fields contain the task of each soul. The character structure can then be seen as a crystallization of the basic problems or personal task a person has elected to incarnate and to solve...[with the basic malady being] self-hatred' (Brennan 1988: 110). Now, as it is to trained healers such as Brennan that many women and men turn, what we find, at least in the Scottish context, is that the healee must learn to recognize for him/herself, based on the healer's interpretative frameworks, what is their 'true life path' and how this can be realized. Further research would be useful here. Are 'life tasks' represented as having gender specificity? What might Brennan regard as key causes for feelings of self hatred? How might a person's individuality be enhanced by following such paths?

The energetic body was represented to workshop participants in the following manner (see Chakra Characteristics).

Chakra Characteristics

Chakra number	Physical place on body	Endocrine Gland	Area of body governed	Meaning to emotional health	Statement made	Colour
1	Base of the tail bone	Adrenals	Spinal column, Kidneys, bladder	Quantity of physical energy, will to live	I want to live	Red
2	Just above pubic bone	Gonads	Reproductive system	Relationship to self and sexuality — feelings of self esteem	I love myself	Orange
3	Solar plexus, stomach	Pancreas	Stomach, liver, gall bladder, nervous system	Intellectual clarity. Who you are in the universe. Feelings towards health	I think	Yellow
4	Heart	Thymus	Heart, blood, vagus nerve. Circulatory system	Love for self and others. Ability to open to love. Openness to life, Ego	I love mankind	Green
5	Throat	Thyroid	Bronchial, Lungs, Vocal Apparatus, Alimentary canal	Communication, Sense of self in life. Connection with the divine.	I connect with divine will	Blue
6	Brow, forehead	Pituitary	Lower Brain Left eye, ears and nose, nervous system	Feels love for all beings. Capacity to visualize and carry out ideas	I love all. I see clearly	Indigo
7	Crown of head	Pineal	Upper brain. Right eye	Integration of life and spiritual aspects of mankind	I know	White (violet)

(Tabulated from information in WMH 2001)

Helen emphasized to us that it is important that each of the chakras is worked with to clear any imbalances for all are of intertwining significance. Yet, I have noted that there also appears to be a tendency with some healees to regard reconnection with 'spirit' through healthy crown and brow chakras as of more initial importance than working on root and 'sexual' lower chakras. And although Helen did state that this sort of thinking was attributable to a 'faulty belief system' it is still, I would suggest, a possible legacy of dualistic notions of 'higher spirit' and 'lower body' so prevalent in Western Christian cultures. Where, to use Helen's words, 'earth based realities' may be passed over or accepted, in favour of 'the spiritual quest'.

In order to obtain 'a visible picture' of energy flowing through the charkas, participants were next shown how to use a dowsing crystal. We were advised that the swing and rotation of the same was indicative of auric states. For, while it appears to be commonly accepted in healing circles that the energetic fields practically exist, to actually 'see' a representation of the same through a visible medium is of considerable importance in the confirmation of energetic ontologies.

Exercises such as dowsing also suggest that the possibility of self-validating certain practices in the healing context is of as much importance as 'healer presented' belief systems regarding the same. For while it is common to hear healers recounting 'privileged wisdom' such as 'what the angels, spirit guides or Ascended Masters have said to me', these appear to often be regarded as a personalized interpretation or addition to the development of 'natural' intuitive healing and divinatory abilities. Therefore what we appear to have in the Scottish healing context is an emphasis on empirical experiential practice, which may, from an insider perspective, open conceptual doorways to 'other levels of awareness'. For example in Brennan's case, she reads the colours of the auric layers as guides to particular 'soul levels' (1988: 238). This she achieves through clearing the mind through deep meditation (1988: 238). Within her analytical framework the colours of the aura have meaning. Accordingly, a lot of green in the aura would indicate a soul level of the nurturing compassionate healer with energy levels applicable to this state of being—this involving the heart chakra and its corresponding 'function' of 'love for self and others'. Similarly, a person with a lot of gold in their aura would be regarded by Brennan as having a 'connection to God and the service of humankind with godlike love' (1988: 239).

It appears then, that working on the self to enable 'a healthy aura' and physical body through the removal of negative emotions or faulty thinking, is also very much about 'communicating and legitimizing changes in social relations in the family and in the community' (McGuire 1998: 167). Healers such as Brennan affirm the correctness of dealing with negative emotions which will have been embodied through interaction with external sources — family, friends, work colleagues etc., — and provide 'appropriate' methods for endogenous healing. That is, emphasis is placed on healing from within. Hence, once again, I would argue that gender should remain of central importance to any evaluation of 'emotional work'.

Also of significance is how Brennan articulates the relationship between the energetic body and the practice of healing. For throughout the fieldwork chapters of this book one will commonly find healers either supporting or critiquing various healing types in relation to the depletion of energy in the healer's body.

An Ethic of Self-care

For Brennan, and indeed for all the healers that I have met, in order to do healing work on others one must first 'work on the self' while having an ethic of self-care. Working on self is generally presented as taking time out each day to do a little meditation or visualization with a corresponding emphasis on 'letting go' of troublesome, often 'ego driven' life issues or 'energetic defence systems'. This is, as I have mentioned, often regarded as being an evolutionary process. Brennan describes the healing act as being one where healing frequencies are passed through the healer's body, these having a particular vibratory rate. Hence, the healer's energetic body is to be regarded as a conduit that should vibrate at the same rate of frequency as the healing energy.

However, according to Brennan, the healer must also 'open and align to cosmic forces...in her life in general. She must be dedicated to the truth and meticulously honest with herself in all areas of her being' (1988: 187). Further, Brennan suggests that in order to do healing work, the healer needs 'some form of spiritual discipline or purification process' (1988: 187). She promotes the idea that meditation and focusing on a mantra such as, 'Be still and know I am God' (1987: 198) prior to the healing process is beneficial, as is some form of physical exercise to stretch and open the chakras.

McGuire also found emphasis being placed among healing groups in the American setting, on the necessity of purification and protection. Here too it was acknowledged that the healer should be 'grounded and centred' and doing healing work in a selfless and non-ego driven manner, otherwise healing energy would be blocked and/or dissipated leaving the healer feeling drained. 'By contrast, using energy properly should be invigorating, according to several respondents. A psychic healer explained, "It's a very vital kind of feeling. Some people I know…said that healing makes them feel drained. And I often wondered why, because it seems to me when you're allowing the energy to flow through you, it's not coming from you personally, and it's just going through you. So I don't feel drained if the energy is flowing"' (McGuire 1998: 177).

And yet Brennan raises, for me, in the above, further questions relating to healing, gender and power. For what exactly is this truth that one must be open to? What are these 'cosmic forces'? In Brennan's case this appears to be dependent on a Christian heritage. For prior to healing she draws energy up the chakras before making 'an affirmation to align myself with the Christ and the universal forces of light' (Brennan 1988: 203). She also prays 'to be a channel for love, truth and healing' (Brennan 1988: 203). Now while she also proposes that the healer should, if not having 'a connection with the Christ' (Brennan 1988: 203), utilize their connection to 'Universal Wholeness, God, the light, the Holy of Holies, etc.,' (Brennan 1988: 203), emphasis still appears to be placed on drawing down healing, 'male, light energy'.

Mary Daly states in *Gyn/Ecology* that 'Western society is still possessed overtly and subliminally by Christian symbolism…Its ultimate symbol…is the all-male Trinity itself' (1991: 37). Within this symbol for Daly, the

> first person, the father is the origin who thinks forth the second person, the son, the Word, who is the perfect image of himself, who is co-eternal and "consubstantial", that is identical in essence. So total is their union that their "mutual love" is expressed by the procession (known as "spiration") of a third person called the "Holy Spirit" whose proper name is "Love" (1991: 38).

Daly further proposes that this sort of symbolism leaves no place for 'female mythic presence' or 'female reality in the cosmos' (1991:

38). These points should be kept in mind in relation to this study of New Age healing in Scotland. For as we shall see throughout this book, again and again healers state that they 'draw down love, light and power' in the practice of healing. From a Dalyian perspective, these symbols could be regarded as eminently male and patriarchal. For Daly argues that,

> It is significant that certain male-defined feminine qualities are attributed to the Holy Ghost of Christian theology. Thus he is called Helper and Healer—which makes him an appropriate paradigm for the "helping professions"...presently [being] perpetuated by the therapeutic establishment in the name of psychological help (1991: 230).

Conversely, do Reiki writers such as Diane Stein (who I shall introduce more fully in Chapters Five and Six of this book) have an awareness of the potentially patriarchal nature of New Age teachings, this being why she locates healing practice within the realm of women's spirituality? And how might women healers respond to Dalyian accusations of their being locked into 'patriarchal systems' of healing practice? Might not they bring with them their own strategies for self-empowerment and self-definition as active agents? I shall engage more fully with these propositions in Chapter Seven. So let us return to the aura and briefly look at how Helen described to us our 'energetic power plays'.

Defences and Masks

Helen advised workshop participants that,

> Communication is only 10 per cent verbal—the other 90 per cent visual (such as body language) and energetic communication through the energy field is very accurate, energy can't lie (WMH 2001: 22).
>
> Because energy can't lie our own energy system always picks up on other people — if we encounter a situation where we are not totally comfortable we will automatically go into our defence pattern. The person or persons we are with will pick up that we are not being authentic and go into their defence patterns and truthful communication can become almost impossible (WMH 2001: 22).
>
> Therefore the more we can learn about our own defences, the reason that we act the way we do, and how not to, can make the world a much easier place to live in. But with this knowledge comes responsibility — we have to be the ones who consciously change how we react in the world, and so help others to move into their own light in safety and confidence (WMH 2001: 22).

From this perspective then, it becomes imperative to understand our own defence systems so that, as Helen put it, 'we can communicate from a position of truth and clarity'. Once again we have here an emphasis on 'truth', where the trained healer is perceived to see others' 'untruths' and then enable these people to go into 'their own light'. Hence, questions should be asked regarding how and why particular sets of representations are utilized in relation to 'our true essence' and the historical background of such interpretations.

Having outlined the defence systems, workshop participants were asked to answer several questions about their own ways of being.

1. Which defense(s) do you normally use?
2. How do you feel when you are using this/these defense(s)?
3. Do you feel safer/less safe when you are in defense?
4. Do you use different defences at different times, i.e. with parents/children/intimates/friends?
5. If so, which ones for different groups and why?
6. If you let down your defences what do you think would happen?
7. What are you protecting by being in defence?
   (WMH 2001: 24)

In conversation with other participants following this self-evaluation, it was commonly voiced that 'in reality we all know that we are coming from one or several of these positions' and that 'if we deny this, we are not being true to ourselves'. Hence, even though none of us had visibly seen our auric 'behaviour' the perception stated was that 'we really do know who we intuitively are, and can change our ways of being and be more responsible to self and others'. Hence, within dialogue such as this above, belief in the visible representations of our behaviour in the aura is based on a trained healer's discursive frameworks. And because the questions above would sit just as easily in the psychological therapeutic context, this being acknowledged by most as scientific and hence as authoritative, then authority might appear to be transferred from this field with the presentation of questions in this way.

This sort of conceptual framework is a familiar one in Scottish healing circles where 'the spiritual' is often psychologised. For example, Barbara Ann Brennan also tends to present her experiences of learning to see and feel auras in a 'scientific' framework. For she proposes, 'More than we want to admit, we are the products of our Western scientific heritage. How we learned to think and many of our self definitions are used by physicists to describe the physical universe' (1988: 21). There appears to be a tension in the above statement with her 'more than we want to admit'. This relates to questions I raised earlier in this chapter with regard to the perceived need for writers like Brennan to couch their healing evaluations — or at least to support the same — within psychological interpretative paradigms. For she, like so many Scottish healers, also regards it to be just a matter of time before, as one healing practitioner put it to me, 'science catches up and proves the reality of what healers have always known'. Yet, Brennan also argues that we need to move from mechanistic, rule-governed Newtonian notions of the basic laws of nature to a position where 'we broaden our frameworks of reality…[and acknowledge that] Our experience exists outside this Newtonian system' (1988: 23). These sorts of propositions will be kept firmly in mind as I progress through further representation of ethnographic material. I shall return to the 'relationships' between science and healing in Chapter Seven, where I argue that New Age women subversively engage with scientific and bio-medical approaches to health.

The Brennan based healing workshop finished with an introduction to how we not only use auric defence systems but also 'present masks to the world'. I am not going to go into these here other than to note that for the workshop facilitator, 'our mask self is a further extension of our energetic defences. We use it to hold back further still from the world and try and protect ourselves from getting hurt'. This occurs because 'you don't want to show your true face to the world because you feel this to be flawed and imperfect'. Helen emphasized that most human beings feel the need to conform to an idealised image of 'what we ought to be' and that this 'keeps us agitated and at a distance from the peace of self-acceptance'. However, we were advised, 'on an energetic basis the more we hide behind our mask the more difficult it becomes to sense the real authentic person…. And so with relationships communication can become from mask to mask, instead of truth to truth' (WMH 2001: 27).

Helen suggested to us that 'when you are using your masks you will find that it will actually cause people to reject you because they can feel that you are not being genuine. This results in exactly what you fear the most—being rejected and feeling unloved'. However, we were also advised that 'the mask or masks that you use are always a distortion of genuine high self qualities. For we do have strong resources of love, power and serenity. These are our natural gifts. We need to be our true selves'.

> The main antidote to the mask is simple—to learn to love and accept our selves, and release our fears around others' views of us—a simple task but one that can take a lifetime to achieve, so be gentle and supportive of yourself. Remember that you do not have to be perfect (WMH 2001: 28).

The final course I participated in at the Salisbury Centre in the spring of 2001 was Maureen Lockhart's 'Healing Circle'. Here too the energetic body was a central theme.

The Healing Circle

This healing circle ran for one evening a week over a six-week period. The facilitator, Maureen, was well-spoken and had been awarded a PhD in Complementary Health some time previously. She had lived for many years in India and appeared to have extensive knowledge of Indian health techniques and meditation practices. Maureen represented the human body in the following manner.

> Each of you has an energy field and this will be…at any one time…in a particular stage of the cyclical healing process. The three positions in this cycle are (a) where you are just surviving often after a major trauma (b) where you are in the middle ground and think that you are OK even though you may not be and (c) where you are thriving. Often when you are thriving you are thrown back to surviving. This should not be viewed negatively but rather be seen as part of the cyclical process.
>
> In the survival stage of healing you will always feel low on energy. This is the dark side…the Mother side…the nurturing side. The healing side is the light side…the Father side…and is about travelling to the light and the sky. This is the inspirational side of the healing process.
>
> The way to connect Father and Mother is to BREATHE. For when you expire, you draw energy down through the body. When you inspire, you draw energy up. Breathing balances the body and is earthing. Healers must learn how to breathe properly in order to heal effectively.

Maureen suggested that many healers often work from the wrong chakra when doing healing work, in that they focus on the solar plexus chakra as the channel through which healing energy travels. This comment ties in with other healers' perspectives in the Scottish field. For I have listened to many discussions about the potential for healers to become drained in the healing process as the client has 'aurically linked in to the healer's solar plexus chakra and leached energy'. For this reason some healers wear metal amulets over this chakra or fasten a belt around this area with a large buckle over the chakra itself. Maureen emphasized however, that rather than healing through the solar plexus chakra the healer should become attuned to the higher spiritual energies. This would be possible once one had developed awareness of 'the six chakras inside the head which are to do with the soul's purpose and mystical experience'. These were described as being in, for example 'the roof of the mouth and the back of the head'. We were also advised that there were several chakras in the aura above the head. Hence 'awareness' and 'the breath' were presented as important elements of walking a 'healer's path'.

For Maureen, it was with an awareness of the chakras above the head that one began the 'dark side' of the healing process. For it was at this 'spiritual level' that energetic imbalance began, this leading to disease. 'Therefore you should start at the eighth chakra [above the head] and work down noting blockages and imbalances in the chakras by breathing through them'. The auric levels were described in the following manner, with level one being the 'furthest away' from the body.

1. The Causal Level, where we contact our spirit guides and those of the client we may be working with.
2. The Soul Body, where we may deal with past life issues, the continuity of life consciousness and relationship issues.
3. The Astral Body which is to do with relationships in the here and now.
4. The Mental Body, where we may engage with states of mind, thought processes and stuck attitudes.
5. The Emotional Body which is the level where we need to engage with unexpressed emotion, fear etc.
6. The Etheric Body which is related to physical processes.

Throughout the six weeks of this course we regularly practised breathing techniques where we visualized drawing breath up 'from the earth', this to be expressed through all the chakras progressively, or drawing breath down through the auric chakras, again expressing in the same manner. The joining point of this exercise was to draw breath/energy up through the root chakra, down through the crown chakra and express both 'streams' through the fully open heart chakra. 'In this way you can send healing to anywhere you want, be this a client, place or situation'.

Spirit Guides

Like many other healers in the Scottish context, Maureen emphasized the importance of 'connecting with your spirit guides'. In order to do this focus was again placed on 'being at one with the breath' and being 'centred and calm'. For when one is in this state the 'greater senses or Mahabuttas' become available, and one can learn to 'hear internally with the inner sense' this being 'at the same level as the spirit guides'. Maureen proposed that all healers need to develop the ability to listen to their inner hearing and 'feel' others (spirits and humans) around them. She also emphasized the importance of 'intention' to the act of healing 'For right intention and sincerity of spiritual purpose along with your spirit guides will protect you while you are doing healing work'.

Maureen informed us that her first 'sense of presence' of having spirit guides was when she was doing osteopathy and bodywork many years ago. For she 'could feel them working through [her] hands...I knew I had a guardian spirit too, even though I hadn't seen him'. She described her guardian spirit as Metatron, 'the fierce king of angels',[3] stating that:

> Metatron is with me at all healings and is as an all-seeing eye. He only actively helps me at times of crisis. At other times my two other spirit guides are present.
>
> The feminine guide always appears at my left when I am healing, the masculine on my right. The male guide's image is as a globe of light, which feels ecstatic. The female guide is always there when I meditate...her purpose being to give love...and both guides are freely available whenever I need them.

The experience of having 'energies' or 'spirit guides' was a commonly voiced fact to several of the participants at this healing circle. Take, for example, the following statement describing these experiences.

From an English woman in her fifties:

3. Maureen confirmed this guide's name by textual evaluation in India.

I have had the experience of seeing Tibetan bowls when meditating. The sound and the energy travels when these bowls are played. The whole room feels full of energy when these bowls are being played. There is a feeling of pure joy and a sense of being in an ecstatic state.

I also have an Indian guide who wears two feathers in his hair. He gave a white one to me as a gift from a sage. Whenever he is with me I feel safe.

As part of this workshop we were also asked to go into a meditative state and, if we had not met our guides already, to allow pictures of these to come. We were to see if our guides wanted us to have a gift from them. Here is what some people experienced.

From a male self-defined shamanic practitioner,

I have met this guide before. He gave me a black feather...I can't remember his name but I think it is something like Black Hawk and he's a Native American tribal chieftain.

From a woman in her sixties,

This time [in this meditation] I was in a forest in the Himalayas. I was in trouble. I was lost. A female guide arrived just as a huge sun came up...and there was golden light coming down from her crown. I was aware of a great sense of gentleness as she gave me a red rope, a crown and a sceptre and she said to me that I was "to step into [my] life mission".

Maureen interjected here that the gifts one receives from a guide might vary according to the 'message to be heard' and 'the work to be done'.

From a woman in her thirties who was a Reiki practitioner,

I saw a sensual green light and a female child. I felt she was telling me that I need to put more fun back into my life. I'm not sure of her name but she gave me a white rose and a chalice.

From a woman in her sixties,

I saw a cow and a milkmaid. This was a flashback I think from childhood. She gave me a gift of self-contentment.

Maureen proposed that images such as these are archetypal and that the 'higher self has wisdom and will tell you things in altered states of consciousness that you wouldn't otherwise know. I want you to go back into a meditative state and ask what these gifts mean'.

Responses to this some time later were that for the English woman who received the gift of a white feather, this meant that she was to work on 'purity of character'. For the male shaman, the black feather meant 'journeying', while for the Reiki practitioner, the chalice symbolized 'purity of spirit'.

We can see then, in the few examples described here that, as Michael Brown has stated following his research among channellers in America, 'Mediums and channels bypass religious specialists to establish direct contact with the spirit world' (1997: 10); although one could, of course, also argue that to some extent the process of 'communicating with your spirit guide' was facilitated and later interpreted by Maureen. However, Brown further proposes that, 'The messages that they [channellers] find there reveal local concerns that have not yet breached the walls of institutionalized religion, which in its search for permanence tends to respond slowly to changing social conditions' (1997: 10). This is of some significance to the Scottish healing context. For here healers do very often call on spirit guides or angels to help them in their healing work. And they do regard these entities to be useful guides who personally assist by 'showing where to place the hands' or by providing 'an energy boost' in the healing process — these being 'activities' that mainstream religions and conventional medicine would not countenance. Hence, emphasis is placed on guides having a practical effect on health by enabling self healing with the fostering of the sense of, as related by participants, 'joy', 'fun', 'safety', 'self-contentment' and 'purpose'.

Healing narratives encompassing spirit entities therefore tell us a lot about how healers see the world and how they 'frame their personal search for meaning' (Brown 1997: 10). For the descriptions above utilize Christian, Native American and Buddhist symbolism and reflect the common New Age tendency of mixing and matching according to need. And though, as Brown has suggested, personally received channelled messages do to some extent bypass mainstream religious institutions, these representations are most certainly historically reconstructed to suit the individual from particular religious and spiritual traditions. Hence, they implicitly tell us about discourses of power.

As I progress through the next two chapters I shall expand from the microdynamics of Salisbury Centre workshops to other contexts and healing networks. As we shall see in the material on Reiki, many of the discourses introduced here fit well. For claims to authenticity in relation to both self and healing practice, holistic connectedness and the nature of reality are central themes in all healing discourse. In Chapter Five I will focus on the construction of Reiki history and begin to ask questions about the construction of the same, while in Chapter Six I shall present material on the nature of Reiki energy and symbol usage. Overall, I shall continue to build up a picture of the construction of gendered identities and their interrelationships to power.

Chapter Five

WRITING REIKI HISTORY

Within the next two chapters I shall introduce a healing practice
that appears to be growing significantly in popularity in Scotland —
Reiki. For in this context it is virtually impossible to go to any New
Age event and not meet several people who are enthusiastic
adherents to this form of healing. Reiki is now also being taught in
Higher and Further Education Institutes such as Perth and Elmwood
College, where the lower fees enable a more open participation.
And one may find advertising material for individual teaching
Masters and practitioners in widespread locations across Scotland.
As Sutcliffe states, Reiki is 'Not just a therapeutic technique but a
pragmatic theology and accessible cosmology — a self contained
spiritual system, in fact — Reiki packages central concerns of holistic
health' (2003: 186). For the individual is taught to engage with life's
events in 'a self-reflexive and self-referential manner' (Sutcliffe
2003: 178). The self becomes the locus for transformation and
empowerment through learning to channel healing energy.

The popularity of this practice is also reflected in European and
American contexts. For, as Gordon Melton states, by 1991 'Reiki
offices and centres could be found in every major urban centre in
North America...through Western Europe and [in] the countries of
the former British Empire' (2002: 77). Hence, I would propose that
Reiki is one of the more significant expressions of holistic healing
to be found in the West at this present time. As such it provides us
with a very useful example of how practitioners renegotiate their
place in the world emphasizing spiritual, rather than materialistic
and rationalistic, frameworks for interactions with others while
emphasizing the oneness of all life and, hence, responsibility for
the same.

In this chapter I shall provide an overview of the ongoing project
of writing up Reiki history and I shall introduce aspects of thought
and practice as found in Scottish Reiki circles. This will provide

necessary background material for the following chapter where I look more specifically at evaluations of Reiki energy (the power that heals) and how healers are taught to work with this energy through attunements and the utilization of Reiki symbols. Correspondingly, in these chapters I shall bring together historical and ontological accounts drawn primarily from emic sources. Hence, I shall utilize the writing of internationally renowned Reiki Masters such as William Rand, Walter Lubeck and Frank Arjava Petter. I shall also draw from Diane Stein's *Essential Reiki*, for within this book she discloses the 'secret' Reiki symbols — an act that has caused considerable ructions in Reiki circles.

Overall I shall be working from a position that historical (from Greek *historia* 'finding out, narrative') investigation of current thought and practice may begin to make 'the contours of the present strange' (Tyler in Peterson and Bunton 1997: 78). For as Foucault has argued, historical investigation may be used as a tool for 'diagnosing the present' (1977) so that we may, in this case, examine why Reiki history is constructed in particular ways and 'disturb the self-evident character' (Tyler 1997: 78) of conceptions of healing and the healer as based on history and theology.[1] Therefore I begin to ask questions here about whether there are normalising, political discourses running through Reiki material and if so, how these are taught and brought to fruition. I shall return to these points in the final chapter of this book where I question whether learning to be an energetic healer can be located within a Foucauldian framework of 'technologies of the self'.

Reiki Roots

The writing of Reiki history is an ongoing process filled with multiple and sometimes competing voices. Several issues have compounded this situation. First, a lot of 'found material' on Reiki is written in the form of Japanese ideograms, these being difficult to translate having multiple levels of meaning. Second, a large percentage of historical Reiki documentation is also written in 'old' Japanese. As the primary Western writers of Reiki history and practice are not native speakers of this language, this has

---

1. Deborah Tyler applies Foucault to child psychology and its object of study, the child, boy, or girl (Tyler in Peterson and Bunton, *Foucault, Health and Medicine*, London and New York: Routledge, 1997: 79).

correspondingly led to interpretative difficulties in relation to the 'accurate' transmission of Reiki history and techniques.

It is also the case that many Reiki writers also reflect a typical New Age emphasis on locating this cosmology in ancient esoteric traditions. For it is common in healing circles to hear dialogues about Reiki's Tibetan or 'Eastern' heritage. Hence practitioners may, for example, engage with Diane Stein's provision of a Tibetan Buddhist definition of the five Reiki symbols (1995: 154), which she also places within a Goddess cosmology. Or they may favour Walter Lubeck's representations of these same 'characters' as having roots in the writing of Confucian philosopher Mancius in 300 BCE (2001: 45). What we should note however, is that while Reiki books of the early 1980s reflected more of an emphasis on teaching the practicalities of 'doing Reiki', by the 1990s equal emphasis was placed on the establishment of 'authoritative' Reiki roots.

However, the Western search for the historical roots of Reiki has also been affected by the 'closed state' of traditional Reiki societies in Japan. For example, one primary Japanese school, the Usui Reiki Ryoho Gakkai (Usui Reiki Healing Society) does not encourage dialogue with Western Reiki practitioners who, they feel, do not practice 'true' Reiki. For within the traditional Reiki schools of Japan practitioners adhere rigidly to a training programme dictated by their Reiki Master where one may spend a lifetime learning the basics, rather than just a few months or years as in the West. These students are also forbidden to disclose Reiki knowledge to 'outsiders'. Hence, the starting point for many Western researchers of Reiki history has been to translate the inscriptions on the memorial stone of the founder and 're-discoverer' of Reiki, Mikao Usui.

The Usui Memorial

The Usui memorial is located in the Saihoji Temple in the Toyotama district of Tokyo, and it is to internationally renowned German Reiki Master, Frank Arjava Petter, that many Western practitioners turn for an initial translation of its inscription. For, while this memorial is written in 'old' Japanese, Petter was assisted in its translation by his Japanese mother-in-law, Masona Kobayashi, and by his Japanese wife, Chetna. Hence, these women have enabled Petter to provide in his *Reiki Fire* (1997) an authoritatively perceived account of the life of Reiki's discoverer Mikao Usui.

Arjava states that at the top of Usui's ten-foot high memorial stone, which he found after a year of searching in 1994, there is the Kanji inscription 'Memorial of Usui Sensei's Virtue'. Petter states that the description that follows of Usui's life was written by Juzaburo Ushida and Masayuki Okada[2] in 1927 — these men being students of Usui. Mikao Usui is noted as being born in August 1864 'in the village of Yago in the Yamagatu district of the Gifu Prefecture'. He is described as 'a talented and hard working student', who as an adult 'travelled to several Western countries and China to study, worked arduously, but did at some point run into some bad luck. However, he didn't give up and trained himself arduously'.[3] His first experiences of Reiki energy and his later healing practice are portrayed in the inscription as follows, which is worth quoting at length.

> One day he went to Mount Kurama on a 21-day retreat to fast and meditate. At the end of this period he suddenly felt the great Reiki energy at the top of his head, which led to the Reiki healing system. He first used Reiki on himself, then tried it on his family. Since it worked well for various ailments, he decided to share this knowledge with the public at large. He opened a clinic in Harajuku, Aoyama-Tokyo in April of the 10th year of the Taisho period (in 1921).[4] He not only gave treatment to countless patients, some of whom had come from far and wide, but he also hosted workshops to spread his knowledge. In September of the twelfth year of the Taisho period (1923), the devastating Kanto earthquake shook Tokyo. Thousands were killed, injured and became sick in the aftermath. Dr. Usui grieved for his people, but he also took Reiki to the devastated city and used its healing powers on the surviving victims. His clinic soon became too small to handle the throng of patients, so in February of the 14th year of the Taisho period (1925), he built a new one outside Tokyo in Nakano. His fame spread quickly all over Japan and invitations to distant towns and villages started coming in. Once he went to Kure, another time to Hiroshima prefecture, then to Saga prefecture and Fukuyama. It was during his stay in Fukuyama that he was hit by a fatal stroke on March 9th, of the fifteenth year of the Taisho period (1926). He was 62 years of age (Petter 1997: 29-30).

2. Hiroshi Doi states that Rear Admiral Juzaburo Ushida wrote the inscription, this being edited by Masayuki Okada, a Doctor of Literature (2000: 46).

3. Rand (2001: 13) suggests that his 'intuitive feeling' is that Usui's 'travels and studies were undertaken more in the style of a wandering monk who depended on personal initiative, flexibility, and divine providence than with the support of wealth [from his family]'.

4. Year dates and comments have been inserted here by Frank Petter.

The inscription goes on to detail Usui's marriage and family members, his personal attributes and general demeanour before stating 'you should follow the five principles of the Meiji emperor... and contemplate them in your heart'. According to the inscription 'Reiki not only heals diseases, but also amplifies innate healing abilities, balances the spirit, makes the body healthy, and thus helps to achieve happiness'.

> The ultimate goal is to understand the ancient secret method for gaining happiness (*Reiki*) and thereby discover an all-purpose cure for many ailments. If these principles are followed you will achieve the great tranquil mind of the ancient sages. To begin spreading the Reiki system, it is important to start from a place close to you (*yourself*), don't start from something distant such as philosophy or logic (Petter 1997: 30 [emphasis original]).

The last part of the inscription deals with Reiki as a transformative force.

> Philosophical paradigms are changing the world round. If Reiki can be spread throughout the world it will touch the morals of society. It will be helpful for many people, and will not only heal disease, but also the world as a whole. Over 2000 people learned Reiki from Dr. Usui. More learned it from his senior disciples, and they carried Reiki even further. Even after Dr. Usui's passing, Reiki will spread far and wide for a long time to come. It is a universal blessing to have received Reiki from Dr. Usui and to be able to pass it on to others. Many of Dr. Usui's students converged to build his memorial here at Saihoji Temple in the Toyotoma district. I was asked to write these words to help keep his great work alive. I deeply appreciate his work and I would like to say to all his disciples that I am honoured to have been chosen for this task. May many understand what a great service Dr. Usui did to the world (in Petter 1997: 30).[5]

We can see in the above inscription that Mikao Usui's life appears to have been represented as, to some considerable extent, a 'seeker's path'. For example, Japanese Reiki Master Hiroshi Doi, suggests that Usui was engaged in a lifelong 'search for the greatest purpose in life' (2000: 47) this leading him to undertake three years of Zen

5. Hiroshi Doi's translation of this memorial while being in essence not dissimilar to Petter's still has some slight variations. For example, Doi's translation starts in the following way: 'What you can realise through cultivation and training is called "VIRTUE", and it is called "MERIT" to spread a method of leadership and practice it. It is people of many merits and a good deal of virtue that can be eventually be called a great founder.... We can say that Usui-sensei is also one of those people' (Doi 2000: 41).

practice. During this period he searched for 'the way to reach the state of mind of accepting our fate and living in peace [sic]' (2000: 47). What many Western writers of Reiki also appear to agree on is that the actualities of Usui's life appear 'to be clouded and filled with mysteries' (Petter 1997: 18). This has led to accounts of the same being either 'blown out of proportion or not properly researched' (Petter 1997: 18). For example, Shuffrey (1998: 11) and Hall (1997: 9) both claim that Usui was the principal of a small Christian University in Kyoto called the Doshisha University. Shuffrey further adding that following his time as Professor of Theology in Kyoto, Usui travelled to America where, after a seven-year period of study at the University of Chicago, he received a Doctorate in Scripture (1998: 11).

It is probably as a result of this confusion that writers such as Petter and Rand have felt the need to travel to Japan to research the 'true' story of Mikao Usui. For as Petter states, nearly all German and English Reiki books are filled with claims to Usui's Christian heritage. This has led Petter (1997:18) to argue, that 'the seemingly Christian aspects of Reiki were added in America to make Reiki more acceptable to Christian countries'. For while, as proposed by his friend and translator Lynn Wakisaka Evans, 'it is possible that Dr Usui may have embraced Christianity for a brief period during his inner search' this 'does not mean that Usui was a Christian in the classical sense' (Petter 1997: 19).

It is necessary to be aware then, that Western Reiki Masters appear to be engaged in a progressive project of rewriting history textually. This as we shall see is a considerable change of methodology from the original transmission of Reiki to the West. For here emphasis was placed on maintaining the secrecy of this practice through the memorised oral transmission of its symbols and techniques from predominantly women to women.[6] Now though, we find that the majority of writers travelling to Japan are male internationally renowned Masters who can financially afford to engage in this project and who can deal with the difficulties of researching cross-culturally. Women appear, to a considerable extent, to be excluded from this Japanese quest. However, for the moment let us return to the memorial inscription.

---

6. Although written material was given to Reiki students in Japan by Mikao Usui.

For many Western practitioners the event of primary importance that is detailed in this inscription is Usui's 'rediscovery' of Reiki energy on Mount Kurama. Rand states that this mountain is held to be sacred. For according to Buddhist literature in the Mount Kurama Temple (founded in 770 AD) it is to here that the Supreme Deity Sonten descended over six million years ago in the form of Mao-son.

> His mission was the salvation and evolution of mankind and all living things on earth. Mao-son is also said to have incarnated as the Spirit of the Earth, residing inside the ancient cedar trees at the top of the mountain. This spirit is thought to emanate from Mount Kurama to this day. Sonten manifests as Love, Light and Power (Rand 1991: A1-5).

It was to this mountain then that Mikao Usui travelled after a period of financial adversity. Rand proposes that at this time he may well have become a Buddhist monk. This is common practice among men in Japan at times of life crisis. In any case, Usui was familiar with Mount Kurama having spent time there as a child studying Kiko, a Japanese form of Qi Gong in a Tendai Buddhist Temple on its slopes. Qi Gong is a disciplined practice where one learns to control the breath, to meditate and through the routine of slow moving exercises develop and use Ki or life energy. In turn one also learns how to build up Kiko as healing energy, which one may then 'transmit' through the hands. However,

> when using the Kiko method, one is also prone to depletion, as it can draw on one's personal energy as well. The young Usui wondered if any way existed to heal without first having to store up healing energy and then leaving one depleted at the end. This was an important question and acted like a seed in his developing mind; a seed that would grow into fruition in a most profound way later in his life (Rand 2001: 13).

Once at Mount Kurama, Usui undertook a twenty-one day retreat. The emphasis during this time was on fasting, meditation and chanting. However,

> Toward the end of his retreat in March 1922, a great and powerful spiritual light entered the top of his head and he had a satori or enlightening experience.[7] The light was the Reiki energy coming to

7. Rand, Petter, Shuffrey, Doi et al. all propose that this occurred after a period of meditation while standing underneath a small artificial waterfall; the fall of water on the head being purported to open and purify the 'crown chakra', a practice still carried out today (see Rand, 1991/2001).

him in the form of an attunement. His awareness was then greatly expanded and he realised that a great power had entered him. He knew it was the power he had wished when he had studied healing on Mount Kurama as a child. He was overjoyed. He knew he could heal others without his energy being depleted (Rand 2001: 14).

Frank and Chetna Petter have collated the following account of Usui's teaching following this event. This narrative is based on their personal encounters with students and family acquaintances in Japan and as such mirrors the typical way that Reiki knowledge is transmitted in Western Reiki circles.

In 1993, Frank Petter and his wife started teaching all levels of Reiki in Japan. 'At that time only the first two levels were open to the public. Many people who had learnt the first and second degree flocked to Sapporo from all over Japan' (Petter 1997: 13). They initiated one Ms. Shizuko Akimoto to Master level. She in turn gave Reiki healing sessions to a gentleman in his late sixties called Mr Tsutoma Oishi unaware that this same man had 'learned Reiki from one of Dr Usui's chief disciples about 40 years ago!' (Petter 1997: 22). She was also unaware initially that his mother had regularly treated polio victims with Reiki throughout his childhood. Mr Oishi had not maintained any contact with Reiki practitioners over the last thirty years but was happy to tell Ms. Akimoto of 'what he knew of Dr Usui and the Reiki movement in Shizuoka' (Petter 1997: 22).

'I carefully sifted through the information, and what follows is an account of what I thought fit for publication in a book' (Petter 1997: 25) According to Petter after the failure of Usui's business venture he decided to 'seek something other than material gain' (Petter 1997: 25) and this led him to undertake, as mentioned previously, his twenty-one day fast on Mount Kurama where he had a satori.[8] He founded the Usui Reiki Ryoho Gakkai (Usui Reiki Healing Society). Some time later he heard about the good reputation of the head of a Reiki centre in Shizuoka, Mr Ogawa. He recognized this man's healing talents and 'elevated him to the highest rank in the organisation' (Petter 1997: 25).

---

8. One should note here that for Petter, 'the Japanese word *satori* cannot be translated as "enlightenment"'. *Sator* traditionally means a fleeting glimpse of a higher order or sudden understanding (1997: 25).

> Dr Usui and Mr Ogawa used to give energy charged crystal balls to
> their Reiki students. These crystal balls were placed directly on the
> patient's diseased area, helping the body to find its equilibrium again.
> After initiation, all students also received a manual that explained
> what Reiki is, described symptoms and gave guidelines for the treatment
> of illnesses (Petter 1997: 25).

Mikao Usui and his teachers carried out estimations of students'
healing potential by asking each person to kneel in the *gasho* position
with hands held at the chest. 'The Reiki teacher would then touch
the student's clasped hands with one hand and estimate their healing
talent and energy' (Petter 1997: 26). According to Fumio Ogawa
(the adopted son of Mr Ogawa), Usui had developed a six level
(degree) healing system in his Usui Reiki Ryoho Gakkai (Usui Reiki
Healing Society).[9]

William Rand's appraisal of Usui's teaching adds some useful
depth to this narrated account above. Having founded the Usui
Reiki Ryoko Gakkai, Usui opened 'a healing clinic in Harajuka,
Aoyama near the Meiji shrine in central Tokyo' (Rand 2001: 14).[10]
The first four levels of attunement were called *Shoden* or *beginning*
level (corresponding to 1st Degree initiation in the West). The fifth
level was entitled *Okuden* or *inner teaching* (corresponding to 2nd
degree initiation in the West), while the sixth level was the master
level, '*Shinpiden* or Mystery Teaching' (Rand 2001: 15).

Approximately one year after Mikao Usui had founded his Usui
Reiki Ryoho Gakkai Japan was hit by the Kanjo earthquake. Due to
the enormous death rate (over 140,000 people were killed) and
physical and emotional injury, the 'demand for Reiki became
enormous and Usui and his students worked night and day to help
as many as they could' (Rand 2001:15). Continued requests for Reiki,
following on from this earthquake, led Usui to open a larger clinic
in Nakano, Tokyo, and to travel extensively. During this period he
trained over two thousand students and initiated sixteen Reiki
Masters (Rand 2001: 16).

Rand proposes that at the time when Usui was carrying out Reiki
practice in Japan 'many other hands-on healing methods were being
taught' (2001: 16). These included the 'Violet Light Healing Method'

---

9. According to Petter this society is also known in Japan as the Usui Shiki Ryoho,
with 'Shiki' meaning 'style, form or system' (1997: 18).

10. This according to the interview material of one of Dr Hayashi's last students
Tatsumi-san, as found by Melissa Riggall in 1996 (cited in Rand 2001: 14).

as taught within 'The Association for The Study of Palm Treatments', this being set up by a former student of Usui. Another centre founded by a Usui student, Toshihiro Eguchi, was the Tenohira Ryoji kenkyu-kai (hand healing research centre). This had, over time, 500,000 students (Doi 2000: 186). Rand also observes that the Japanese derived religions of Mahi Kari and Johrei also emphasize healing. 'Interestingly, both use the same symbol that Usui sensei chose for the Master symbol. I do not know if any connection exists between these healing systems, but their nearly simultaneous beginnings indicate a sudden interest towards healing all over Japan at the time Usui sensei discovered Reiki' (2001: 16). This would be a useful area for further research and one initial question might be how, precisely, Usui was able to 'choose' a Master symbol when these are represented by Reiki writers as being of a 'revealed' nature.

It appears that Usui was also concerned that Reiki should remain a system of healing available to everyone. He emphasized that as Reiki travelled across the world it could enhance Reiki practitioners' lives. For once they had 'experienced the divine' they would be 'more willing to work together to create a better world' (Rand 2001: 16). After Usui's death in 1926, Mr. Ushida took over the leadership of the Usui Reiki Ryoho Gakkai as shown in the table below. This is drawn from Hiroshi Doi's *Modern Reiki Method for Healing* (2000: 183).

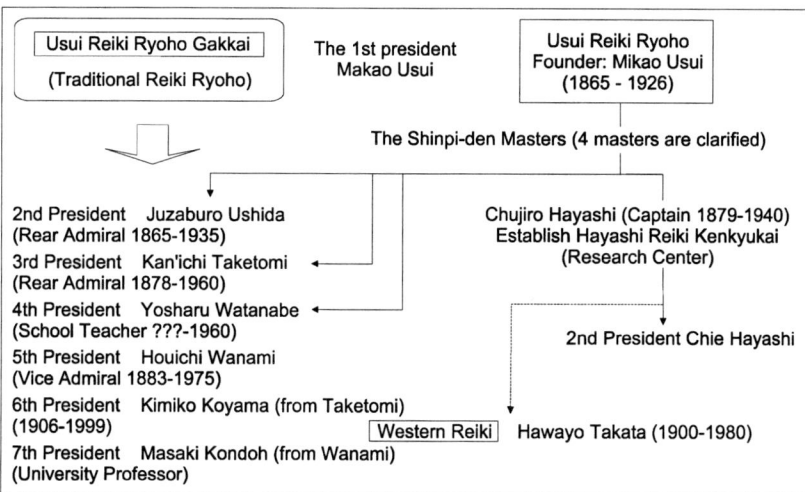

Successors of Traditional Reiki Ryoho

Reiki in the Western World

Of the sixteen masters initiated by Usui it was through Chujiro
Hayashi's teaching that Reiki first spread to the West. After Usui's
death, Hayashi set up his own Reiki organisation and developed a
teaching manual. It was to Hayashi that a Mrs Hawayo Takata
turned when diagnosed with severe illness in 1935.[11] Takata was a
Hawaiian emigre of Japanese origins. Rand states that after four
months of treatment by Hayashi, Takata was completely healed —
this being confirmed by hospital tests. 'She wanted to learn Reiki in
order to continue treating herself and also to take it back to Hawaii
to share with others. Dr Hayashi allowed her to work at his clinic
and also began to give her Reiki training' (1991: 1-29). Rand states
that Mrs Takata worked in Dr Hayashi's clinic for over a year
carrying out Reiki treatments before returning to Hawaii in 1937.
Shortly after her return, Dr Hayashi joined her and 'together they
travelled around Hawaii giving lectures, teaching Reiki, and giving
treatments. On February 21, 1938 Hawayo Takata was initiated into
Shinpiden [Master level] by Dr Hayashi' (2001: 18).

Following the advent of World War Two, and particularly after
the attack on Pearl Harbour in Hawaii, many Japanese were placed
in internment camps and, as Rand suggests, it must have been a
difficult time for Takata to promote a Japanese healing practice (2001:
24). He argues that this was why she stated that she was the only
living Reiki Master in the world — all of the Japanese Reiki Masters
having died in the war. It was also Takata who first started the
mythology that Usui had been at one time a Christian minister and
that he had taught in Christian Universities in Japan and America
(Rand 2001: 25).

By promoting herself as the only living Reiki Master and source
of information about this healing practice Takata located herself in
a position of significant authority. And though some were doubtful
about her claims to be the sole inheritor of the Reiki tradition the
majority of people accepted her claims 'because it was the only
information available' (Rand 2001: 26). She set up several large Reiki
clinics in Hawaii and initiated many students up to the second-

11. These have been listed by Vera Graham in *The (San Mateo) Times* (1975) as a
tumour, gallstones, appendicitis and asthma, these being reported as being 'completely
cured' in Patsy Mahura's article in the *Honolulu Advertiser* entitled 'Mrs Takata and
Reiki Power' (1974, in Rand 1991: 1-28, 29).

degree level. Gordon Melton states in his 'Reiki: The International Spread of a New Age Healing Movement', that these people were all Japanese Americans. It was only with her first visit to Puget Sound in mainland America in 1973 that she first initiated to First and Second Degree level those of any cultural heritage, rather than Japanese emigrants (2001: 79). She also 'often initiated members of her clients' families so they could give Reiki as well' (Rand 1991: 1-29).

However, it has only been in the last two decades that researchers such as Rand, Petter and Lubeck have begun to build up a picture of Reiki history from Usui to Takata. It is also only post-Takata's death in 1980 that Reiki has grown significantly in popularity in Western circles. Three factors have been responsible for the initial curtailment of this healing practice. First, Hawayo Takata 'stated that the official fee for Reiki Mastership was $10,000 and that if one did not charge this amount one was not practising the Usui system of Reiki'[12] (Rand 2001: 30). She initiated twenty-two Reiki Masters, fifteen of these being women. Each of these new Masters had been made to 'take a sacred oath to teach Reiki exactly the same way as she had taught it. This made it difficult for most of them to change, even though some of her rules seemed to go against the nature of Reiki and made it more difficult to learn' (Rand 1991: 1-30).

Secondly, Takata insisted that 'one must study with just one Reiki teacher and stay with that teacher the rest of one's life' (Phaigh cited in Rand 1991: 1-29). Her final command was that all Reiki teachings and symbols must be memorized. Reiki was to be an oral tradition. However, after her death some of these same Reiki Masters started issuing their pupils with training manuals and allowed the taking of notes in class (Rand 2001: 27).

In general, these Masters felt that they should follow their own inner guidance and enable, rather than hinder, the spread of Reiki by moving away from restrictive practices such as prohibitive fee structures, in the spirit of Usui. It also became common for Reiki initiates to move between various Reiki teachers. For Rand, this is because 'Reiki students are guided to the teacher right for them. Because of this the fee the teacher is charging is exactly the right fee for the student to pay; (2001: 20). He states that there are 'at least 200,000 Reiki Masters in the world today [as of 1991] with

12. Rand states that Takata first initiated Reiki Masters in 1970 (1991: 1-29).

well over 1,000,000 practitioners and the numbers continue to grow!' (Rand 1991: 1-31). However, considerable emphasis is also still placed, within Reiki circles, on finding a teacher of good lineage. For good lineage is perceived as being directly related to efficiency when giving attunements; this in turn enabling the student to 'do' healing work. As he states, in relation to the 'four unique qualities that identify the class of healing techniques appropriately called Reiki' (Rand 2001: 22):

1. The ability to perform Reiki comes from receiving an attunement, rather than developing the ability over time through the use of meditation or other exercises.

2. All Reiki techniques are part of a lineage, meaning the technique has been passed from teacher to student through an attunement process, starting with the one who first channelled the technique (Rand 2001: 22).[13]

Reiki Lineages

In Japan there are now six Reiki lineages independent of Usui's Reiki Healing Society and of Western influence (Melton 2002: 85). After Takata's death 'the Western Reiki Movement also split into two directions, The "Reiki Alliance" led by Phyllis Furomoto and the "Radiance Technique" led by Mrs Barbara Ray and based in the USA. Several other branches grew out of the "Reiki Alliance" such as the independent Reiki Masters (Petter's line) and Osho Reiki' (Petter 1997: 21).

Academic writer Gordon Melton also provides a useful overview of how some Reiki practitioners have integrated Reiki with other spiritual traditions, these becoming internationally well-known. For example, he describes how one Kathleen Milner took a Reiki course in 1983 in the 'hope that it would improve her art work' (2002: 85). Following two car accidents, which left her in considerable pain, she turned to William Rand, founder of The International Centre For Reiki Training. She received her Master's training from him in 1989 'primarily for her own benefit. The experience greatly assisted her in finally overcoming her pain' (Melton 2002: 85). However, she did eventually start to give classes in Reiki. At this time she

---

13. The other two qualities are that Reiki is 'guided by the higher power' (Rand 2001: 23) and does not require the mind to direct energy, and 'Reiki can do no harm' (Rand 2001: 22).

was also practising meditation and forms of divination such as 'the runes and the Egyptian Cartouche' (Melton 2002: 85).

Milner taught Reiki to Marcy Miller a disciple of Sai Baba. Miller travelled to India to meet this guru and 'made contact with a non-corporeal entity described only as a "Higher Being" who told her that Takata had left out one attunement symbol and much of the initiation procedure for each of the degrees' (Melton 2002: 85). Upon her return she relayed this information to Milner and stated that this entity 'wanted to meet them both' (Melton 2002: 85). The following day,

> "the Higher Being revealed the missing symbol and initiation procedures" (Melton 2002: 85) which Milner taught to her former students. They in turn reported an increase in energy. Milner "soon established her own direct contact with an array of Higher beings...They told her it was time to go public with what they had taught her and would be teaching her in the future. These additional teachings, now integrated into the Reiki training, became the basis of the new Tera-Mei Reiki Tradition" (Melton 2002: 85).

William Rand, Milner's original teacher, began to meditate on 'her' new symbols. This resulted in him 'slightly altering the uses of certain symbols as well as the attunement process. It was his experience that the energy of the entire system had shifted. He claimed that Reiki energy as a whole had become very heart centred, and he named his new approach Karuna, from the Sanskrit word meaning "compassionate action"' (Melton 2002: 87). Rand promoted Karuna Healing energy as being 'much more definite and focused' (Melton 2002: 85). In turn Rand trained Ellen Kahne, whose initial voyage into Reiki had been a result of her wish to improve her own health and live a productive life in her old age. Her initial Reiki teacher had been Josephine Miranda, a Master of the Furimoto tradition. Kahne took her Masters level and Karuna initiation with Rand. She considered herself to be an intuitive person and developed what she called Point of Focus techniques which 'use[d] intensified, focused, and grounded Reiki techniques' (Melton, 2002: 88). Kahne has therefore promoted this form of Reiki as having the ability to enhance 'all other healing skills and disciplines (including massage, physical and occupational therapies, nursing, psychological counselling and all allopathic and alternative medical modalities)' (in Melton 2002: 88).

The styles of Reiki I have briefly introduced above are but a few examples of the diversity of this practice. And although there may be tension between some of these lineages, they do show how Reiki is utilized by practitioners alongside other healing modalities and within other spiritual frameworks. Emphasis appears to be placed on the evolving nature of Reiki, as found in symbol usage and practice. For example, in the International Centre for Reiki Training's website, Rand espouses the benefits of Karuna Reiki, as mentioned above, this being taught only to those who have had Master Level Reiki training. He states 'most students find it more powerful than Usui Reiki. The energy has a more definite feel to it. It works on the emotional and spiritual levels and can also help one become more grounded. Those who receive the attunements report experiences with their guides, angels and higher self and feel the healing presence of other enlightened beings...Karuna Reiki opens you to work more closely with enlightened ones who are physically present as well as those in spirit' (www.reiki.org, 2006).

What we appear to have then, in the writing of Reiki history is two differing areas of emphasis. On the one hand we have writers such as Rand promoting—from Usui's 'mystical' experience on Mount Kurama where he saw revealed the Reiki symbols—an *original* healing tradition. We can see this also in Usui's own handbook the *Reiki Ryoho Hikkei* in which he states that 'Our Reiki Ryoho is something absolutely original and cannot be compared with any other [spiritual] path in the world...our Reiki Ryoho is an original therapy, which is built on the spiritual power of the universe'.[14]

However, when practitioners develop 'new' and 'more powerful' ways of doing Reiki, focus is also often placed on locating healing practice within older traditions and then trademarking the new 'form' as Rand has done with Karuna Reiki. Hence, although Rand states that 'Karuna' as 'compassionate action' is 'the motivating quality of all enlightened beings who are working to end suffering on earth' (www.Reiki.org, 2006), this 'work' appears to come at a price; the fees for Rand's class in 2006 being, for example, $875.00. This surely must have the potential to exclude those of limited financial means. Further questions might be asked with regard to Rand's aforementioned assertion that 'Reiki students are guided to the teacher right for them. Because of this the fee the teacher is

14. This handbook has been published in the West by Frank Petter in 1999.

charging is exactly right for them' (2001: 20). Or do Reiki writers/ practitioners who charge fees for services regard money as 'morally neutral raw material...[a view inherited] from nineteenth century self-help movements that promoted the power of positive thinking'? (Brown 1997: 11).[15]

Reiki and Health

However, underlying all of the debates within Reiki circles is a concern with health. For many Western grassroots practitioners 'the search is on' for more efficient ways to incorporate Reiki into all aspects of their daily lives. Located right at the centre of this quest is, according to Rand, Petter, Lubeck *et al*, 'the five principles'. For the practitioner is expected to voice these principles daily, once in the morning and once in the evening. They are promoted as enabling the practitioner to deal with life's daily challenges in a positive manner, rather than feeling at 'the will of others' and disempowered. The following translation of the principles comes from Usui's memorial, contemporary teachers giving roughly similar versions.

1. Don't get angry today.
2. Don't worry today.
3. Be grateful today.
4. Work hard today (as in meditative practice).
5. Be kind to others today.

Walter Lubeck explains the meaning of these principles more fully in *The Spirit of Reiki* (2001). He proposes that, in relation to the first principle, when 'we feel angry with ourselves, we should get to the bottom of this feeling as quickly as possible and clarify the purpose for which our Higher Self has sent this powerful energy to the body and mind at this moment. Then we should think how this power can be meaningfully translated into actions and get to work' (2001: 250). The second principle relating to worry is concerned with us learning precisely what it is we fear. Hence, a person should look at their worries closely and move through them by giving themselves Reiki. 'Reiki tells us: "recognize your strengths! Get up and walk your path in your own way! Set a good example for those that are weaker, and help them find their personal path and take it seriously!"' (Lubeck 2001: 252).

15. For Brown found this to be the philosophy held by middle-class American channellers.

For Lubeck, the third principle 'be grateful today' relates to 'recognition of the special grace, the divine blessing received in everything that is given to us, no matter how small or large it is' (2001: 252). The fourth principle, we should work hard at Reiki as a spiritual path, for to do so is to work on ourselves. 'This life principle reminds us to truly get involved in life, not waste our time, and use our opportunities' (Lubeck 2001: 255). The fifth principle is about treating each other lovingly and is 'perhaps the hardest challenge of all. Why? True spiritual love wants the best for everyone involved—not the well-meant but ultimately superficial adaption of behaviour' (Lubeck 2001: 256).

What we find throughout these life principles is an emphasis on wholeness. For if 'you truly get to the bottom of them, you will learn to experience the unity between the surface of separation. Make the effort, and you will find less separation and more unity within yourself' (Lubeck 2001: 257). Working at these principles is then reflected in giving Reiki treatments in that, for example, if either client or healer feels anger or fear — *which can manifest as physical dis-ease*—these may be resolved by using Reiki 'constructively [to] deal with these feelings' (Lubeck 2001: 259).

What we find in the above is a continued emphasis on spiritual practice being intimately related to the body and health with, as Sutcliffe has proposed, the individual being taught to engage with life's events 'in a self-reflexive and self-referential manner' (Sutcliffe 2003: 178). An example of this may be seen in the promotion of 'positive affirmations'. The following brief account is drawn from material gathered at a Frank Arjava Petter, Reiki Techniques workshop held at the Salisbury Centre in Edinburgh in 2001.

According to Arjava, 'people who have suffered have the potential for enormous strength' in that only they know what it is to 'be free from suffering'. For once you have experienced this 'you know inside what is your true self'. It is this knowledge that drives us forward'. For Arjava, affirmations are a useful and empowering way of remembering to live consciously in the present rather than continually looking backwards into the past where suffering has occurred. Hence, a positive affirmation made by a person helps them to focus on what is important in the here and now. For Arjava,

> affirmations are a useful way of dealing with desires that come from negative positioning. For example if a person comes to me with a stated affirmation "I want to be enlightened" then I would say to that

person that they needed to look at their dark side, accept their negative habits and learn how to love themselves more freely.

Another example might be of someone coming to me with an affirmation "I want to be more successful". Here, I would advise them that underneath this affirmation they have a greater fear of failure.

For Elaine, a workshop participant, her need was for a positive affirmation that enabled her to deal with her concerns 'about not having enough', for she felt that her concern with material things was derived from her childhood experiences of financial scarcity following the break-up of her parents' marriage. Correspondingly, she felt she had been left with the sense that she had to 'continually squirrel for hard times'. Arjava asked her to work through some affirmation possibilities until she arrived at the positive affirmation of 'I am here. That is enough'. He then suggested that 'perhaps a more useful affirmation for you might be "I am still here", simplicity being the key to empowerment'. Elaine agreed with Arjava that this affirmation enabled her to have 'feelings of abundance' which lessened her 'fear of starvation based on lack of money'.

So 'suffering' is an important theme underlying healing practice. It is often voiced that healers who have suffered are better able to have an empathetic relationship with their clients. Tied to this is the perception that the healer, in dealing with self-suffering, has empirically tested various forms of practice for him/herself and is now also able to utilize this expertise for the client's benefit. This is an ongoing process with clients' perceptions of healing work being drawn from by the healer in a mutual interplay of 'voiced feelings' and empirical testing. Of course, definitions of suffering may well vary, but then healers do not appear to be overly interested in defining suffering. Suffering is a personal experience of feeling perhaps limited in some way, or devalued, dis-abled and in pain. And how does one define pain which is, in itself, also a subjective experience? Here we see the potential for tension between academic and holistic fields of knowledge. For while the 'academic mind, whether of the scientific or humanist persuasion, thrives on distinctions and particulars...New Age thought seeks connections and universals, which are pursued with an enthusiastic holism that disorients thinkers trained in highly specialized disciplines' (Brown 1997: 10). This occurs because healers continually reinvent and re-imagine themselves by drawing from their own and their clients' experiences of suffering and the acknowledgement and sometimes alleviation of the same. In turn, this experiential knowledge is then taken out into other social spheres which means that since *women* predominate at the grassroots level of healing practice, we need, not wishing to state the obvious, to listen to their voices and include them when writing up healing thought and practice.

One ought to also be aware however, that men and women may not experience and deal with suffering in the same way. For women 'have been told for centuries that they are incompetent in matters of the world' (Isherwood and McEwan 1994: 57) and have correspondingly been excluded by men in the public sphere and driven into the private. Yet 'The private sphere, the paradigmatic women's sphere, [was] not created by women; women were assigned to it, backed up by divine commands and public legislation' (Isherwood and McEwan 1994: 57). Once located 'as less' supported by 'the sexism pervading society, whether in its crass forms of wife-beating, incest, rape, and pornography or in the less crass but more sweeping forms of women being abused by ridicule, groping and suggestive language' (Isherwood and McEwan 1994: 57) it is a long hard battle for women to relocate themselves as 'of worth'.

> It is clear that many women find the task too daunting; they are up against peers, subordinates, superiors at work; they are inexperienced in claiming their rights publicly and they turn a blind eye. They do not want to be a "bad sport" *and so internalise their suffering in silence.* They find it very difficult to resist patriarchal patterns of authority (Isherwood and McEwan 1994: 57) [italics mine].

Therefore of necessity, one should apply a feminist hermeneutic of suspicion to any claims of 'mutuality of suffering'. For although a female Reiki Master may well have a basis for similar claims to her mainly female students in that she too has 'lived experience' of being located relationally as sister, wife or mother, would 'aristocratic' Frank Arjava Petter (his claim) be similarly able to empathically relate to, for example, a single parent healer from a small community in Scotland; my Reiki Master? What is Petter promoting when he states that a positive affirmation for her would be 'I am still here'?

I would like to close this chapter with some responses to questionnaires as handed out at the above workshop 'with Arjava's approval' because these give us some idea of why Reiki is growing in popularity. They are useful illustrations of how Reiki practitioners 'see the world' as a place for reflection and active engagement through 'walking the Reiki path', this being intimately tied to 'being healthy' and alleviating suffering.

In the initial questionnaire I asked, apart from basic information such as age, gender, home location and length of involvement in Reiki practice, two 'primary' questions (a) 'What first drew you to Reiki as a healing practice?' and (b) 'What do you perceive to be its primary benefits?' The first question elicited various responses such as 'the universe drew me to Reiki'...'I've always been interested in healing arts and suddenly the time was right and the correct Reiki Master was there as if by magic', 'Reiki finds *you* and works in mysterious ways' to, 'I knew there was something missing from my life', 'after a family crisis', 'curiosity' and 'inner guidance'.[16]

Many practitioners stated that they had 'got into Reiki' while practising another complementary therapy — reflexology being a commonly cited example here. A second reason given was that, 'I have experienced chronic ill health myself' such as 'asthma', 'physical disability' or 'repetitive strain injury'. This in turn led these persons to visit a complementary therapist who 'put me on to Reiki' as a useful 'self healing technique'.

My second question, 'What do you perceive to be Reiki's primary benefits?' drew out answers such as Robert's 'It is a path for spiritual development. You can share the energy with others...and it's a totally new and fresh way to live'. For Peter, practising Reiki was a way of 'helping others to heal/help themselves, leading ultimately to a better world', while for Rhona, Reiki is good for 'clearing blockages which lead to physical illness and neurosis, psychological and emotional problems. It is also good for working to balance energies in people, situations and buildings etc.' When asked for additional comments Rhona stated that, 'Reiki has become an integral part of my life and has led me into other spiritual experiences such as daily meditations. It has totally transformed my attitude to life and I no longer worry about anything or let anything wind me up'. While for Peter, 'The gentle art of Reiki can be learnt so quickly and easily that it is an easy method to enhance other healing abilities such as nursing and other therapies, and it reopens the latent ability for everyone'. The following is the narration of one Reiki practitioner's story as compiled from a later interview.

16. The questionnaire may be found in Appendix B.

Susan is a paediatric nurse in Edinburgh and is in her early forties. She was brought up in the Western Isles of Scotland where "religion not politics rules" through the ministrations of the "Wee Free" [Free Church of Scotland]. "My parents were quite liberal Church of Scotland, but we still went to Church every Sunday and I also went to Sunday School. However, we were allowed to play outside on Sunday while many of my friends were not. I left the Islands when I was seventeen and came to Edinburgh to do my nurse training. I have been doing this for twenty-four years now. In the last three or four years I have become interested in the spiritual part of my life. I didn't hear about Reiki from anybody but just started feeling it in my hands. Then I had my Tarot cards read and was told that I had healing hands and had I heard of Reiki?

I started Reiki training and it brought structure into my life. I was trained by Poona and she is a follower of Osho. She is a very spiritual person, though it is strange that you do meet some Reiki people that are not spiritual at all...they just teach the craft. For me, Reiki encompasses everything. It is the Universal Life Force that exists around all of us...but we can lose this through stress or bereavement. Reiki reconnects a person to this energy which can be a very emotional time as Reiki unblocks energy blocks.

I use Reiki on myself in my working environment. I do Reiki to clear a room before treating someone [as a paediatric nurse] and am aware of using Reiki when with babies. It just flows where it's needed during my work. I also do Reiki on staff at lunchtime...sometimes. This makes a lot of people less stressed. Reiki is a really powerful energy and really amazing.

My Reiki Master had worked with Frank and Arjava Petter so the new techniques that we learnt at this workshop weren't all that new to me. They were incorporated into my training. So my First and Second Degrees are Osho-Neo-Reiki in that the teachings of Osho are incorporated into daily practice...meditation is really important for instance. I'm not a follower of Osho though.

I didn't intend to become a Reiki Master but a lot of people said that I was going to be a healer. I think life just manifests this sort of thing to you. And Poona said that I should do my Master's.... and I feel so much richer now...it's the best present that I have ever got!

The account above is fairly representative of the views held within the field of Reiki practice in Scotland. For Reiki healers acknowledge that one of the primary benefits of Reiki as healing practice is that it is beneficial for oneself initially, in that you need to 'heal yourself' before you can 'heal others'. However, it is also acknowledged that practising Reiki regularly may enable a transformation of the self through reawakening of one's latent healing abilities (which everyone has) and that this in turn enables healing to spread throughout the community. The view is also held that eventually, when enough people become awakened to the benefit and universal 'truth' of Reiki, there will be a planetary shift in consciousness towards a more spiritual planet. Hence, though many people's experience of Reiki is initially because of personal health issues, there appears also to be a steady progression from this perspective towards a feeling that Reiki is a pragmatic and empowering resource for day to day life 'to keep one healthy'.

> In order to continue to build a picture of Reiki thought and practice I shall in the next chapter, look at how Reiki energy is variously described and perceptions of how 'doing Reiki' can lead to a fuller and dis-ease free life.

Chapter Six

Doing Reiki

In the last chapter I introduced the historical background of Reiki practice and perceptions of its origination. As we saw, debates abound with regard to the actualities of Mikao Usui's life and his 'rediscovery' of Reiki in Japan in the 1920s, following which he founded the Usui Reiki Ryoho Gakkai (Usui Reiki Healing Society) and several healing clinics prior to his death in 1926. And I flagged up the perceived significance of lineage to efficiency of practice, in relation to initiating (attuning) Reiki Masters in the Western world as here, one will find forms of Reiki 'in every major urban centre in North America...through Western Europe and [in] the countries of the former British empire' (Melton 2002: 77).

In this chapter I shall continue to build a picture of Reiki healing by focusing more specifically on representations of the nature of Reiki energy and symbols. For these are central to healing practice and have, for example, been 'reclaimed' to their female roots by influential Reiki writer and practitioner Diane Stein, to whom I shall also return in the final chapter of this book in relation to her representation of Reiki as a powerful resource for women.

Reiki Energy

As with all things Reiki, representations vary about 'the nature of Reiki energy'. These representations are intimately related to the Reiki symbols or characters and their historical roots. Within Reiki circles this is a huge field of debate and as such one could write an entire book about such matters. For influential writers such as Walter Lubeck propose that a deeper understanding of the 'tool box — the symbols and their mantras — of the Usui System of Natural healing contain some important statements about the method [of walking the Reiki Path] through working with these symbols'

(2001: 43).[1] I shall merely provide here a review of some of these representations, as the use of Reiki symbols to 'draw down' Reiki energy is an integral part of healing practice. Initially, I will provide key teachers' representations of the nature of Reiki energy and their experiences of being attuned, this being the starting point for learning to 'do' Reiki as we have seen in the last chapter.

William Rand

One of America's most respected Reiki Masters is William Rand. Rand has written training guides for First and Second Degree Reiki practice, these being commonly used in Scottish healing circles and later more evaluative material on the form of Reiki symbols and energy etc. Rand states that his personal interest in spiritual matters and metaphysics began when he was at high school leading him to join the Rosicrucian Order where he learnt, over twenty years, that 'the best way to learn about life and especially about metaphysics was from experience' (Rand 2001: 61). He also spent a year studying with a Hawaiian 'Kahuna'.[2] All of these experiences deepened his awareness that underpinning all life is the energetic life force, or Ki, and that any depletion of this would lead to illness or even death (Rand 2001: 62).

Ki is a living energy. It is also known as the vital force or the universal life force. This is the non-physical energy that animates all living things. As long as something is alive, it has life energy circulating through it; when it dies, the life energy departs. If your life energy is low, or if there is a restriction in its flow, you are more vulnerable to illness. When it is high and flowing freely, you are less likely to get sick. Life energy plays an important role in everything we do. It animates the body and has higher levels of expression. Ki is also the primary energy of our emotions, thought and spiritual life. (Rand 2001: 1-2).

1. Questions might be asked here in relation to whether 'walking the Reiki path' may be regarded as the promotion of a holistic way of life which produces its own health needs, in that in order to be a 'whole person' one should learn to carry out Reiki practice and adhere to its Principles (see last chapter). Or, might Reiki be better regarded as a valuable and empowering resource for the individual to draw from? I shall engage with these issues in Chapter Seven.

2. Rand states that the word 'Kahuna' means 'Keeper of the Secret', and that he 'was very fortunate to have been given some of the Kahuna's teaching when [he] was with him' (2001: 63).

For Rand, human beings become sick when negative thoughts and intentions about oneself 'influence personal Ki in a negative way…[for] negatively directed Ki will form around the organs of the body and in the chakras and the aura, slow[ing] down healthy activities of the body' (2001: 64). Therefore health is dependent on developing and maintaining a 'positive self-image' through the 'releasing' of 'all negative thoughts and feelings from our mind' (2001: 64).[3] However, Rand also argues that what we have experienced in past lives affects the mind and subtle energy fields in our present life. 'This effect, called karma, is carried into life in the aura when the soul first enters the physical body at birth' (2001: 65). Hence, throughout our life it is this auric past-life karma that 'attracts experiences to us, which in turn strengthens the karmic charge in the aura…[which then] move[s] into the chakras, and eventually into the physical body' (2001: 65).

> As it [the karmic charge] works deeper into the energy system, the effects become more pronounced and, depending on whether this karmic energy is either positive or negative, it can affect us in different ways, attracting good fortune or bad and also having a similar range of effects on our health. This is the basis of poor health and sickness (Rand 2001: 63).

For Rand then, illness is caused by blocked or low levels of life/universal energy. This may occur if one holds on to negative thoughts and intentions, through faulty thinking, or it may be caused by negative past-life karma. These themes are common in the Scottish context, an Edinburgh healer saying to me for example, 'You're in good health so you obviously aren't carrying lots of bad karma from previous lives'. Conversely, as McGuire has proposed, 'Because the concept of karma includes reaping effects of previous "lives"' behaviour, it is a useful theodicy for the suffering, illness, or death of a good person' (1998: 107).

Rand first experienced Reiki energy when he was initiated or *attuned*, by Bethal Phaigh in 1981. During this attunement he experienced 'a new energy coming down from [his] crown chakra

---

3. This positioning is of course very similar to that expressed by Paul Heelas in his (1996:19) *The New Age Movement* where he evaluates the primary themes of New Age self-spirituality, namely how we have been 'brainwashed' – by mainstream society and culture. The [competitively materialistic] mores of the established order…[leading to] 'self limiting images and images that make us feel we are not terribly worthwhile' (cited by Wallis 1984, p. 32).

and then into [his] heart where it exploded out' (Rand 2001: 66). Following this attunement 'he noticed a new energy flowing within [himself]...[and] knew that Reiki was real and that the attunement had created an important improvement to [his] energy system' (Rand 2001).

Influential German Reiki Master, Frank Arjava Petter, similarly attributes his attunement to 'energy'. Arjava was initiated into Reiki in Berlin in 1982 by his brother who 'serendipitously thought that it might enhance our development'. We can see here, as mentioned in earlier chapters, that healing is all about beneficial mutual interplay. Petter undertook First, Second and Masters Degree level initiations in a period of three months — the speed of these initiations leaving him feeling 'unbalanced'. He felt that 'this might have had something to do with a problem with my brother's lineage as his connection could have been stronger'.[4] Following these initiations, Arjava returned to Japan where he and his wife were running a language school. He initiated his wife into Reiki and began to teach all levels of Reiki in 1983.[5] For 'At that time only the first two degrees were available to the public. Many people who had already learned the First and Second degree flocked to Sapporo from all over Japan. We've been busy teaching ever since' (Petter 1997: 13).[6]

Let us return to Rand for he also states that although all healers utilize Ki energy in their healing practice not all use Reiki life energy, this being guided by the Higher Power. Rand's preferred esoteric interpretation of the Japanese kanji for 'Rei',

> as it is used in Reiki, is more accurately interpreted to mean higher knowledge or spiritual consciousness. This is the wisdom that comes from God or the Higher Self and is the God Consciousness which is all knowing. It knows the cause of all problems and difficulties and knows how to heal them (Rand 2001: 1-1).

Rand proposes that as Reiki is guided by God or the higher power 'it knows exactly where negative Ki exists in the person's subtle

4. Arjava suggested that a lot of people 'are bothered' by lineage breaks. There seems to be considerable emphasis among Reiki masters that their lineage is strong and 'genuine' through historical connection to a valued Master, s/he ideally being from Mikao Usui's lineage.

5. Hiroshi Doi notes the arrival of Petter's Reiki teaching in Sapporo. He states that this was the birth of Western style Reiki in Japan and that 'Since then...the number of who [sic] learned Reiki is approximately 30 thousand' (2000: 53).

6. This is rather interesting. For in my local area, most Reiki practitioners are Second Degree and only go on to Master's level if they wish to initiate others on a fee paying basis.

energy system' (2001: 68). Hence it will flow to that area raising the rate of energetic vibration so that negative Ki is released or is transformed to a positive state. It is 'positive Ki which restores and maintains health' (2001: 68).

If then, our whole physical and emotional being may be affected by higher realities or power as Rand proposes — and this is a commonly held perception among Scottish Reiki practitioners — and if this higher power or dimension may be experienced in a Reiki attunement or treatment, then one might also expect there to be a similar emphasis on the transformational potential of this healing practice. Indeed, this appears to be the case. For as Rand puts it,

> The great beauty and value of Reiki is that it connects us to the part of the universe where all is guided by the wisdom, love, and peace. When we receive a Reiki treatment, we get a taste of the higher dimension; at the same time, Reiki points us towards a greater experience. If we listen to the consciousness of Reiki, we will realize that it is offering the possibility that this higher dimension could be our continuous and unending reality. Every aspect of our mind, our lives, our entire being, could be continually surrounded and guided by the love, beauty, wisdom, peace, and grace of the higher power. It is the creation of this state of consciousness within each person that is the deeper intention of Reiki. As we discover this deeper intention for ourselves and open more and more to it, our lives will be transformed (2001: 70).

For Rand then, and indeed for Lubeck and Petter, once we learn to allow our lives to be directed by our spiritual core then we will be less affected by selfish drives from our ego. A person will become healed and live life more joyously, harmoniously and in a loving manner. This perspective is apparent in Scottish healing circles as we saw in the previous chapter where Rhona responded that 'Reiki has become an integral part of my life and has led me to other experiences such as daily meditations. It has totally transformed my attitude to life and I no longer worry about anything or let anything wind me up'. Questions might well be asked here as to whether this is an empowering position for a woman or whether becoming a Reiki practitioner leads towards disengagement with the public sphere and societal issues.

But for the moment let us revisit the writing of German Reiki Master, Frank Arjava Petter and his evaluation of energy systems and attunements.

Frank Arjava Petter

Petter proposes that if one wishes to gain a deeper understanding of Mikao Usui's Reiki techniques then one should have some knowledge of the Chinese system of 'meridians', for as Mikao Usui was a Buddhist scholar who had learnt about Chinese medicine and Qi Gong, he 'did not base his Reiki system on the Indian theory of the chakras' (Petter 2002: 77).[7] Petter proposes that the energy pathways in the Chinese system of meridians enable the flow of vital energy to the physical and subtle bodies; this also relating to the flow of yin and yang.[8] 'Yin and yang are not only opposites like black and white and day and night, they are also seen as complementary elements. They are dance partners like man and woman, like high and low tide. Without the one the other does not and cannot exist' (2001: 80). Hence, Petter argues that the Reiki practitioner should, in similarity with other 'Eastern' healing practitioners, aim to restore the balance of the opposite dependencies of yin and yang enabling a state of perfect equilibrium and harmony and a healthy body (2001: 81).

Petter's emphasis on the centrality of the meridians, rather than the chakras, in Reiki practice is a considerable shift in positioning. For in his 1997 *Reiki Fire* he provides an evaluation of the 'Eastern' chakras in relation to Reiki hand positions. 'The 12 Reiki hand positions are located "above" those centers and help the energy flow freely to and through the chakras for an individual's optimum health and well being' (1997: 100). This is yet another example of ontological frameworks being reconstructed as a result of finding 'new' historical information. It is also an excellent example of how as practitioners 'walk the Reiki path' by doing Reiki 'as spiritual practice' new insights may be seen to be 'provided from the higher

7. It should be noted that Reiki healing in Scotland however is very much based around clearing energy blockages in the chakras within an eclectic interpretative framework where mixing Indian and Chinese energetic frameworks appears to be the normative procedure. For example, Rand proposes that the 'chakras are like subtle energy transformers [that] take the Ki or life force that is all around us and transforms it into the various frequencies we need…[hence] understanding them [chakras] can be helpful when giving Reiki treatments' (2002: 83).

8. Petter states that the Chinese medical system also regards everything in the universe as corresponding to the five elements of the earth (earth, fire, water, wood and metal). Hence with regard to the human physical body 'earth' corresponds with the stomach, spleen and pancreas, 'fire' with the heart and small intestine, 'wood' with the liver and gallbladder, 'metal' with the lungs and large intestine and 'water' with the kidney and bladder (2001:81).

source', this causing a shift in perspective. For as Petter argues, at the Reiki initiation (attunement) universal life energy is transferred to the student by the teacher which helps the student to 'absorb more cosmic energy for his personal wellbeing' (1997: 108-109). 'Profound understanding of the Reiki system is something that comes with time and practice to the sincere seeker' (1997: 108-109). This is why Petter regards Reiki to be a spiritual path. For as Usui founded the Usui Reiki Ryoho Gakkai in the same year that he had a satori on Mount Kurama then this system of healing is born out of religious experience (2001: 93).

'Such was the greatness and genius of Dr. Usui: the ability to channel the divine into a form that can be experienced and practised by his fellow human beings' (2001: 93).

Walter Lubeck

German Reiki Master, Walter Lubeck, also regards Reiki as a form of spiritual path, which in its practical elements is intimately related to Chinese esoteric and medical systems. Lubeck's personal path of 'living with Reiki' (1994: 13) has enabled him to 'develop his personality and to attune his life to the rhythms of the universe' (1994: 13). On this path his experiences of studying the ancient Chinese oracle the I Ching, the chakra teachings and the more inward style of martial arts in Asia (1994: 13), have assisted him in now walking the 'Reiki-do' – the path of healing love. For, he states, by travelling this path each person comes to realize that it is the divine universal life energy within oneself that gives life. 'In a certain sense everyone is God, because his or her innermost core is divine' (Lubeck 1994: 16). He proposes that the continual practice of Reiki enables each individual to 'grow into their own identity without external pressure' and experience fewer blows delivered by 'fate' as 'life force energy' is raised. His defining of 'the essence of Reiki as love; an all embracing divine vibration, emanating joy and life' (Lubeck 1994: 14) enables him to suggest that once this energy is drawn into the body, then each person will experience a more vitalized life.

> The Universal Life energy relaxes those parts of the body it is allowed to enter.[9] Tension brings anxiety and hostility into your life; wherever

9. Lubeck proposes that if a human being decides that he or she does not want to receive Reiki energy due to 'feelings of guilt or the conviction of being too "evil" or too "sinful" [then that person]… will not let anything come near [him or herself] that could bring about [his or her] healing' (1994: 28).

there is love, hostility and tension cease. This is why acute inflammations [of the body] ease under the effect of Reiki, for they are the symptoms of a conflict bound to erupt when you resist life, and blockages occur. Reiki opens other, more harmonious pathways, and in flowing the blockages will be dissolved (Lubeck 1994: 17).

Lubeck proposes that Reiki can have very positive effects on our generally hectic modern lifestyles where emotional highs and stressful situations alternate at frequent intervals, placing 'too great a strain on our nerves and organs' (1994: 24).The practice of Reiki, he suggests, balances out these highs and lows leading to a lifestyle where we learn to look inward as well as outwards.

> By becoming more in tune with your inner Self, stress and the feeling of being out of touch simply disappear. The quality of life improves as you more easily integrate the experiences you cross in your path. A sense of peace arises as you realise that the lessons you have learned enrich your personality. Physical and mental conditions improve and often disappear or are suddenly cured by medical means, which so far may have not been effective without the boost Reiki provides. Reiki supplies a continuous flow of energy which causes the Third Eye, which is responsible for the recognition and realisation of the ideal path for each of us, and the energy center, the root chakra, to work together in harmony (1994: 25).

Here then, we find an emphasis on the complementary nature of Reiki healing in that biomedical and/or 'alternative' approaches to health can be supported by 'spiritual power'. This positioning is common in healing circles and relates well to McGuire's findings in the American context, in that while some ideals of health — as holistic for example — may be relatively commonplace in society at large, 'other aspects are peculiar to the groups distinctive belief systems' (1998: 32). In Reikian circles this specificity/originality is located with the ability to channel spiritually guided *Rei* to affect universal energy, *Ki*. As put by my initiating Reiki master,

> Reiki means Spiritually Guided Universal Life Force Energy. The life force is the same energy that is present in all living things. In a Reiki treatment large amounts of this energy from the universe flow through the hands of the healer and it is guided by the spirit of the person receiving the treatment. The Reiki is a very loving energy which flows to wherever in the body it is most needed at the time of the treatment. The treatment is holistic i.e. it benefits the client mentally, emotionally, physically and spiritually. This means that the cause of a person's condition is addressed, not just their symptoms.

> Reiki treatment is safe for almost anyone to receive. It is an excellent complement to other forms of treatment, whether orthodox or complementary (FRW1 2000:1, see Appendix A).

In the above, we also can see that healing is represented as occurring because 'the spirit of the person' guides the life force energy within in an endogenous process — healing occurs within. In turn, a person's whole *condition* is addressed. This is a core theme in all energetic circles and relates to perceived shortfalls in biomedical systems, as we have seen, in that they only treat symptoms. Hence, ideas of health are constructed in the social sphere based on 'energetic norms', which in turn links 'the cause of illness to the necessary treatment'. And if a person's condition is not physically improved, then within these aetiologies there is also emphasis on providing meanings for such an occurrence; karma or past life trauma being a common example here.[10]

I would like to close this section with one last Reiki theorist and practitioner, Diane Stein, and her perceptions of the nature of Reiki energy. Stein is a significant figure in Reiki circles. She has disclosed in print the form of the Reiki symbols — a highly controversial act — and has written about the techniques of 'doing' Reiki'. For as Petter states,

> The Reiki system, including the hand positions and all the symbols, does not work without initiation, since the channel for the universal energy has not yet been opened. That is why Reiki is so bathed in secrecy: It simply cannot be talked about openly with people other than initiates (1997: 108).

Diane Stein

Stein, although acknowledging that one cannot become a Reiki practitioner without being initiated by an attuned and trained teacher of the same — and that her book is a Reiki practitioners' and teachers' guide — also feels that,

> In this time of change and crisis for people and the planet, healing is too desperately needed for it to be kept secret any longer. Always have respect for the sacredness of the information that follows and for the Goddess's gift of Reiki (1994: 1).

10. Although even these may be resolved. For example, Frank Petter informs the Reiki practitioner that it is possible to resolve one's own and others' karmic situation by sending 'the mental healing system and afterwards the power symbol. Ask for forgiveness or forgive' (1997: 45).

Stein states that she first experienced hands-on healing and several other healing techniques at the Michigan Women's Festival in 1983. From this point she knew that she wanted to devote her life to healing and spent many years learning various healing practices. However, she also felt as she progressed along this path 'that there was a piece of information missing, something that would increase the effectiveness of hands-on healing plus make it easy and simple as I suspected it could and should be' (1995: 2). Here then, we find continued emphasis on seeking out new modalities of healing practice, these enabling more effective 'work' on the self and others.

At a metaphysical gathering where she was demonstrating healing, two men approached her and asked from whom she had learnt Reiki. Despite her assertions that she knew nothing of this practice, the two men 'having felt her hands' (1994: 2) insisted that it was Reiki that she was doing. A little later they gave Stein a 'full body Reiki healing' (1994: 2) in her home and she knew that this was the simple healing system that she had been looking for. So Stein looked into the possibility of learning Reiki in 1987 and was appalled to learn of the high costs of being taught this practice—$10,000 for Master-teacher training (1994: 2).

Soon after, however, she managed to persuade a Second Degree practitioner—despite considerable resistance, for he had not received his Master's attunement—to initiate her into Reiki.[11] She immediately felt a major shift in her healing ability. 'I felt light and filled with energy I had never before experienced or dreamed existed. I was filled with light and with love for all Be-ings' (Stein 1995: 3).

By 1990 Stein was initiated to Second Degree Reiki and had started trying to pass attunements, having received a page torn from a Reiki Master manual (anonymously) upon which was written the Traditional Reiki III Master's symbol. When she informed her Reiki teacher of this 'Her anger was immediate and intense' (Stein 1995: 3). However, she later telephoned Stein back and stated that if she was going to attune people anyway she might as well have the right methods to do this. 'She then gave me the method for passing Reiki attunements over the phone' (Stein 1995: 3).[12]

11. I am interested in how this occurred. For in Scotland you are only given three Reiki symbols and it is the Fourth that is necessary (apparently) for successful attunements.

12. I shall return to Stein and 'disclosed attunements' later in this chapter.

In 1991, Stein asked a friend to channel for Reiki's historical origins. This woman,

> described Reiki as having originated with the planet that also brought the many-armed goddesses to Earth, the root culture of what became pre-patriarchal India. The Indian god we know today as Shiva, female at that time, brought the energy here and s/he wants to be remembered for this gift. When the human body for this planet was designed Reiki was incorporated into the genetic coding as a birthright of all people (1995: 8).

Stein also states that Reiki was known in India at the time of Gautama Siddharta (1995: 10) and that the technique of Reiki (but not known by that name) was familiar to Jesus as a reincarnated Bodhissatva, or Tulka; he having retained memories of previous lives and psychic and healing abilities (1995: 10).[13] Jesus, she argues, survived his crucifixion later living 'a very long and well respected life as a holy man in India' (1995: 12). As he had taught his disciples the healing art of Reiki, this spread around the globe as they travelled. She also proposes that by the fifth century Jesus' healing method was largely lost to the West, only remaining active with Buddhist adepts 'who used but did not publicize its existence' (1995: 12).

It was Mikao Usui then who found the texts describing the healing formula in their original Sanskrit in a Zen Buddhist monastery (Stein 1995: 12). He knew that, as this text was 2,500 years old, and as its meaning was concealed, he would have to work hard to translate it. Following his period of meditation on Mount Kurama where he saw, after twenty-one days, '"millions and millions of rainbow bubbles" and finally the Reiki symbols as if on a screen. As he saw each of the symbols, he was given the information about each of them to activate the healing energy. It was the first Reiki attunement, the psychic rediscovery of an ancient method"' (Stein 1995: 12).

It should be noted at this point that Stein also bases some of her interpretation on the writing of Hawayo Takata, she having been critiqued by Petter and Rand *et. al.*, for incorporating Christian elements and historical 'facts' into Usui's life story. However, Stein is still representative of the many Western Reiki practitioners who emphasize the intimate ties healers have cross-culturally to Jesus, historically and in the present, for they all have/are utilizing the same life force energy to heal.

13. Questions might be asked here, then about Reiki's earlier espoused 'originality'.

Mikao Usui left Mt. Koriyama knowing how to heal as Buddha and Jesus had healed (Stein 1995: 12).

Stein provides a comprehensive evaluation of the significance of Reiki energy and argues that, 'The nature of this energy and how it moves through the body is the nature of life itself' (Stein 1995: 77). A summary of her positioning will suffice here. According to Stein, *Ki* is life force energy and it circulates around the body, being known as Prana in India and Ch'i in China. Prana is symbolized in yogic traditions 'by the Mother Goddess called Shakti-Kundalini, the feminine quality of existence that births consciousness into form' (Stein 1995: 77). She argues that in Japan and China, 'the movement of Prana or Ki is based upon intention, this positioning also being held in Buddhist teaching' (Stein 1995: 77). Further,

> The "Ki" in "Reiki" is the Goddess of Consciousness, the life force energy, and the connecting link between the physical, energy and spirit bodies. The intention to move Ki is expressed when a Reiki healer puts her hands down to do a healing — it turns the energy on...Ki comes from the Heavens and the Earth, and is the enlivening form of Be-ing (Stein 1995: 79).

In the above Stein clearly articulates that Ki is of the Goddess and may be drawn from the heavens and the earth to enable healing, adding that each individual also is born with 'Original Ki, the life force instilled in us at conception' (Stein 1995: 77). Might one presume that for Stein, this is also of the Goddess?

As part of working with Reiki energy, Stein promotes meditation on, for example, Reiki symbols or Mandalas, this latter being common practice in Buddhist traditions. 'In Vajrayana Buddhism, this is done to gain mind control, skill in creating mental images, to contact Goddesses and other psychic forces (also mind created) and to achieve altered states of consciousness' (1995: 134). According to Stein then, it is by meditating and focusing on Ki and the Reiki symbols that the Reiki practitioner withdraws the ego and enables her 'Buddha Nature or Goddess Within [to] come forward' (1995: 134).

It is outwith the scope of this book to evaluate Stein's interpretation of Buddhist thought and practice, however overall Stein appears to argue that the Goddess is within and without, for 'it is in the heart that Tara or Kwan Yin reside' (1995: 138). She locates Reiki as of the Goddess and of the Buddha, its special qualities being that 'Reiki brings enlightenment into the body, instead of taking consciousness out of the body to achieve it (1995: 139). For Stein, the Goddess is both an external and internal reality and not just a symbol for empowerment. We shall see later in this chapter how Stein re-interprets one of the Reiki master symbols as being 'of the Goddess'. This, I shall argue, is an action which relates very much to a sense of re-empowerment for women and relates to the development of de-centralized narratives of power and a politic of reclamation.

For as we have seen in this chapter, Reiki literature is alive with debates surrounding the origins and usage of symbols, the historical background to Reiki and the specifics of energy pathways and practice. And I shall return to Reiki in the final chapter of this book where I reflect further on my time in the field and relate healing practice to other forms of gendered spirituality and to theoretical standpoints. For the moment, let us return to an event of primary significance in Reikian circles.

Learning To Do Reiki

One of the most significant initial events for the intending practitioner is, as observed earlier, the attunement or initiation which the student receives from the Reiki Master. Having experienced this for myself I find it extremely difficult to put it into words. This is why I am in accord with Young and Goulet when they propose that:

> Extraordinary experiences force one to deal with the possibility that reality is culturally constructed and that instead of one reality (or a finite set of culturally-defined realities), there are multiple realities — or at least multiple ways of experiencing the world, depending upon time, place, and circumstances (1994: 8).

My starting point for a journey into healing was responding to the following advertisement, this being placed in the local Dunfermline Press[14] in 2000.

Learn Reiki
– change your Life!
A hands on healing art that anyone can learn
For self healing or healing others
– no previous knowledge required

14. Dunfermline is a small town in Fife approximately twenty miles north of Edinburgh.

As I had already met numerous Reiki practitioners at various healing workshops in Scotland, all of whom had promoted Reiki to me as being personally self-empowering, this advertisement seemed like a useful entry point into developing an experiential awareness of the same. I secured 'the last free space' for the following weekend and duly found myself at a hotel in Dunfermline with five other women.[15] As all of us were rather unsure of what to expect of this weekend, there was, I felt, an air of somewhat nervous anticipation.

We were shown to a room 'regularly booked for Reiki' carrying our pillows, blankets and large bottles of water as requested. Initially, it felt odd to be starting out on such a potentially 'transforming' path within the confines of a hotel function room rather than at a holistic centre such as The Salisbury in Edinburgh. Once inside however, emphasis appeared to have been placed on fostering of a sense of 'different space' with a lit candle in one corner, burning incense and oriental sounding Reiki mood music. Tables were arranged around the walls for later healing work.

Fiona was an attractive young woman in her thirties simply dressed in trousers and a jersey. She asked us to draw some chairs into a circle and to introduce ourselves in turn. Ann, Marianne and Isobel (these women being aged between thirty-five and sixty) told Fiona that they were interested in learning Reiki to see if it could help them with chronic health problems that had not been relieved by bio-medical approaches to health. Susie, an expectant mother in her early twenties, wished to be able to use Reiki on herself during pregnancy and in labour for she had heard from friends that this practice was very relaxing. Lynn wished to learn Reiki 'to add another string to [her] bow' and 'to see whether Reiki strengthened [her] Bio-Energetic training'.[16] I disclosed that I had been interested in complementary therapies for many years and that I was also researching healing at the University of Stirling. We have here typical examples of the sort of people that take up Reiki. They are

15. Of the five women present one was in her twenties and in the mid-stages of a first pregnancy, while the other four were aged between thirty-five and approximately sixty.

16. Bio Energetic therapy is based on a six month training course in Ireland. Within this system practitioners are taught to heal energy field blockages, which allows the client to return to a state of balanced health. This system of healing works from the premise that all humans are energetic beings surrounded by an aura. It is this aura that displays states of dis-ease as blockages.

predominantly white, middle-class and with a good standard of education which enables them to ask questions about and seek alternative forms of health care.

As part of this period of initial introduction, Fiona told us about her journey into Reiki. She informed us that she had a two year-old daughter and that she was trained in clinical aromatherapy and massage, having a client base in Dunfermline. She had learnt Reiki initially having felt 'personally drawn to this healing art' over eight years ago. Since that point she had taken her First, Second and Master level degrees with Richard. This Reiki Master was, I later discovered in conversation with Fiona, also a follower of Osho. Fiona regarded Reiki as a lifelong spiritual way of life and hence her view is very similar to the writers I have presented earlier. Her disclosures also appeared to work on several levels, in that she located herself first as a mother and then as a working therapist with clients. By doing so, she appeared to minimize the potential for a hierarchy to be set up of teacher/student and fostered instead a sense of empathy with participants. We were all mothers or mothers to be, we all worked, and we subscribed to holistic frameworks of interpretation. In this sense 'being a woman' felt empowering as there was a perception of mutuality of experience.[17] This feeling did not dissipate throughout the weekend even when we were advised that in order to do Reiki one had to be attuned by a Master. For, in this case, it was still a woman that was going to fill this role.

The Attunements

Fiona explained that 'the attunements will raise and balance your energetic bodies so that you can become open channels for Reiki energy'. Describing what actually happens during the attunement is very difficult for the simple reason that we all had to have our eyes shut and were seated in a circle facing outwards with our bare feet 'flat on the floor for grounding'. Sensory input was hence limited to one's own perceptions 'of being blind', an interesting experience as vision is often prioritised as the sense that provides us with an awareness of objects and others and indeed our selves. As Grosz, writing on Merleau-Ponty explains,

17. I am however, also aware of the difficulties of engaging with 'women's experience'. For these are particular to the individual and are not normative — as in all women experience life in the same way.

Since the earliest days of Greek philosophy, vision was considered superior to the other senses. Knowledge itself was generally described in metaphors derived from vision and optics. Thus it has tended to function not only as the model for knowledge but also as representative of all the other senses…Its role is generally regarded as that of unifying and hierarchically ordering the other senses, taming and toning them (1993: 97).

For the attunements[18] we were asked to breathe 'as in Gassho meditation'. In order to do this we were to put our hands together in the prayer position and with 'your awareness focused at the meeting point of the two middle fingers…breathe in with the tongue touching the roof of the mouth and breathe out with the tongue relaxed. This we were told 'really opens up the heart chakra and puts you into a good state of being for doing Reiki'.

I next sensed Fiona standing behind me for a few moments while I breathed as directed. I felt her hands move above my head and lightly brush my crown. She walked to my front and pulled my hands directly forward and opened my palms as if I were holding a book before clearing the hair from my forehead. After a few moments she raised my clasped hands over my head and then lowered them, finally crossing them over my chest. Within a minute or so of her having carried out my attunement I began to experience a feeling of great heat flowing through my body and uncontrollable whole body shaking. This was completely unexpected and was also experienced, I later discovered, by three other women in the group. This shaking lasted several minutes before gradually easing off. I felt unsettled by what had happened for the whole experience was outwith my analytical frameworks and control. I quite simply did not know what had happened to me. Four attunements were carried out over this weekend with progressively decreasing body shaking but similar levels of waves of heat. After each attunement we were shown the correct hand positions and techniques for physical healing, these to be practised for the rest of the weekend.

At this point I feel it would be useful to evaluate what appeared to be occurring during the attunements. The actualities of this event are shrouded in secrecy, the Reiki Master in general regarding this as a sacred rite of initiation. Hence, here I draw from textual material.

---

18. Four attunements were carried out for this First Degree workshop within what appeared to be an identical ritual format (apart from the use of Master symbols).

I have chosen to utilize initially Reiki author William Rand's description of this 'process' in *Reiki, The Healing Touch, First and Second Degree Training Manual* (1991). For Fiona advised us that this was 'one of the best books to learn about Reiki from' and that it was this text that she had utilized throughout her own training.

According to Rand, Reiki is believed to be a special kind of healing energy that can only be channelled by a person that has been attuned to it. People who already do healing work may, apparently, experience 'at least a fifty per cent increase in the strength of their healing energies after taking Reiki classes' (1991: 1-3). He describes the attunement process in the following manner:

> Reiki is not taught in the way other healing techniques are taught. The ability is transferred to the student by the Reiki master during an attunement process. During the attunement the *Rei* or God-Consciousness makes adjustments to the student's chakras and energy pathways to accommodate the ability to channel Reiki and then links the student to the source of Reiki. These changes are unique to each person. The attunement energies are channelled into the student through the Reiki Master. The Reiki Master does not direct the process and is simply the channel for the attunement energy flowing from the Higher power (1991: 1-4).
>
> Rand also proposes that for most people the attunement is a powerful, often spiritual event, where many have reported mystical experiences, 'an opening of the third eye', flashes of past lives, healings and visions. The attuned person may also experience 'increased intuitive awareness' (1991: 1-5). Further attunements may lead to 'healing of personal problems, clarity of mind, increased psychic sensitivity and a raised level of consciousness' (1991: 1-5). Rand suggests that: 'The attunement is also attended by Reiki guides and other spiritual beings who help implement the process' (1991: 1-5) and that the attuned person will "have Reiki" (1991: 1-5) for the rest of his or her life.

The attunement is hence promoted as affecting the individual on several levels. Self-healing is enabled on physical and emotional levels by the 'clearing' of life energy. In turn the individual's life will be affected as s/he becomes a clearer energetic channel and most probably, more engaged in 'spiritual practice'.

Rand's evaluation of the effects of being attuned were, I found later, to be in accord with those of many of Fiona's students. Many of these attunees reported noticeable 'energy fluctuations', 'heightened perception' and 'hot hands' as Reiki energy flowed.[19] One should note here that students had been advised by Fiona prior to attunement that they might experience tiredness, lack of appetite and mood swings as blockages were released from the energetic field and that this might be amplified after the Second Degree attunements. It was for this reason that Fiona told potential second degree attunees that they must accept this initiation with a conscious awareness of Reiki's purpose, that of 'healing with love'.[20] On a more positive note, the ability of attuned Reiki practitioners to self-heal was promoted as a blessing in itself. For as the practitioner must self-heal on a regular basis so that s/he can channel Reiki energy freely, s/he then should enjoy the personal benefit of a more 'balanced' life as 'giving a treatment always increases one's energy and leaves one surrounded by loving feelings of well-being' (Rand 1991: 1-7).

What we appear to see in the above, is an emphasis on Reiki as a worldview that can be drawn upon in good times and in bad and in sickness and in health. As McGuire found in the American healing context, 'adherents used their beliefs and practices as an *active* and comprehensive perspective from which to understand the non-problematic as well as the problematic, the positive aspects of life as well as the negative, and health as well as illness' (1998: 211) [italics mine]. The new Reiki practitioner will actively engage in learning to heal self and others and will empirically test the efficiency of healing thought and practice, while holding the perception that

19. Shuffrey provides a concise evaluation of the Reiki energy pathway after attunement. For Shuffrey, once the student has agreed to receive Reiki into his or her life and given a gift of exchange, a gateway is created. 'The body has seven major centres of concentrated energy that are called *chakras*. These are located on the crown of the head, the brow, the throat, the heart, the solar plexus, the navel and the reproductive organs. These natural healing centres are neither open nor closed but realigned in such a way that the energy access is made available and does not revert to its original form. The initiations are the essential part of the Form, the difference between Reiki and all other forms of healing. They allow the path of Reiki to be drawn down through the top of the head, through the heart, into the solar plexus and out through the hands' (1999: 28).

20. In describing Reiki as 'loving energy' Fiona locates herself alongside writers such as Doi, for he states that ' "Reiki-ho" is a technique to heal everything you see, come across or touch by being a passage of Reiki-Universal energy as well as the wave of love'. Being a passage means to receive the wave of love by uniting yourself with the consciousness and the rhythm of the universe and to purify and transmit it as it is' (Doi 2000: 26).

by doing healing work on others one will also benefit the self. These are central concerns of holistic healing.

Before I move on to take a further look at Reiki practice in Scotland I am going to present Diane Stein's evaluation of passing attunements, for in her *Essential Reiki* she describes these as 'the major "miracle" of the Reiki healing system' (1995: 104). Stein is the only Reiki author to date to have released details of the process of attunement and the usage of symbols as part of this, for by Reikian tradition, the 'Second and Third Degree symbols should be kept absolutely secret…it is all right to write them down but they should be kept away from uninitiated eyes' (Petter 1997: 43). Hence, I have had to think very carefully whether I too am prepared to face potential censure from Reiki authorities by reproducing already printed material. For Reiki symbols are only disclosed to the student after the Second Degree attunements which cannot be taken less than six weeks after the completion of the First Degree.[21] I have, after careful thought, decided to risk doing this for similar reasons to Stein (and also because it does not involve the passing on of information given to me in confidence). Namely, if everyone has the ability to heal and if Reiki powerfully enhances this ability, then it should be available to everyone and not just those who can afford to pay the fees for training courses. I also tend to feel that if, as is promoted, Reiki can do no harm and is divinely guided, then knowledge of the same must be of value to all interested parties allowing for 'what you send out returns to you multiplied manyfold' (Stein 1995: 1). Hence, I will look first at Stein's evaluation of the process of attunement which I shall abridge. More specific information on the symbols will be presented later in this chapter.

Disclosed Attunements

Stein first states that the Reiki Master carrying out the attunements should do so while holding the 'Hui Yin position' (1995: 113). This is where the tongue is positioned at the roof of the palate, the breath is held and for women Reiki Masters the vagina and cervix is fully contracted 'closing an additional energy gate. Ki immediately begins to move upward in the body along the Hara Line, and energy can no longer move downward in the body through the feet and internal

21. No symbols are given at the First Degree attunements, so by the Second, a student will have already devoted considerable time and effort to learning the basics of 'how to heal' and will have generally accepted the need for non-disclosure of Reiki symbols.

organs. Connection is made to Earth energy, which is drawn upwards...[So eventually] Ki moves from the crown downward, as well as from the earth upward' 1995: 91).[22] At this point the Master should be centred and in contact with his or her Reiki spirit guides and standing behind the seated student. 'Some very complex things happen in the Reiki initiation, but the Master doesn't even need to know what they are. She just does the attunement. The Reiki guides and Reiki energy will take care of all that follows' (Stein 1995: 112). Stein proposes that the Master stands first behind the seated student and opens the Crown chakra primarily by visualization and hand movement. The Master symbol is drawn over the crown. The Master then reaches over the student's shoulders and takes hold of the hands. The Crown is blown into before the breath is re-held. The three other Reiki symbols are next traced over the Crown, the student's hands once again being held and the Crown blown into (1995: 114).

The Master then moves in front of the student and opens his or her hands like a book. The power symbol, the Cho-Ku-Rei is drawn over both palms and the hands tapped three times. This is repeated with the emotional/mental and distance healing symbols. The hands are then refolded and held in one hand while the Master blows from root to heart chakra and then takes a deep breath, this being held (1995: 114). Upon returning to stand behind the student the Master closes the aura with the Reiki symbols now drawn inside it while leaving the Crown chakra open. The Hui Yin is released as is the breath (1995: 113).

Stein proposes that the Reiki initiations may be 'made into a beautiful ritual, or done, as I do it, swiftly and in a matter of fact manner' (1995: 115). However, the Master should wear comfortable and loose clothing for you 'will heat up tremendously during the attunements and for a while after' (1995: 119). The Master should also be careful not to attune too many people at one sitting as this can have very draining consequences on that person's energetic levels.

I feel that this description of the Reiki attunement, which Stein proposes is a 'nontraditional' (1995: 116) version, fits well with what

---

22. Stein provides a much fuller evaluation of the Hui Yin than could be accommodated here. But in general this relates to the flow of energy or Ki around and through the body travelling along the meridians, the chakras and the Hara line – all of these being esoteric pathways.

I felt and experienced in the Scottish context. For Fiona did ritualize the procedure by carrying out a guided meditation before seating us for attunement and music was played throughout. Stein suggests that this meditation and music should induce a 'deeply altered state' (1995: 116). So let us move on and now look briefly at the actualities of learning to practice Reiki in the Scottish context.[23]

The Scottish Healer

After the first attunement as previously described, Fiona demonstrated to the rest of the students the various hand positions on my body.[24] As she did this I felt a deep sense of relaxation while she in turn expressed that, 'I can feel lots of heat coming from Jude and I sense that she has well developed psychic and intuitive abilities'.[25] Fiona also told us that she uses the following prayer prior to healing as 'it sets the right mood'.

> I give thanks to the source of Reiki for this healing. I call upon my guardian Angel and (client's name) Guardian Angel to be present. I also call upon Archangel Michael, Archangel Raphael, Archangel Uriel and Archangel Gabriel to be present. I ask them to please cleanse, bless and sanctify this room. I ask the angels to protect and guide us during this healing and to assist in any way they can. I thank the angels for their help. Amen (FRWI)

I must admit that, having 'psychic abilities' or not, it was with some trepidation that I paired up with Isobel to try for the first time to 'do' Reiki. As I placed my hands over Isobel's main chakras I kept my eyes closed as advised by Fiona having 'grounded myself' (through the visualization of my feet as rooted in the earth) so that I didn't become 'light headed', 'spacey' or 'unbalanced by the higher

---

23. I have a much fuller archive of ethnographic material but have here chosen to draw selectively from this.

24. There is some debate surrounding the 'correct' hand positions. But in general the First Degree Reiki practitioner will place her hands on or over the seven main chakras in the body to carry out a healing of the physical body. Second Degree practitioners use additional hand positions around the head for emotional and spiritual healing. These students are also advised to learn to trust their intuition, in that this will show them where areas of the energetic body are manifesting blockage or imbalance.

25. From a cynical perspective one could think that this is just 'telling the student what s/he wants to hear'. However, this sort of comment, where the emphasis is laid on 'utilising our intuitive and psychic abilities' is common within not just Reiki but all fields of healing.

vibration energies that you are channelling'. Throughout this first healing I was surprised to be able to feel different amounts of heat and cold coming from the various chakras. When I mentioned this to my partner Isobel it appeared that when I felt a chakra 'as hot' she correspondingly felt 'cold' coming from my hands. When I placed my hands on her knees she stated that she felt 'a lot of heat' at this place and that she had problems with painful knees. I too, in similarity to most of the other students, felt extremely hot while 'working with the energetic body'. Fiona explained that this was because the Reiki energy was clearing out toxins from the body and also opening the Reiki channels. And indeed this feeling of intense heat was further amplified after the second attunement where these energetic pathways were 'further cleared'. This second attunement also resulted in what appeared to be more 'sensing' hands. For when I 'worked' with Fiona on Susie, the expectant mother, I could feel 'waves of energy' running up and down Susie's body between Fiona and myself.

The rest of the weekend involved learning, as Fiona put it, 'to feel the energy flowing through the chakras' and to see whether we felt 'heightened sensitivity' after attunements. For 'receiving each attunement helps to speed up the rate of vibration of the physical body, which tends to increase spiritual awareness as well as promoting healing'. The second-degree attunements 'further increase the students' healing power, and often sharpens intuitive and psychic abilities' (FRW2 2000: 3, see Appendix A).

Fiona advised us that a Reiki healing treatment should usually take about one hour and that it is carried out with the client lying fully clothed on a treatment couch. 'The treatment usually feels deeply peaceful and relaxing for the client and the healer, who also receives some of the Reiki energy and is never drained by the treatment'.

I participated in the Reiki Second Degree workshop some six weeks after completing the First Degree weekend, having practised Reiki on friends and family in the intervening period. Fiona advised Isobel, Ann, Marianne, Susie and me[26] that 'the two further attunements you will receive today will enable you to do emotional

---

26. Lynn did not return to the Second Degree workshop as she had not felt any increase in her Bio-energetic healing ability.

and spiritual as well as physical healing'.[27] Rather than describing the totality of this workshop I will focus on an integral part of Reiki healing from Second Degree, the three Reiki symbols, these being used to enhance physical, mental/emotional and absent healing, I shall draw from Fiona's notes for Second Degree Reiki where she categorically stated that 'these secret symbols are not to be revealed to those not attuned to Reiki'.[28] And I shall then move on to Diane Stein's much contested disclosure of the same.

The Symbols in Healing

At the Second Degree weekend Fiona carried out two attunements on each of us in turn, again in the same large room. Following the attunements, these being carried out in the same way as those in the first workshop, but utilizing different symbols, we were again asked to pair up and take turns at healing each other. I did not experience any body shaking at these attunements but still felt the same sensations of increased heat in my body.

Fiona advised us that all that is needed to activate Reiki energy is 'right intent' and that she usually says to the person being treated that 'You are a beautiful being of light. This Reiki is being sent to your highest essence. Take what you need for perfect body, mind and spirit knowing that it is sent with the greatest of love'. Fiona also informed us that this treatment 'gives access to the client's subconscious mind so positive affirmations are particularly powerful when used by the healer during this part of the treatment, e.g., "I know that I am healed and whole", or "I have chosen to heal" can be very effective' (FRW1 2000: 2, see Appendix A). Once again then, we see an emphasis on the transformatory power of affirmations.

We were also told that it was necessary to do 'an auric cleansing—a Ken-Yo-Ku or dry bathing—on yourself if you intend

27. Although the splitting of emotional/spiritual and physical healing sounds more dualistic than holistic this may not actually be the case. For First Degree practitioners are encouraged to use 'body' Reiki primarily for themselves, for as this Reiki energy flows more freely through their 'energetic body' both mind and body will be progressively healed. This, Fiona advised us enables 'students to take the Second Degree attunements (which nearly all practitioners do) while being more balanced and open. This means that you can channel Reiki more effectively and heal better'.

28. Fiona informed us that there is considerable debate as to whether the Reiki symbols should ever be written down. For example, Rand proposes that 'Since the power of the symbols comes from the attunement, showing them to those who have not received the attunement will not help them and could cause confusion' (1991: 11-5).

to do a Reiki healing'. This technique can be used 'before and after treatment to disconnect from the client, to clear ourselves of negative emotions, to clear ourselves from negative thought' and 'in order not to bring work home' or 'after shopping in town' (FRW1 2000: 6, see Appendix A). Here, we have continued emphasis on the relationship between mind and healing work, with healthiness being partly attributable to a 'right' state of mind.

After lunch and another period of visualization Fiona introduced us to 'the symbol used for absent healing and directing the energy' stating that 'this is a particularly effective way of sending healing to a person, place or situation both in the past, present and future…the Reiki being directed by intention if sent to a situation'. We were advised that 'absent healing should be sent only with the receiver's consent and it is best to arrange a time when the person is resting as the treatment can make them sleepy'.

I must admit that I had my 'sceptical hat' on with regards to the possibility of any effectiveness of absent healing. However, all of the practitioners that I have spoken to propose that absent healing can be much more effective than hands-on as 'it knocks out the ego of the healer relating to the client'. A small illustration might be of use here hence I shall first (a) relate how Catherine experienced one 'absent healing', (b) describe my father's responses to an 'absent healing' as sent by myself and (c) present a healer from Tayside's description of a 'sent' absent healing as received by her elderly mother.

Catherine

Catherine is a Reiki practitioner from Fife and she related the experience of receiving an absent healing to me during an interview.

> Well, I laid on my bed and I'd got the house nice and quiet and put some…you know...sort of nice music on. Well, I was just lying there and all of a sudden it was like I could feel someone's hands on my head and I felt all warm and sort of cosy. I've been having problems with my back so I had said to Jessie [the sending practitioner] to send me Reiki there [her back] and I think it helped. No, I really feel it did because I got up afterwards and it was nowhere near as sore you know …like down at the bottom…and during the healing I could feel like hot hands and my back felt all warm and…hmm…sort of tingly.

Jude

> My father has suffered from arthritis in his hips and knees for several years and, having found that I was learning Reiki, suggested jokingly

that I should "send him some for his legs to see if they would work any better". My father is from Yorkshire and, to use one of his euphemisms, "calls a spade a spade", while prior to retirement also being a financial administrator for a large health board. He regards himself as being eminently practical and subscribes to conventional medicine because "I've paid for it all my life so I'm not going to use anything else". So as requested I "sent him Reiki" at his designated time and place and waited to hear from him. The following day he rang to say that he had lain on his bed at the time Reiki was to be sent and "much to my surprise felt lots of heat and tingling in my hips and knees". He also informed me that he "felt much less stiff" and could "now tie [his] shoelaces more easily". I repeated the healing for him over the next two days and he suggested that while the feeling had not been so intense on later occasions he had still experienced continued improvement in his ability to get about.

The down side of this healing was that he felt so much more comfortable in his legs that he went outside without his stick, slipped on the step at the door and twisted his ankle. He has not asked for Reiki since!

Maggie

I carried out an absent healing for my mother and she said to me afterwards "Maggie…it was just like you were in the room with me…I felt that if I had opened my eyes I'd have seen you there…it was just incredible". Maggie explained to me that "my mother had broken some bones in her foot and when I was doing the healing I could feel throbbing in my hands when I got to her feet.[29] My mother also said to me that when she got up to go to the toilet later, her feet felt great…and I said to her, she'd go to the toilet a lot as Reiki would flush out the toxins in her body".

Maggie then explained that she had carried out another absent healing for her mother two days later and "had felt a lot of heat when I worked on her shoulders [on the teddy bear]. And afterwards…you know, she said to me 'what a heat I felt on the back of my shoulders and how did you know they were sore?'… and I'd said to her "it's Reiki going where it's needed". Maggie also added that her mother had been on sleeping tablets for the last twenty years and had been able to sleep without them since receiving Reiki.

These three brief narratives of the experience of receiving absent healing illustrate well the sense of surprise that the healee often

---

29. A teddy bear is often used in absent healing as representative of a person's body. Correspondingly, Maggie would have her hands on the teddy bear's feet, when she felt 'throbbing in her hands'.

feels when they experience sensations in areas of the body where there is a physical problem. For the promoted benefit of Reiki is that, as it is God directed, healing will always go to the area that it is needed—even if the healer has no awareness of this location. And as the uninitiated receiver may well also have no awareness of energetic healing, then the experience may appear bizarre or unreal. For while most people receiving absent healing do this because it is coming from a friend or family member and hence might be more receptive to the possibility of its occurrence, this is not always the case. Belief is not necessary for healing to occur. It just appears 'to work' and provide practical benefits.

Now while Fiona has proposed, in accord with Reiki authors such as Rand (1991), Lubeck (1996), Petter (1997), that the distant healing symbol can be used to send absent healing to past, present and future situations, it can also, according to Rand:

> be used for exorcism and spirit release work. This is a simple process that is very powerful. It is not based on a contest between you and the spirit therefore it does not drain your energy or place you in harm's way. Just use the distant healing symbols to send Reiki to the spirit, then call on the Ascended Masters and ask them to take the spirit up into the light. Continue for a few more minutes until you feel the process is complete. The Ascended Masters will do all the work and deal with the spirit in exactly the right way to create a healing both for the person and the spirit (Rand 1991: 11-12).

Once again, we see in the above an emphasis on locating healing within larger New Age frameworks of belief. For the Ascended Masters are commonly perceived to be significant sources of knowledge and revelation in these circles. They are, in the Scottish context, frequently channelled by healers and tend to be described as 'the Christ' or 'the Buddha' or 'the entity Michael' and they, along with personal spirit guides, may assist with 'difficult' healings. Indeed, I have also heard one Edinburgh healer claim that he himself was an Ascended Master who had returned to earth 'to help others to come home'. It is rare however, to hear descriptions of these 'beings' manifesting in female form. This is why writers such as Monica Sjoo (1994) and Mary Daly (1991) would regard these sort of representations to be eminently patriarchal, leaving little space for women to reconnect with the Goddess and the spirits of nature. However, as I shall argue in Chapter Seven, spirit guides of a female or androgynous nature may also be 'utilized' as 'vehicles' for women's personal growth, with channelled information also providing new sources of gendered empowerment.

But let us for the moment return to the interpretation and usage of the Reiki symbols. Here we find that there is considerable diversity of thought and a multiplicity of interpretations of the Reiki symbols and their historical background. Many of these locate the rediscovered symbols as being of Sanskrit or Chinese origin, as we saw with Lubeck's interpretation in the last chapter.

Diane Stein

For Diane Stein, the Reiki symbols are part of the 'Mahayana Sutras and the Vajrayana [Tibetan Tantric Buddhist] mystical interpretations' (1995: 133). A brief review of Stein's interpretation and usage of the same will be useful here as I am interested in her location of these in particular frameworks and traditions and whether this affects levels of empowerment.

The five Reiki symbols are the five levels of mind that lead to Enlightenment. They are familiar to Buddhists as the Path to Enlightenment itself (1995: 131).

> Together the five Reiki symbols are the non-duality of mind and object and the emptiness from ego that achieves Buddhist Nirvana. Once attained, the formula and the process of Reiki releases the soul from the wheel of incarnation. The symbol system's original use was not for healing but spiritual—Enlightenment for the purpose of helping others, the Bodhissatva Path (1995: 132).

In the five symbols are the five stages of this path. The Cho-Ku-Rei is the beginning stage and represents the physical/etheric double level. The Sei-he-Ki is the transformation of emotion and ego (the emotional body), the Hon-Sha-Ze-Sho-Nen is the creation of the true reality by the understanding of the pure mind on the mental level. The Dai-Ko-Myo is the attainment of the Bodhissatva Path and represents the spiritual body. The Raku is enlightenment itself, transcendence and Nirvana, the beyond-the-body Transpersonal level (1995: 133).

Stein's interpretation of the symbols in this way is based on discussions with a Mahayana Buddhist nun, she being familiar with these symbols in her daily practice. Since then Stein has researched Mahayana and Vajrayana Buddhism extensively and feels that this philosophy and Tantric Buddhism underpins 'virtually all religions' (1995: 129). Questions might be asked here with regard to the 'originality' of Reiki as promoted by Rand, Petter *et al.*, and my Reiki Master's assertion that 'Reiki is not associated with any religion, but it is a spiritual practice and can facilitate personal and spiritual growth' (FRW1 2000: 1).

Stein also states that 'the Reiki symbols are Sanskrit-derived Japanese forms, at least 2,500 years old' (1995: 133) and that these representations as such, according to the Buddhist nun, are cultural variations. However for Stein, irrespective of which way these symbols are presented to the student, his or her primary problem is their memorization for usage in healing work as they become easily distorted. She is right in this assertion. For while the first and second symbols are fairly straightforward to memorize, the third is rather more complicated and for many Scottish practitioners

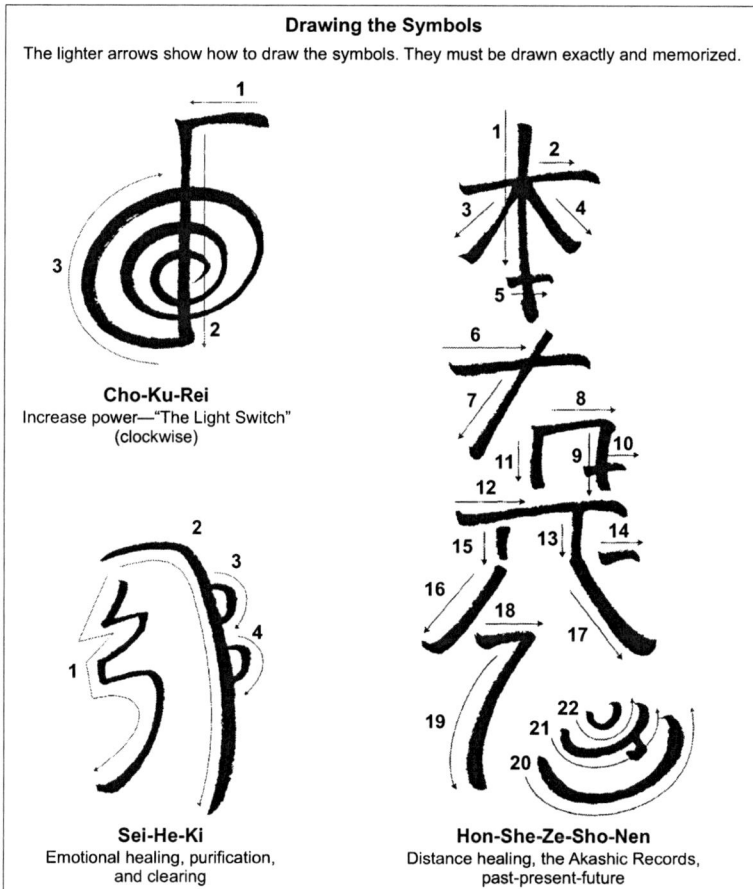

Drawing the Symbols

The lighter arrows show how to draw the symbols. They must be drawn exactly and memorized.

Cho-Ku-Rei
Increase power—"The Light Switch"
(clockwise)

Sei-He-Ki
Emotional healing, purification,
and clearing

Hon-She-Ze-Sho-Nen
Distance healing, the Akashic Records,
past-present-future

(Stein 1995: 58)

this results in them using a drawing of the same when absent healing (at least initially) — this being usually carried out from the healer's own home. The symbols used by Second Degree practitioners are as follows with instructions showing how they should be drawn.

Stein states that the first symbol, the Cho-Ku-Rei /cho ku ray, is most probably used in all healing sessions, as by visualizing this 'your ability to access Reiki energy is increased many times' (1995: 57). She notes that she was taught to draw this symbol clockwise while the traditional Cho-Ku-Rei is drawn counter-clockwise. (I was taught to draw this symbol in the latter fashion). Having experimented with the strength of flow of power along with her students, Stein now feels that one should draw this symbol clockwise as this is the correct way for the Northern Hemisphere. 'In any metaphysical work, including Wicca, clockwise motion in the Northern Hemisphere is the direction of invoking and increase, and counter-clockwise is the direction of decrease and dispersion. In the Southern Hemisphere it is the opposite' (1995: 57). However, she also adds, again in accord with all practitioners, that the key to doing Reiki is 'intent', therefore the healer should try both ways and see which works best for them when they intend to increase power in healing.

However, Stein presents a major interpretative shift in relation to this symbol typical of the Reiki practitioner's 'pick what feels right for me' approach. For she argues that when one uses this symbol one is focusing Reiki in a particular spot by,

> calling all the energy of the Goddess Universe into the healing. The spiral and pathway shape of this symbol is the design of the Labyrinth, an initiation space at the ancient temple of the Palace of Knossos on Crete. In the archaeology of the planet, spirals always represent Goddess energy (1995: 57).

Stein effectively appears to reclaim this central Reiki symbol back to its 'female' roots for women and at the same time downplays the 'male' overlay so prevalent in Reiki writing and teaching practice, as for Stein, the 'Buddha nature or Goddess Within' (1995: 134) are one and the same. This sort of reappropriation has proved itself to be highly popular with women Reiki practitioners who are also involved in aspects of feminist spirituality.

Now when Stein was taught the second emotional healing symbol that works on the subconscious, the Sei-He-Ki, this was defined for her as 'God and man coming together…[for this symbol] brings divinity into human energy patterns and aligns the upper chakras' (1995: 59). Stein was rather offended by this portrayal, for why should this not be 'Goddess and women coming together' or 'Divinity and people' (1995: 59). Hence, I would agree with her implicit assertion that as this symbol is primarily utilized for emotional healing—in that it may be used to heal long held 'painful emotion or trauma' (1995: 59) this having caused dis-ease—then having a 'female' symbol of power may be empowering as the 'symbol brings Divinity into human energy patterns and aligns the upper chakras' (1995: 59).

Stein also argues that this symbol may be utilized to 'seal the space or person's aura from encroachment from any form of negativity' (1995: 74) and in combination with the Cho-Ku-Rei may be used for manifesting abundance or 'boosting positive qualities' (1995: 72).

The Universe is comprised of abundance, with every goodness available for those who ask and are ready to receive. Receiving is not easy for most people, especially women—we have been taught that we do not deserve to have or to ask for good things. Of course we do. While many situations are karmic—and patriarchal—manifesting is a skill that can be learned (1995: 72).

Overall, Stein proposes that healers who work frequently at the Second Degree level will begin to become 'aware of realities beyond the physical plane. She will come to know her spirit guides and be able to "access other worlds for information and help in healing"' (1995: 66). She will find after attunement that a process of mental and emotional clearing will take place where long held damaging thought patterns are challenged and removed.

> The process of emotional/mental clearing is never easy. One woman may decide that her primary relationship is no longer right for her and leave her partner. Another may finally deal with the abuse or incest memories that she has pushed aside for years. Someone else may choose to stop working for other people and go into business on her own. Dreams that seemed only fantasies now become daily life, and what were once unacceptable risks become things to reach for routinely. Everyone is stretched by Reiki II, everyone grows. At the end of a year or so, the healer looks at who she once was and who she is now. She is amazed to realize that she is stronger and more whole, though the path getting there seemed chaotic. She is pleased with who she has become (1995: 66-67).

Although the above appraisal might be somewhat optimistic, it is also however, the case that many women do change their way of life having become Reiki practitioners and do also deal better with the trauma or life change which occurred—this leading them to Reiki in the first place. I have heard stories from so many women in Scotland of how they got involved with healing and New Age thought because their lives had 'hit rock bottom'. Nearly all of these women perceive themselves to be more empowered and healthier. It is to these perceptions of empowerment that I shall turn in Chapter Seven, where I shall revisit issues raised throughout this book and consolidate my positioning that within healing circles, women appear to be engaged in a politics of reclamation and work within 'fluid fields of force'.

Chapter Seven

POWERFUL BODIES

Within this book I have provided the first empirical academic study of energetic healing and Reiki as it is in central Scotland. I have placed emphasis on exploring how participants learn to heal in specific workshop settings, the teachings and issues that underpin healing practice and students' responses to the same. Throughout this work, I have drawn selectively from ethnographic material and have supported this with textual examination of New Age healing literature and workshop manuals etc.

This is also the first exploratory study of how gendered spiritualities may be actively constructed in the above settings in relation to, for example, the internalization of healing concepts. It is hence, I would argue, another step towards addressing the historical imbalance of writing about New Age beliefs, practices and location from a predominantly androcentric positioning. For as Dominic Corrywright states, 'the web of New Age spiritualities is crucially sustained by the individual and collective weavings of women and this is particularly evident in healing and therapies' (2003: 131).

In the Scottish New Age setting, as we have seen, women's predominance in healing circles has a lot to do with personal projects of redefinition and self-transformation. This sort of 'work on the self' does not occur under, as radical feminists Daly (1991) and Sjoo (1994) would state, overarching patriarchal paradigms. Rather, 'healing of the self' is located within 'fluid fields of force' (Foucault 1980). Hence, in order to build up a more decentralized narrative of power I have related this particular research to other empirical studies of healing, Meredith McGuire's (1998) *Ritual Healing in Suburban America* being a key example here, and to feminist writers in general. I have also drawn from research in the parallel fields of Goddess and women's spirituality. For here we do find useful examinations of how women re-inscribe their bodies as sacred and practice outwith the confines of institutionalized religion and bio-medical approaches to health.

Therefore within this chapter I shall consolidate my work by returning to key themes introduced in earlier chapters. These will include evaluations of my politicized location as a *bothsider* (an academic writer and Reiki practitioner), the multivalent discourses of power within healing circles themselves and examinations of how gendered identities are substantively constructed within specific healing contexts. For questions need to be asked about why women predominate in healing circles and networks and these must be related to empirical contexts as well as to textual material. To this end let us first return to feminist historian Joan Scott's positioning on gendered identities, as this can be usefully situated alongside the work of Meredith McGuire *et al.*

Scott (1986) states that feminist historians of religion have tended to feel more comfortable writing descriptively rather than theoretically. However, she argues that progressively this standpoint has shifted as these writers have become aware of the need for, in relation to case studies of women's history, 'some synthesizing perspective that can explain continuities and discontinuities and account for persisting inequalities as well as radically different social experiences' (1986: 1055). For Scott, we must apply gender as an analytical category so that we can analyse 'the relationships between male and female experience in the past [and] also the connection between past history and current historical practice' (1986: 1055). She defines gender as an analytical category in the following manner:

> Gender is a constitutive element of social relations based on perceived differences between the sexes, and gender is a primary way of signifying relationships of power. Changes in the organisation of social relationships always correspond to changes in the representation of power, but the direction of change is not necessarily one way. As a constitutive element of social relations based on perceived differences between the sexes, gender involves four interrelated elements: first culturally available symbols...second, normative concepts that set forth interpretations of the meanings of the symbols [and] that attempt to limit or constrain their metamorphic possibilities (1986: 1067).

Scott's final two subsets relate to the gendered relations to be found in kinship circles, these encompassing political and economic 'issues' and the development of subjective identities (1986: 1067).

Scott argues that by applying gender as an analytical category in the above manner we can move away from earlier feminist effort, which attempts to 'explain the origins of patriarchy' (1986: 1057). For these theories of patriarchy are problematic in that they 'assert the primacy of that system in all social organisation' (1986: 1058) and hence provide 'endless variations on the unchanging theme of fixed gender inequality' (1986: 1059). This is most certainly the standpoint of radical feminist Mary Daly.

For Daly, a writer who, in her own words, found that her creative process of forming *Gyn/Ecology* involved the flinging open of doorway after doorway in her imagination as she 'raced through the labrynthine passages of [her] mind, Facing and Naming the myths and actual atrocities of Goddess-murder all over the planet' (1991:xx). Patriarchy is without doubt primary in all social organizations.

> Patriarchy appears to be "everywhere". Even outer space and the future have been colonized. Nor does this colonization exist simply "outside" women's minds, securely fastened into institutions we can physically leave behind. Rather it is also internalised, festering inside women's heads, even feminist heads (Daly 1991: 1).

Daly holds the basic premise that no matter where one travels in this world of polluted 'phallo-technic societ[ies] (1991: 9) one will find 'mind/spirit/body pollution inflicted through patriarchal myth and language at all levels' (1991: 9). Of particular relevance to this research is her proposition that 'soul doctors (priests and gurus), mind doctors (psychiatrists, ad-men, and academics), and body doctors (physicians and fashion designers) are, by professional code, causes of disease in women and hostile to female well-being' (1991: 10). Men want to possess 'female energy' (1991: 12) in all its creative aspects. Daly argues that, for women, the way out of this patriarchal morass is to remember who they are and reclaim their own power. Women must become aware of how women have been erased (as witches and in patriarchal scholarship), reversed in mythology (as in Adam giving birth to Eve), falsely polarized where 'male-defined "feminism" is set up against male-defined "sexism" in the patriarchal media' (1991: 8), and divided and conquered. In this latter 'token women are trained to kill off feminists in patriarchal professions' (1991: 8). Once women have remembered 'the games of the fathers' (1991: 8), she posits, they will live beyond patriarchy as 'Survivors having cut through the multiple layers of deception' (1991: 8).

What Scott and Daly would both agree on is that women and men's sense of identity is intimately related to complex webs of social relationships. These interrelationships are therefore indivisible from discourses of power. For an individual is affected by 'authoritative' discourses from the fields of science, medicine, religion and politics etc., in relation to 'how one should be as a human being'. Correspondingly, the 'experts' in these fields promote standards of 'acceptable' behaviour for the individual in relation to *gendered* bodies, minds, and souls. So let us now look more closely at theoretical investigations into New Age spiritualities themselves.

Dominic Corrywright has provided us with a useful evaluation of such investigations to date. He argues 'that the New Age emerges *both* out of the historical conditions and processes that have constructed unified theories *and* is a product of postmodernity with its fractured, deconstructed models of knowledge' (2003: 24, italics original). It is a dynamic and evolving field built on complex relationships with historical roots. Hence, if the academic tries to locate the same within a typology – this also being based on multiple layers of epistemological and ontological assumptions – then one will be faced with major challenges. For a 'typology is…perforce, static' (2003: 23) and if the scholar constructs the same then 'she or he begins to create a framework of shadows, of closure' (2003: 23). This is why I have noted initially that McGuire's categorization of 'healing types' might be better located as constitutive elements of healing practice.

Corrywright also states that New Age spiritualities as theories of knowledge are not 'monolithic attempts to define how we really know the world' (2003: 23) but rather that they search for 'the cracks and fissures of the reified systems of modern scientific epistemology' (Corrywright 2003: 23). In this assertion he is correct. For New Age theories of knowledge are often built up in messy, unstructured ways with individuals picking and mixing according to need and personal applicability. Correspondingly, a person may draw from science or any of the world religions and spiritualities and appropriate the parts 'that work for them'. Hence, although New Agers may be critical of science as reductionist and rationalistic, they will equally happily adopt scientific theorists who appear to support their own theories — Fritjof Capra (1977), David Bohm (1980) and Rupert Sheldrake springing to mind here.[1]

At the same time, when the New Ager begins to question 'absolute truths' she or he engages in a project of disrupting the normative concepts that attempt to fix such 'truths'. 'These concepts are expressed in religious, educational, scientific, legal, and political doctrines and typically take the form of a fixed binary opposition, categorically and unequivocally asserting the meaning of male and female, masculine and feminine' (Scott 1986: 1067). Hence, we need to examine the founding presumptions and methodological criteria that underpin such theories of knowledge. This is of particular importance to those feminists who wish to challenge 'the traditional patriarchal forms that knowledge has taken thus far' (Grosz 1993: 187). For once we become aware that 'knowledges are but perspectives — points of view of the world — [then we can] acknowledge that other, quite different positions and perspectives are possible' (Grosz 1993: 194). New Age women are but one example of a 'group' who have become aware of the multiple possibilities for redefining and re-empowering the self. I shall return to specific redefinitions of the gendered embodied self later in this chapter.

However, another of the key difficulties in 'accurately' representing New Age theories of knowledge is the historical prioritization of text in academic circles. I would argue that when engaging with this field of enquiry we would do better to work from a more flexible positioning — where text is not seen as the sole provider of 'truth'. For text is not the sole medium for New Age theories of knowledge.

Experiential touch, and particularly *the energetic touch*, is also of central significance. This is why my position as a *bothsider* has been useful. I have learnt to feel energetically and have an appreciation, politicized though it is, of 'what it is to do healing work' and the sense of transformation that this fosters. Hence, I am in accord with Corrywright when he further argues that,

> the most successful and accurate hermeneutic in the study of New Age
> spiritualities is one which is practically orientated to participation

---

1. Capra wrote *Tao of Physics*; Bohm, *Wholeness and the Implicate Order*; and Sheldrake, *A New Science of Life: The Hypothesis of Formative Causation*. All of these develop new theories of the world (and its inhabitants) as holographic, energetic and interconnected.

and qualitative approaches, rather than observing and quantitative approaches. More radically, it adopts some of the very challenging ideas of New Age spiritualities themselves in order to capture the dynamic and manifold nature of the phenomena adequately (2003: 45-46).

Another problem arises with the prioritization of text as 'source of academic knowledge'. This is of particular relevance for the first time ethnographer who very often is researching to gain a PhD. This new fieldworker will be working in an 'original field' and will be relatively new to the difficulties of descriptive writing and of representing events (such as initiation into Reiki) in a textual format that satisfies academic criteria for objective analysis. Such an event is also a subjective, embodied and very personal experience. Correspondingly, I have found myself enmeshed in a task of not appearing to write defensively for an academic audience about a different form of knowledge. I have had to ask myself questions with regard to levels of personal disclosure. Would I, for example, admit (defensive stance) that as part of this research I have learnt to see the basic levels of the aura and have hence found myself in 'a whole new world of possibilities' (positive healer's standpoint). As Horsfall succinctly observes: 'Our knowings, our understandings are often multifaceted, multidimensional and sometimes chaotic. And yet we are required to explain ourselves in one dimension [the written word]; there is no room for the multitude of voices, thoughts and feelings that occur in the meaning-making of bodies' (2001: 88). Prioritizing text also means that demonstrations of practices such as Reiki are excluded from knowledge transmission in academic circles. Hence, a significant form of 'religious' bodily expression is 'silenced' and excluded.

On the other 'side of the coin', I have also discovered that my own bodily state—and historical experiences of dis-ease—has been a significant medium for mutual understanding. For, by having turned to holistic therapies myself, I was seen to acknowledge healers' own ways of 'knowing the world'. McGuire had similar experiences during her research in Ireland in the late 1970s. Here the local women came to her aid and McGuire reciprocated by providing transportation to markets, handing down baby clothes and by helping a sick neighbour. In this process 'My women neighbours and I discovered our commonalities, which then became a foundation for a better understanding of their social worlds'

(McGuire 1992: 202). She also observed that her own experiences of mothering, and the Irish women's experiences of McGuire's mothering 'allowed for a closer mutual identification' (1992: 203). This, too, I experienced in the Scottish context for I was regularly asked whether I had children and indeed whether they had been initiated into Reiki. The point McGuire makes overall is the significance of mutual understandings based on physicality and that memories are not just experienced in the mind 'but also as a bodily experience' (1992: 205), her 'later studies of illness and healing [convincing her] of the possibility and validity of this way of knowing' (1992: 205).

> Ours was not exactly the same experience [of nursing an infant]. We could not, for instance, experience the other's memories. But the shared physical experience was a critical bridge that enabled me to understand the neighbour more deeply, drawing from my own body/mind experience. It strikes me that this may be an unexplored avenue by which ethnography goes beyond the purely personal knowledge of the ethnography (McGuire 1992: 205).

I agree with McGuire most wholeheartedly. For until I was initiated into Reiki, I could not *feel* doing healing work. Being initiated enabled me to have a better understanding of healers' narratives of experiencing the same—even if experiential appraisals differed somewhat in content.

One writer who, according to Elisabeth Grosz, has made a significant contribution to theorizations of the body and experience is Merleau-Ponty. I shall draw very briefly from Grosz's engagement with his work here, as I am interested in her perceptions of his usefulness for feminist writers.

> Merleau-Ponty begins with a fundamental presumption, not of Cartesian dualism of mind and body but of their necessary interrelatedness. He claims that phenomenology wants to understand the relations between consciousness and nature and between interiority and exteriority. The body and the modes of sensual perception which take place through it are not mere physical/physiological phenomena; nor are they simply psychological results of physical causes. Rather, they affirm the necessary connectedness of consciousness as it is incarnated; mind, for him, is always embodied, always based on corporeal and sensory relations (Grosz 1993: 86).

Primacy is hence not to be given to 'mind' within Merleau-Ponty's frameworks, for one cannot stand back from the body as 'it is through this that we perceive and receive information of and from the world' (Grosz 1993: 86). The body is hence the medium through and in which we have relations with others and experience life as meaningful. In turn, perception and experience are located 'midway between mind and body and require the functioning of both' (Merleau-Ponty quoted in Grosz 1993: 94-95). For Grosz, it is Merleau-Ponty's 'emphasis on lived experience and perception, his focus on the body subject, [which] has resonances with what may arguably be regarded as feminism's major contribution to the production and structure of knowledges—its necessary reliance of lived experience, on experiential acquaintance as a touchstone or criterion of the validity of theoretical postulates' (Grosz 1993: 94).[2] So while Merleau-Ponty acknowledges that experience is itself 'implicated in and produced by various knowledges and social practices' (Grosz 1993: 94):

> his understanding of the constructed synthetic nature of experience, its simultaneously active and passive functioning, its role in both the inscription and subversion of socio-political values, provides a crucial confirmation of many feminists unspoken assumptions regarding women's experiences (Grosz 1993: 94-95).

So how does my positioning as a feminist relate to my experiential knowledge as a healer? Spickard and Landres have succinctly observed that analysis of women's experiences in the world—my own might be included here—require an ethnographic approach so that we may chart a 'new religious landscape' (2002: 4). They also argue that ethnography in general has been impacted upon by feminism and that 'it is not an accident that many—not all—of the most prominent contemporary ethnographers of religion are also feminist women' (2002: 4). For feminism, as a critical method of study is engaged, in part, in the unmasking of areas where women are silenced. Academic writing on the New Age is just one such area where I have argued that this occurs. Similarly, Wendy Griffin tells of the difficulties of obtaining funding into Goddess spirituality (see Chapter One of this book). Hence, questions must be asked

---

2. Grosz flags up here that one must also be aware that 'experience' is not an unproblematic category but is 'of course implicated in and produced by various knowledges and social practices' (1993: 94). She also states that Merleau-Ponty's work 'remains inadequate for understanding the differences between the sexes' (1993: 109) though remaining a valuable resource for rethinking the body outside of dualistic notions.

here with regard to the perceived significance of some fields of study by those with academic power and the downplaying of others as academically of 'less significance'. Or are these 'to be unfunded' areas seen as potentially dangerous and threats to long held patriarchal bastions, as Mary Daly proposes? And in the same way that feminist writers continue to evaluate the patriarchal underpinnings of much 'recognized knowledge' (science and religion being two key examples here) so too do many feminist women in New Age and Goddess spiritualities negatively evaluate the same. Both feminisms critique '"the rules" and "boundaries" of acceptable knowledge and behaviour… [as] historically conditioned by social constructions' (Corrywright 2003: 63) while also providing new and positive visions for the future (Corrywright 2003: 63). In turn these 'positive visions' themselves are situated within fluid fields of force. They are embodied visions tied to, in New Age circles, healing practices. These are carried out in the social world. The Reiki practitioner hears of conflict or suffering and does Reiki, often with others, to 'raise the energy levels at that place, time or situation' to effect actual change. And even if working on the self, the vision remains the same. Focus is placed on the spiritual development and transformation of the self so that that embodied self can actively bring about change. The healer's social interactions and 'moral' way of being becomes in its own right (it is hoped at least) an instrument for promoting harmony and 'positive growth' with the maximising of one's own potential *so that one may help others*. This includes the negation of internalized representations of the woman's body as less in favour of positive redefinitions of the same as spiritual and sacred through, in Wiccan and some women's groups, the imminent tie to the Goddess.

As a *bothsider* I am now more aware of these dialogues than I was before I began this research. I acknowledge just how fortunate I have been to be able to spend years in academic study and become a healer. I am just one example of a woman, healer, academic, mother, who walks in a world full of other 'multitasking' others. However, I have not forgotten that I have also been taught precisely how I should *be* in each of these roles. My engendered body is both an instrument of power and the site of struggles over power.

Take, for example, the aforementioned prioritization of text in academic circles. I have been trained to write academically yet my 'new religious landscape' (Spickard and Landres 2002: 4) as healer is, as I have mentioned, experientially based on energetic touch — a different framework of meaning based on intuitiveness and spirituality rather than rationality and science. And it is I who also have to decide how to 'accurately' represent 'others' healing practices. Here I put on my 'academic cap' and subscribe to discipline-bound conventions. I have to write and make myself visible. Debbie Horsfall elaborates on this dilemma rather well.

> There are many tensions in writing, tensions that can be silencing. Many of these surface as we struggle with writing to the people who may read our work. "The act of writing is addressing the silence of the unknown reader" (Morgan 1992: 193). I am one of the readers for whom I write. In writing I clarify my thoughts, understand and know myself better. I also take a risk as I make myself visible to you and myself. In writing I make myself vulnerable. Imaginary readers in "authority" who will judge this work threaten nebulously ...The tension, then, is being true to myself and being accessible to others while at the same time being able to connect with, be understood and validated by those in authority. I experience this tension as a never-ending compromise. I have to be accepted, if I am to be heard, from both within and without. Thus I very rarely end up saying what I want to; the sharp, adversarial edges have by necessity been rubbed smooth (Horsfall 2001: 86).

Horsfall's comments may be usefully related to feminist ethnography. For example, Woolf asserted that feminists need to be sensitive 'to power as a factor in all our research' (1992: 135). This most certainly appears to be the case. For I too (as feminist ethnographer) have had endless debates with myself with regard to the applicability of 'intense reflexivity in [my] research and writing [as to whether it] will be evaluated as being in the post-modernist mode or as tentative and self doubting' (Woolf 1992: 135) by those in positions of academic authority. I have pondered on the difficulties of writing about a field as diverse as New Age healing with its shifting sand of individual epistemologies and ways of being. Where should one start? Where finish? Who am I to define such boundaries in the first place? However, I am a healer and I want to tell the stories of other women healers in Scotland. Therefore throughout this work I have also become very aware of the difficulties of writing up 'the other' — for the other is also me. And I have attempted to 'design [a feminist] research project[s] that women want and need' (Mascia-Lees, Sharpe and Cohen 1989: 23). However, I have not forgotten that my writing is only 'truth-in-the moment…[for I know that] "there is no absolute truth when it comes to how we remember the past"' (Horsfall quoting hooks 2001: xix). I have written about lived experiences in the field. These are not fixed on paper until I put them there.

So let us now return to the wider evaluation of the linkage between healing and gender roles, which I shall relate to my findings in the Scottish context. For as McGuire has stated, religions, quasi religions and healing movements all 'raise some interesting interpretative questions about the linkage between religion and gender role, between religious practice and the socializing of emotions and bodies, and about diverse religious responses to fluid or uncertain societal and cultural definitions of maleness and femaleness' (McGuire 1994: 273).

Gendered Spiritualities

Meredith McGuire proposes that many 'religious and quasi-religious groups are addressing adherents' gender concerns by offering new images of what it means to be a man or a woman and creating rituals and other opportunities for gender identity transformation' (1994: 274). She focuses particularly on groups where the gendered self is seen to be intimately tied to the spiritual self. Correspondingly gendered spiritualities allow room for the individual to re-interpret, revise and transform their own biographies. However, she argues, these gendered spiritualities are not accidentally formed with eclectic picking and mixing from 'spiritual supermarkets'. Rather 'they are closely linked with the changing locations and functions of religion, as a social institution, in modern society' (McGuire 1994: 274).

> Specifically I would argue that emerging gender issues are the epitome of contemporary gender concerns. Sociological analysis of gendered spirituality may shed light on new patterns of individual-to-society relationships, the changing nature of identity and autonomy in modern contexts, and how religion (in both traditional and new forms) shapes and reflects these changes. Gendered spirituality may be a prime example of what Hervieu-Leger (1990) has identified as a "new work" for religion to accomplish (1994: 247).

In order to examine the development of new and empowered gendered identities in New Age networks in Scotland, I am going to return to the questions I raised at the beginning of this book. Gender, 'as an analytical category' will, as Scott suggests, remain central throughout this project of constructing a decentralized narrative of power relations in healing circles (Scott 1986: 1055). My four questions were:

1. If New Age healers promote the balancing of 'masculine' and 'feminine' elements within the individual, then who promotes this sort of standpoint and why? How does this relate to representations of the body 'as energetic'?

2. If healers promote new forms of gender identity, how does this relate 'to assertions of power, authority and privilege' (McGuire 1994: 284)?

3. How do healers/healees form new conceptions of health and disease? How does this relate to re-inscriptions of the body and discourses of power?

4. Are New Age women engaged in a politics of reclamation with regard to healing practice and theologies of the same? How does this relate to the corresponding development of new and empowered identities 'as healer'?

In order to begin to address these questions — and this *is* just a beginning for there is enormous scope for further investigation — I am going to review representations of the human body as provided by healers in the Scottish field and as found in textual material. I shall commence with Barbara Ann Brennan's representations of the human body, which she couches in terms of 'reading the aura and the chakras' and 'life and world tasks'. And I shall refer to her gendered descriptions of sending healing energy of particular colours, the creator and channelled spirit guides. My first question was,

> 1. *If New Age healers promote the balancing of 'masculine' and 'feminine' elements within the individual, then who promotes this sort of standpoint and why? How does this relate to representations of the body 'as energetic'?*

Barbara Ann Brennan

In Chapter Four of this book I presented a primarily descriptive account of energetic workshops as held at The Salisbury Centre in Edinburgh. The first of these was based on the interpretative frameworks of Barbara Ann Brennan and very much emphasized experiential practice. Participants would learn to see or feel the energetic body and become able to detect blockages and damage in the same. Key themes here were that 'the aura shows all thoughts and emotions' (WMH 2001: 2, see Appendix A) and may be seen as a flowing field of colours. Negative emotions cause dis-ease to manifest in the body. Healing and therapeutic practices such as reflexology may help to clear the body of such negative emotions and return the body to 'a state of balance and health. In most instances we are unconscious of what is happening, and healing is about us becoming conscious of what we are holding and doing in life' (WMH 2001: 2, see Appendix A).

The process of healing was couched very much in an evolutionary sense. The person (with the guidance of a healer initially) must learn the task that they were reincarnated in this life to learn. Each person has a life or personal task where the aim is to 'express a new part of one's identity' (Brennan 1988: 109) and a world task. 'The world task is a gift that each soul carries into the physical world to give to the world' (Brennan 1988: 109). Hence, as McGuire has suggested, new images are provided of what it is to be a man or a woman. For from Brennan's perspective, health is intimately related to all of the energy flows in the body being balanced and in harmony. When this occurs, 'The soul has learnt its particular lesson and, therefore, has more cosmic truth' (Brennan 1988: 109). Brennan argues that the healer (and in turn the healee) can see in the aura what the life and soul tasks actually are. This can be achieved once the mind is cleared through a process of deep meditation.

For Partridge, this type of 'New Age meta-narrative…arises directly out of the modern belief in evolutionary progress the particular interpretation of which, in many cases, can be traced back to late-nineteenth century theosophy' (Partridge 1999: 80). At this time Romanticism also held sway with emphasis being placed on feelings, imagination and inituitive abilities as valuable mediums for discerning 'the metaphysical within the physical' (Partridge 1999: 81). 'Hence for New Age epistemology, the self becomes supremely significant: not only is the self able to discover truth, but the truth it seeks is within the self' (Partridge 1999: 81). Within Brennan and her colleague Pat de Vitalsis's ontological frameworks, the colours of the aura have meaning. Accordingly, a lot of green in the aura would indicate the soul level of a healer with a lot of healing and nurturing energy. In turn, healing energy will be sent of a particular colour, this having very particular qualities. For example 'Purple helps the patient connect to his spirit…Velvet black brings the patient into a state of grace, silence and peace with God. Purple-blue takes away pain when doing deep tissue work and work on the bone cells. It also helps expand the patient's field in order to connect to her task' (Brennan 1988: 238). However, Brennan also adds here that she herself does not generally choose what colour of energy to send, though she can 'sustain a color that comes through [me]' (Brennan 1988: 238).

> At a certain point in my healing career, the guides suggested that I start using black light. This seemed unusual to me, since the dark colours in the aura usually are associated with illness. This black however was not the black of cancer, but a velvet black, like black velvet silk. It is like the life potential held in the womb. It is the black mystery of the unknown feminine within all of us, which teems with undifferentiated life. Sitting within the black velvet void is another way to be at one with the creator, but this time without form. To sit within the black velvet void means sitting in silence and peace. It means completely being there, in fullness and without judgement. It means going into a state of Grace and bringing your patient into that Grace with you. It means completely accepting everything that is in that moment. Heyoan and other healing guides often sit in this place with cancer patients or other very serious illness for a whole hour at a time. It is very healing. It brings the patient into a state of oneness with the Divine (Brennan 1988: 240).

In the above discourse we see themes that resonate across Scottish healing circles.

- Living in the present (and not holding on to damaging thought processes).
- Living life in as full a manner as possible (by not being judgemental or holding on to judgemental critiques from another).
- Being at one with the creator as much as possible (by remembering who you are and doing your life and work tasks).
- And in listening to other sources of authority (such as spirit guides).

Michael Brown, having researched channelling in America, proposes that,

> channelling is dominated by women who find in communication with spirits a refuge from mainline religions that even today offer little scope for spiritual aspirations. Not only can female channels achieve the religious authority denied them elsewhere, they are free to embody male spirits or "energies" in ways that many find liberating.[3]

---

3. Though I am intrigued as to why Brown feels that embodying male spirits may be more liberating than female entities.

Increasingly, both men and women involved in channelling are drawn
to androgynous spirits that have moved beyond gender altogether
(Brown 1997: 11).

Barbara Brennan has just such an androgynous spirit guide whose
'unseen hand' has led her through her life as a healer. The
importance of such guides to Brennan – and to many Scottish women
and men 'doing' healing practice – should not be underestimated.
Working with guides is regarded by many as being an integral part
of healing self and healing others.

> We are all guided by spiritual teachers who speak to us in our dreams,
> through our intuition and eventually, if we listen, they speak to us
> directly...These teachers are full of love and respect for us. At some
> point along the way, you, too, may be able to communicate with them
> as I do. This will change your life, for you will find that you are fully
> and completely loved (Brennan 1988: 16).

But let us for the moment return to Brennan's description of 'the
creator'. In her discussion of healing colours she clearly signifies
that 'velvety blackness' is of a 'feminine nature'. When one sits in
this black void one is with the creator, a creator who embodies life-
giving potential and mystery. We need to remember here that this
is not an external deity. Deity resides within as without and is central
to one's growth. This is a considerable move from mainstream
Christian religious representations of deity and indeed of women's
nature. For by locating the 'divine feminine' within, women are
provided with a simple and profitable, sacralized, model for life.
By getting in touch with the inner feminine as nurturing and life
giving, women feel empowered. Their bodies become vessels of
growth not constraint. Agency as 'spiritual being' is accomplished
through the body. So while I have asked questions with regard to
Brennan's framing of cosmic healing power within a Christian
context (as noted in Chapter Three) it appears that she may well
just be drawing from Christianity the 'symbol' of Christ as healer
so that she can 'add' this to her experientially developed 'sense of
self' as balanced masculine and feminine energy.

> The Goddess/God force is both black and white, both masculine and
> feminine. It contains both the white light and the black velvet void
> (Brennan 1988: 25).

Is Brennan then, promoting the Goddess/God force as creative
principles invalid without each other? Might she be referring to

deity from an androgynous perspective which 'in its broadest sense can be defined as the One which contains the Two, namely the male (*andro-*) and the female (*gyne*)' (Singer 2000: 4)?[4] Might she be in accord with Singer who argues, in 'Androgyny as Guiding Principle of the New Age', that:

> For the spark of creation to be engendered, the male and female must come together in all their sexual maleness and femaleness. Before they can be joined they must have been apart, differentiated, separated from one another. Before they were separated they were bound together in one body, and that body was the Primordial Androgyne (2000: 5-6)

Or might we do better to take on board Boyarin's evaluation of the basis of androgyny? According to this writer early Judaic thought was heavily influenced by Philo, a Jew from Alexandria. Philo's work 'was a generative and important source for later Orthodox Christian thinking, to the extent that Philo is frequently listed as one of the fathers of the church' (Boyarin 1998: 119). Boyarin informs us that Philo was interested in the creation of humanity and sexual difference as found, for example, in biblical accounts. Here, the reader is informed, see Genesis 5.1 and 2, that Adam was created in the image of God and as both male and female, whereas in Genesis 2.7, God causes Adam to fall asleep and removes one of his ribs which he forms into a woman. 'In the interpretation of Philo, the first Adam is an entirely spiritual being, the noncorporeal existence of whom can be said to be male and female, while the second chapter first introduces a carnal male Adam from whom the first female is constructed' (Boyarin 1999: 120). For Philo, this meant that 'only the first one is called "in the image of God," that is, only the singular, unbodied Adam-creature is referred to as being in God's likeness and his male-femaleness may be understood spiritually' (Boyarin 1999: 120).

Boyarin puts Philo's argument into 'more secular terms...the essence of the human subject precedes its accidental division into the sexes. The "true self" — we would say the "subject" — exists before being assigned a gender' (1998: 120). Hence, 'the unsexed being is superior to the creature marked by sexual difference' (1998: 121). A hierarchy of value is hence set up wherein humanity 'as divided

---

4. Singer's work is published under 'The Jung on the Hudson Book Series', where emphasis is placed on exploring the relevance of Jung and his psychological ideas as a practical resource.

into male and female is corruptible, always already fallen, while humanity undivided by sex is immortal' (1998: 121). And this is where things become interesting, for Boyarin elaborates that while opportunities for parity between men and women did exist (as depicted by Philo) in the spiritual sphere, this was dependent on women renouncing 'both sexuality [in favour of celibacy] and maternity' (1998: 121).

> Insofar as the myth of the primal, spiritual androgyne is the vital force for all of these representations [of celibacy, spiritual immortality, falleness etc.,] androgynous status is always dependent on the notion of a universal spiritual self that is above the differences of the body, and its attainment is *necessarily* a renunciation of the body and its sexuality (Boyarin 1998: 125) [italics original].

We appear to have a conflict of standpoints here. For we appear to have in Singer's writing, an emphasis on the value of the sexual gendered body rather than negation of the same with an initial positive valuation of being male *and* female. I have a sense that Brennan would subscribe more to Singer's positioning than to Boyarin's. This would indeed be an area worthy of further research. But let us move on to another workshop at The Salisbury Centre in Edinburgh as facilitated by Maureen Lockhart.

Maureen Lockhart

In Maureen Lockhart's Healing Circle, emphasis was placed on the cyclical nature of healing. Healing was also couched in the terms of the feminine and masculine. For in 'the survival stage of healing, energy will be low…this is the dark side, the Mother side'. In the inspirational side of the healing process you are 'in the light side…the Father side'. Health would occur, we were advised, when both Mother and Father 'sides' were energetically united in the body through practices such as correct breathing. Descriptions of spirit guides in these workshops also included both male and female entities and non-gendered 'images' of "Tibetan singing bowls", green and golden light and gifts of black feathers. The personal search for meaning then, reflects the historically constructed nature of the person involved and the areas to which the person will turn for spiritual guidance — shamanism, Buddhism and Native American being just a few examples here. The emphasis throughout learning to heal is that in order to affect positive change externally in one's life, there must first be an inner change towards harmony and balance of masculine and feminine. In general, in similarity to Goddess spirituality, Wicca and women's spiritual groups, there is 'a systematic deconstruction of the traditional perception of Western culture and religion as the universal norm for humanity and the epitome of human progress' (Hanegraaff 2002: 295).

So what about Reiki, the healing practice 'rediscovered' in Japan in the 1920s? Do we find representations of balancing the masculine and feminine here?

Reiki

As I noted in Chapters Five and Six of this book, Reiki is a rapidly growing form of healing practice in Scotland.[5] In relation to representations of the masculine and feminine, these were not usually explicitly referred to in Reiki healing circles. For when I asked one female practitioner if gender had any significance to healing practice, the response was 'No, I don't think that it does. Both men and women make equally good healers. It's more down to practice and intention...the more you practice, the better you get at channelling energy'.[6]

In order to find out more clearly whether masculine and feminine elements of the human being are represented in Reiki — if there are such things, and if so, how does one move beyond essentialising

5. It is very difficult to quantify numbers of Reiki practitioners because most are not on 'registration lists' or in groups which are formally counted — and also because of the tendency by practitioners to mix Reiki with other healing modalities. However, during the time I conducted this research, in my immediate rural area there were four initiating Reiki Masters, two complementary health centres where Reiki is on offer and a beauty salon with two practicing Reiki therapists (in combination with other treatments). As there are only ten thousand inhabitants in this particular area this suggests a high level of interest in this form of healing. In addition, local further education colleges (in Perth and Cupar) both offer courses in learning to become a Reiki practitioner. All of the Reiki Masters and the vast majority of Reiki practitioners noted above are women.

6. My couching of the question in this way was problematic in that it was not specific enough in relation to 'the definition of gender' and the definition of 'practice' (and about every word in between). On looking back at this, I recognize just how important it is to try and state things 'correctly' — not always easy for a newcomer to the field learning qualitative methods 'on the hoof'. But it also made me reflect on the potential for 'silencing' in questionnaires. My own questionnaire was very simple and was followed up with some phone interviews (see Appendix B). But even so, I set the agenda for what would be discussed and I am the one reporting the findings. My interpretation of the same will obviously also depend on my academic training and my ability to 'accurately' represent such findings in the written word.

the same—I turned to 'teaching texts'. For this is one form of healing practice where texts are often used as a forerunner to experiential practice. It is also an area where a theological superstructure is being rewritten primarily by men, a point to which I shall return in the latter stages of this chapter where I engage with narratives of power.

In my early readings of Reiki training materials—from Fiona and William Rand, the founder of the International Center for Reiki Training—I again found no specific emphasis on Reiki as a form of gendered spirituality. Rather, focus was placed on the nature of healing energy and the energetic body, the Reiki symbols, Reiki history and the basics of healing practice. As I showed in Chapter Five, *Reiki* is represented in the following manner.

> It is the God-Consciousness called Rei that *guides* the life energy called Ki in the practice of Reiki. Therefore, Reiki can be described as spiritually guided life energy. This is a meaningful interpretation of the word Reiki. It more closely describes the experience most people have of it; Reiki guiding itself with its own wisdom, rather than requiring the direction of the practitioner (Rand 1991: 1-3 [italics original]).
>
> Because Reiki is guided by God-consciousness, it can never do harm. It always knows what a person needs and will adjust itself to create an effect that is appropriate. One never needs to worry whether to give Reiki or not. It is always helpful (Rand 1991: 1-6).

As I also observed in Chapter Five, the writing 'of Reiki' is an ongoing process. It was not until 2001 (the year following my initiation) that *The Spirit of Reiki, The Complete Handbook of the Reiki System* was published. The authors of this text, William Rand, Walter Lubeck, and Frank Petter are described as world renowned Reiki Masters. Each interprets Reiki in their own distinct way while emphasizing the need to transcend differences of opinion regarding the same. For tensions do arise between various Reiki traditions as to the most effective forms of healing practice, usage of the term Reiki itself, interpretations of history and significance of lineage. If we look at representations of the energetic body in the aforementioned book, we find healing ontologies based on Traditional Chinese Medicine and Qi Gong (Petter), Indian Chakra Systems, (Rand) and Japanese systems for describing Life Energies (Lubeck).

This sort of appropriation of non-Western medical and religious traditions is common in Scottish healing circles and has strong resonances of Orientalism. For once transferred and translated out of 'native' contexts distortion often occurs in relation to foundational 'truths' and methods of practice. As Waterhouse states, 'When words that express Buddhist truths are translated into English, they take on connotations which may be unintended and which are usually associated with the Christian doctrinal heritage' (2001: 119). For example in Scottish healing circles it is very common to find meditation being promoted as a transformatory tool 'in its own right'. Yet few healers/healees attend organized classes in the same (at least not in rural settings) and seem to prefer self-teach approaches to this practice. This they then mix with communing with Christian angels and the texts and the teachings of, for example, Sai Baba or Osho, these themselves being primarily aimed at Western adherents. It is also rather usual to find particular aspects of Buddhist or Hindu thought being mixed and matched with psychological interpretations. This we saw with Brennan in her *Hands of Light* where she refers to 'masochistic' or 'schizoid' (1998: 111) character types.

In relation to the practice of Reiki, here too we find Orientalist tendencies. For when Usui 'rediscovered' the Reiki symbols following his meditational fast on Mount Kurama, these have been described by writers such as Stein as being of Sanskrit origin and translations of the healing teachings of Jesus while in India. However, while at the 'higher' level of Master teaching and writing authors such as Rand, Lubeck, Petter and Stein do emphasize the significance of deeper symbol interpretation as a transformatory path in its own right, (See Chapter Six of this book), we also found that this was not necessarily the case with the 'grassroots practitioner'. For at the local level Reiki symbols are utilized for practical healing and not theological debate. Therefore, though 'world renowned' Reiki Masters such as Lubeck, Petter and Rand continue to rewrite Reiki theology, often locating this within older religious traditions such as Buddhism — which have been evaluated by writers such as Campbell (1996) and Grosz (1993) as patriarchal in nature and practice — this is not to say that women cannot re-appropriate for themselves elements of the same which they find personally empowering. Therefore I would argue that the appropriation of aspects of non–Western medical and religious traditions has a lot to do with re-significations of power and re-defined individual-to-society relationships.

However, let us return to Reiki practice for a moment. When I first commenced my journey into this form of healing, although I found no particular emphasis being placed on textual constructions of 'the masculine' and 'the feminine' this was somewhat different when it came to doing healing work. For example, my Reiki Master noted that sometimes women found it easier to learn to do hands-on healing work as they were more used to touching, holding and stroking the body due to their experiences of mothering. As Reiki Master Frank Petter puts it 'women are ahead of us men in the art of touching. Because of their maternal instincts, their basic nature leads them to be willing to touch others, as well as themselves, in a loving way and without any sexual ulterior motives' (1999: 20). We appear to have here interesting Reikian assumptions about the underlying nature of gender and sexuality. For are women being represented as sexual beings in relation to procreation only? If so, this is a significant difference to Goddess spiritualities where, as I observed in Chapter Two, the 'Mother [is regarded as being] sexual, powerful, loving and demanding…a whole integrated adult' (Griffin 2000: 18). Is Petter, in his defining of the norms of the female body, also suggesting norms of the masculine, in that women are tactile, men not? Is this not a rather essentialising discourse in that women are to be seen as bodily orientated while men are 'of the mind'? Or is Petter trying to break down such 'traditional' assumptions with his promotion of touch and mothering, rather seeing these as the way forward for growth of both men and women? Certainly the women I have spoken to in healing circles would support the latter. And might this not leave space for a celebration of the female body as *more* rather than as less, than the male. Could this be a potential starting point for the breaking down of hierarchical dualistic notions?

In order to continue to engage with these issues, I am now going to draw in my second question as raised in Chapter One:

> 2. If healers promote new forms of gender identity, how does this relate to 'assertions of power, authority and privilege' (McGuire 1994: 284)

Let me first return to Paul Heelas in relation to the above question. For he has argued that underpinning much New Age thought and practice are three 'self-ethics', which I introduced in Chapter Two of this book. These are, Heelas states, 'your lives do not work, you are gods and goddesses in exile and let go/drop it'

(1996: 18-20); and that these relate to New Age teachers' emphasis on 'religions of the self'. Correspondingly, New Age teachers set up contexts where a person may look within him or herself for sources of authority, rather than turning to traditional forms of religion (1996: 23). In this he is correct. But it must also be noted that it is not uncommon for these same teachers to be repeatedly visited at considerable financial expense in order to clarify 'the authenticity' and 'correct' way of following 'self as own authority'.

In relation to Heelas' 'your lives do not work' self ethic, I argued that all of the points he raised related to the motifs of 'power', 'desire' and 'lack' and that these motifs must be approached from a gender perspective. For example, Heelas proposed that a common refrain running through New Age thought was that human beings malfunction because they have been 'brainwashed' by society and find themselves located within societally ordained roles. Here emphasis is placed on competitiveness, materialism, behaving as one has been taught by parents, educational systems and other institutions. In turn, it becomes impossible to live as authentic human beings (1996: 18).

For radical feminist Mary Daly, this sort of 'lack of authenticity' would relate to a patriarchal society where women are constrained and contained within misogynist systems—these occurring in all aspects of life. I, however, would argue for a more decentralized and nuanced narrative of power. For while without doubt patriarchy may be found within most countries' religious, educational and societal systems, they are often vigorously and/or subtly contested by women and indeed by some men. For example, in non-medical and 'spiritual' healing circles, people do appear to resist traditional bio-medical and religious (in Scotland, predominantly Christian) significations of the body, emotions and ways of being. In turn, new conceptualizations of 'what it is to be a human being' are developed and these intimately relate to agency and authority. Hence, as Scott has argued, changes in social relationships also lead to changes in significations of power and new forms of subjectivity.

As I have already observed throughout this book, men and women in healing circles have also developed new ideas of being healthy and whole. These are often based on getting back in touch with 'the intuitive self' often aided by spirit guides, these guides in turn assisting in healing practice. This is not to say, as McGuire also observes, that bio-medical approaches to health are rejected in totality. Rather, a synthesis is developed between the two with healing practice being regarded as 'an enabler' for the body to self-heal, with for example, healing work being promoted as a way in which to enhance bio-medical approaches to health.

> In seeking healing, most respondents make no clear distinctions among physical, emotional, relationship or other problems. Healing was the appropriate response to virtually every problem; holism reduced the boundaries and made it meaningless to segregate, for example, emotional from physical healing (McGuire 1998: 186).

Therefore all 'healing work' is linked to power and authority as located within the self. It goes without saying then, that for the New Ager, once power and authority *are* located in this way, then one becomes responsible for 'the right use' of such power. For healers commonly acknowledge that they are in a position of privilege in relation to the unenlightened mainstream of society and hence hope that their ways of being as 'informed healers' will have a positive effect on society as a whole. This standpoint, as I have noted, was of particular relevance to Reiki healers. For Reiki is very much regarded as a spiritual path and as a way of life. Therefore lifestyle choices become significant factors in the healing process. Note, however, how Walter Lubeck represents Reiki.

> As a healing method for the body and mind, Reiki requires at its basis the participation in the appropriate initiations and training in the use of spiritual life energy. This training includes the following, among other things: the whole body treatment, aura work, intuitive Reiki, harmonization of the chakras, special positions for the specific treatments of certain health disorders, as well as rules for a healthy diet and a constructive lifestyle.
>
> However, if you would like Reiki to bring harmony to your soul and guide you on the path to the light, something else will be necessary: knowledge about the mystic aspect of the Usui System of Natural Healing (Lubeck 2001: 245).

In the above we find represented a very particular way of negating—or at least appreciating—why 'your lives do not work' (Heelas' first self-ethic). In order for life to work, that is, for it to be a harmonious holistic whole, one needs to follow the Reiki life path. In order to no longer be 'gods and goddesses in exile' (Heelas' second self-ethic) one must learn Reiki as a 'path to the light' (Lubeck 2001: 45). One must let go and drop (Heelas' third self-ethic) faulty ways of living and replace these with knowledge of Reiki as a mystical path. This sort of thinking is a significant departure from bio-medical approaches to health and is an implicit critique of the same in that 'the whole person' is not treated, just the body or the mind. But let me add a little more to the above quotation. Lubeck continues, in relation to the mystic aspects of Usui Reiki, that:

> Up to a few years ago, very little was known about this in the West. But through intensive research, a significant amount of which was based on the work of Frank Arjava Petter, it was possible to also shed light on this foundation of Mikao Usui's lifework. In addition to the life principles, the central themes of the mystic path of Reiki include meditation, the esoteric meaning of the Reiki symbols, and the *waka* that Mikao Usui used to teach his students; these are the spiritual diadetic poems written by the Meiji emperor, who Mikao Usui greatly valued (Lubeck 2001: 245).

Here we see that assertions of authority are located in several tiers: Frank Petter's interpretation of the mystic path and life principles (these being written on Usui's gravestone in a Buddhist cemetery in Toyko), interpretation of the Reiki symbols (Lubeck's evaluation being rooted in 300 BCE Confucian philosophy), correct meditational practice (Buddhism), and Usui's *waka* (the Meiji Emperor, nineteenth century Japan). It appears therefore, that though authority may lie within the self, according to these male writers, the self must be developed by subscribing to older traditions where patriarchy had a considerable hold at all levels of society. For Reiki is very much a product of a particular historical context.

For example, following on from Mikao Usui as President of the Usui Reiki Ryoho we find four high-ranking officers in the Japanese Navy, including two Rear Admirals and one Vice Admiral. On the other hand, Japanese society today is still firmly hierarchical with women being firmly associated with the family and the home. Will there be—if women are located in such a way—a progressive shift in emphasis for Western women Reiki practitioners, to be similarly located? Will this mean that the role of carer and nurturer is presented by male Reiki writers as the 'correct' mode of being for women healers? How does this relate to representations of the woman as 'naturally maternal' as noted earlier in this chapter in relation to Frank Petter? For as I observed in Chapter Five, Japanese Reiki Master Hiroshi Doi, stated that the absent healing symbol 'can be sent to your children studying upstairs…[and to] your husband sleeping in the living room' (2000: 88).

As I also noted earlier, I found little emphasis on the masculine and feminine in Reiki theology. What, then, does this say about a 'new religious practice' where women predominate at the grass roots level? Is this a positive step towards androgynous spirituality in similarity to the earlier noted significance on androgynous spirit guides? For as Brown has noted, these androgynous guides were regarded as empowering for men and women in American channelling circles.

> The purpose of channelling—and by extension, other forms of New Age spirituality—is to bring together elements ripped apart by Western civilisation: science and religion, body and soul, culture and nature, male and female, reason and intuition, thought and matter. Where one half of a dichotomy has overpowered the other, channelling tries to strengthen the weaker partner (1997: 48).

I feel that a lot of New Age healers in Scotland would very much agree with Brown's findings. For considerable emphasis is placed on 'strengthening the "weaker partner"'. Those of a feminist persuasion, however, might be a little more wary. For by inference, the 'weaker partner' is woman. Yet again woman is located as intuitive, natural and matter bound while men are to be seen as of the intellect, rational, and coming from traditions of reason, science and culture. Therefore it would be wise to keep a very close eye on practices such as Reiki in the future to see just what happens in relation to the empowerment of women and the rewriting of Reiki theology.

This continued observation might also take as a referential starting point feminist critiques of Christianity and 'the lack of female presence'. Mary Daly, for example, argues that,

> Western society is still possessed overtly and subliminally by Christian symbolism, and this State of Possession has extended its influence over most of the planet. Its ultimate symbol of processions is the all male trinity itself.[7] Of obvious significance here is the fact that this is an image of the procession of a divine son from a divine father (no mother or daughter involved). In this symbol the first person, the father, is the origin who thinks forth the second person, the son, the word, who is the perfect image of himself, who is "co-eternal" and "consubstancial" that is identical in essence. So total is their union that

7. Daly emphasizes that 'patriarchal society revolves around myths of Processions. Earthly processions both generate and reflect the image of procession from and return to God the father' (1991: 37).

their "mutual love" is expressed in procession (known as "spiration") of a third person called the "Holy Spirit" whose proper name is "Love". This naming of "the three Divine Persons" is the paradigmatic model for the pseudogeneric term *person*, excluding all female reality in the cosmos (1991: 37-38).

Or we might engage with Monica Sjoo's critiques of the New Age movement as being full of patriarchal thinking, for emphasis is placed on 'light gods and light sons...[and] Brotherhoods behind the scenes pulling the strings' (1994: 22). Sjoo further states that within New Age networks we will find deity being represented as 'light and shining' (1994: 25) as 'transcendent, disembodied male father spirit, god...[and] not of the earth' (1994: 25). I would agree that there is considerable emphasis in Scotland on 'love, light and power' – particularly in Reiki. However, this is not the picture in totality as we have seen. For within Reikian circles we also find practitioners following on from Diane Stein in 're-appropriating' a modern variation of one of the Reiki symbols – the Master Symbol, the Dai-Ko Myo. This is the symbol that is both used for healing and the transmission of Reiki attunements (initiation into Reiki). Stein states that after she had received the traditional symbol from her Reiki teacher, this woman then suggested that she try this modern form. Stein states that she was initially reluctant to use this new symbol since the older form worked well for her. However once tried, she 'never returned to the Traditional form' (1995: 96).

> The new symbol required no memorisation – it was as I had always known it – my first thought upon seeing it was, "Of course, it's the Goddess' spiral". In using it for attunements, I discovered it to be far more powerful and vastly more easy-flowing than the original Dai-Ko-Myo. When I used both on students and asked them to compare them, everyone liked the newer symbol better. It felt clearer, simpler, stronger to them, as it did to me (1995: 97).

For Stein, when she uses this symbol in healing sessions, 'life changes' and 'miracles' (1995: 98) most often occur as this symbol heals disease from the 'highest source...[for] its focus is healing the soul' (1995: 98). Its focus is on healing the spiritual level of the etheric body.

However, Diane Stein has also disclosed the Reiki symbols – including the Master's initiation symbols – and the techniques for Reiki initiations/attunements in print (as we saw in Chapter Six). For she has argued that the 'Goddess gift of Reiki' (1995: 2) should be available to all and not solely to those initiated into Reiki. This disclosure has been heavily critiqued in Reiki circles. For at the present time in the West, a Master may only transmit these symbols to the initiated student in a vertical hierarchy after 'correct' training. The initiate does not see this process, and will only be shown the first three symbols upon initiation to Second Degree Reiki. They are then clearly told not to disclose these symbols to the uninitiated. As Rand puts it,

> By keeping the symbols secret you demonstrate respect for them…Since the power of the symbols comes from the attunement, showing them to others who have not received the attunement will not help them and will cause confusion (1991: 11-5).

It is not immediately apparent why this secrecy is so necessary and why seeing the symbols would cause confusion to the uninitiated. For if, as Rand has stated 'without the attunement the symbols don't appear to do much' (1991: 11-5), then perhaps this portrayed need for secrecy has a lot more to do with the dynamics of power and authority in the teaching context than with the symbols themselves. Further, as my Reiki Master had also informed me that she had drawn Mickey Mouse — rather than the Reiki symbols themselves — when doing a healing, and that this 'had worked just as well', then one wonders about the need for symbol usage in the first place. And, if all people can heal, this being commonly stated in New Age circles, and if initiation into Reiki just heightens this ability, then this discourse may really be about representing Reiki as 'better and more powerful' than other healing practices. For tensions do abound with regard to the efficiency of various healing practices in the Scottish context. For example John MacManaway, an influential healer at the Westbank Centre in Fife, did not regard Reiki favourably, for he saw 'many Reiki healers with energy depletion problems'. Now this is a very significant critique of Reiki, for one of the primary 'selling points' of this healing modality is that 'personal energy' is not depleted in the healing process as the person is purely a channel for God guided Ki, as I observed in Chapter Five.

But let us return to Diane Stein once more. For it is predominantly Reiki Masters who critique her disclosure of the symbols and not the grassroots practitioner. For many women Reiki healers, her *Essential Reiki* is a focal point on their own healing journey. In fact,

I lost count of the number of women practitioners who recommended this book to me as an inspirational read. Why? Because she couches the significance of healing practice very much as 'coming from the Goddess', while her critiques of power, authority and privilege are wide-ranging. Stein regards the earth and all its inhabitants as going through a process of rebirth. 'We are in a time of death, and in a time when new life is beginning. The leaders of nations are helpless as are medical authorities to ease the change and pain that no one is exempt from. Misogyny, homophobia, religious intolerance, every sort of discrimination and racism are reactions to this pain and helplessness—futile attempts to find someone (anyone) to blame for it' (1995: 141). However, she argues that a new awareness is now being born and that this can be seen in the shift in authority from '"out there" in government and medicine to power from within' (1995: 141). Here women's voices are of particular significance 'Women are refusing to accept the rape of their own bodies, their children and the Earth, and they are insisting on equality, common sense, sustenance and healing' (1995: 142). Her critique of medicine is a position commonly held in Scottish healing circles. For she argues that it is over-technological, aloof and lacking in compassion, 'treating the body as a dead machine' (1995: 141). Correspondingly,

> There is a resurgence of methods taken from women and the common people by the Inquisition in the thirteenth to seventeenth centuries, and a resurgence of other non-invasive methods of the present and past...They are effective tools and often succeed where the medical system fails...Reiki is one such method, a major and important one. No tools or products are required, only the healer's hands, and it can be used as part of any other method of healing...Simple and profound, Reiki teaches a basic treatment useful for any dis-ease—emotional, mental, physical or spiritual. It is easily taught. It is part of women's empowerment in an age of powerlessness and fear. Reiki is a return to the ancient past and a birthing of the unknown future.
>
> This is a call to action, for women and aware men, for healers, peace workers and light/information workers. This is a call to action—to bring Reiki back to people and make it universal as it was meant to be. Heal the people of this planet, heal the animals, heal the Earth. Heal human awareness. Do Reiki and teach Reiki to manifest peace, healing, wellbeing and change. The techniques are now in print for the first time, there is no more secrecy or exclusiveness ...Remember the qualities of kindness, compassion and oneness that are the basis for Reiki and all healing (Stein 1995: 142).

So let me round up so far how new forms of gendered identity as 'holistic being' in Reiki circles relate to assertions of power, authority and privilege. There appears to be, as we have seen, an emphasis for male Reiki writers to evaluate the Reiki symbols in their older Chinese, Japanese or shamanistic forms. These are hence based in systems where patriarchy held sway. At the same time these same writers critique Western, predominantly American, representations of a 'Christianised' Reiki as we saw in Chapter Five. Here, I told how Reiki writers such as Shuffrey (1998) and Hall (1997) emphasize Mikao Usui's involvement with Christian universities in Japan and America. This led Petter, for example, to argue that 'the seemingly Christian aspects of Reiki were added in America to make Reiki more acceptable to Christian countries' (1997: 19). Reiki's transmission to the West was through a Japanese woman immigrant in Hawaii, Hawayo Takata. She emphasized the oral nature of the Reiki tradition and the memorization of symbols. It was not until the mid-1980s that Reiki teaching moved into a written format. Takata also charged high fees for Reiki attunements hence restricting the number of students. This also altered in the 1980s with initiation fees being lowered to encourage more students to learn Reiki. Japanese schools of Reiki remain closed to Western practitioners as Western forms of Reiki are regarded as 'corrupted'.

Reiki is passed to the student in the attunements/initiations. The efficiency of the Master in transmitting the symbols to the initiate is assessed in relation to their Reiki lineage. For the most authoritative Masters are perceived to be those that have come down from the Usui or Hayashi or similar. As Shuffrey puts it: 'The Lineage Bearer embodies the essence of the system and with great conscience maintains its purity, simplicity, and upholds to inspire others to their own integrity, as indeed I do' (1998: 31). This is why I and several other Second Degree practitioners were asked to leave the room when Masters symbols were discussed at The Salisbury Centre Reiki workshops.

On the other hand we have women, like Stein, who implicitly critique the secrecy and symbol usage in Reiki by returning to the Goddess as a central 'power figure' in their Reiki practice. For Stein subscribes to the viewpoint—based on channelled information — that 'Reiki was brought to Earth with the first people to incarnate in bodies. Shiva brought the healing energy and wants to be remembered for it' (1995: 140). Hence, she opens up the doors for those who wish to learn Reiki but are financially unable to do so.

It is perhaps within the realm of channelling then, that New Age women and men find an area of considerable possibility for personal empowerment. For, as we have seen, channelling appears to provide individuals with the opportunity to create their own realities. For, as described in Chapter Three, teachers such as Barbara Brennan and Maureen Lockhart both espoused the merits of listening to spirit guides to enable growth on one's spiritual path. They also promoted the benefits of having such guides' help while doing healing work. Hence, individuals who have the ability to channel build for themselves new worlds of energetic meaning and an expanded sense of self. For, as Brown has found in the American context, channelling also provides women with the opportunity to 'achieve the religious authority denied them elsewhere, they are free to embody male spirits or 'energies' in ways that they find liberating. The complex play in sexual identities in channelling offers unexpected insight into the emotional struggles of middle-class Americans as they try to survive the gender wars of our times' (1997: 11).

Yet, some Reiki Masters also critique the authenticity of channelled information. Frank Petter, for example, argues that 'Channelling has nothing to do with Reiki. With Reiki we channel universal life energy, not entities, gods, or spirits. In order to channel Reiki energy, no preparation other than the Reiki initiations is necessary' (1997: 93). This is a position often held in Scottish healing circles. For not all practitioners receive channelled information. However, we need to remember that Reiki is often carried out as part of other 'treatments', where it is regarded as enhancing. Hence we find Reiki practitioners 'doing Reiki' alongside reflexology, Indian head massage and, in my immediate area, as part of beauty therapies. I noted, for example, in Chapter Three of this book, that at Maureen Lockhart's Healing Circle we found a woman Reiki practitioner in her thirties called Sue. This woman experienced a 'spirit visit' from 'a female child' who gave her a 'white rose and chalice' which she felt symbolized 'purity of spirit'. In turn, Maureen interpreted these 'images' as archetypal and to be found when one connected to the Higher Self while in an altered state of consciousness following meditation. Therefore for Sue, having now 'discovered' her spirit guide, she had a 'helper' to assist in Reiki practice. This she felt to be empowering and proof of her ongoing 'spiritual development.'

However, Frank Petter also suggests that if 'channelling happens to you…it would probably be best, too, to find a spiritual master to verify your experience or at least find a true and experienced channeller to help you on your way' (1997: 94). Hence once more we find emphasis being placed on finding an authoritative teacher to ascertain whether 'self experience' is authentic. I would argue therefore, that discourses of power are a central feature of all healing practice in the Scottish context, for here, power is not 'unified, coherent and centralized' (Scott 1986: 1067) but fluidly malleable and discursively constituted. Healers are not subsumed in totality in patriarchal systems, rather they develop personal 'ways of being' based on experiential practice as 'active healing agents'. They are perennialists. They go beyond traditions as normally conceived to find the 'inner esoteric core' (Heelas 1996: 28). Hence, even though Reiki Masters such as Lubeck, Petter and Rand rewrite Reiki theology it is still up to the individual 'to discern — by way of their own experience, their gnosis or experiential knowledge — those spiritual truths which lie at the heart of, say, Vedanta or shamanism. And although these truths — by virtue of their intrinsic nature — exercise authority, they do not curtail the authority of the New Ager's Self: the truths within the "traditions" and within the New Ager are the same' (Heelas 1996: 28).

For it is in the field that healing takes place and not in the pages of a text. So while, yes, one could argue that in the macro context Reiki symbols are being reinterpreted by men predominantly for teaching purposes, women vastly outnumber men in healing practice at the micro level and can utilize symbols, spirit guides and develop forms of healing practice as they wish. At the 'grassroots level', healing is 'done' by women for women. I am now going to bring in my third question as voiced in Chapter One of this book, namely,

3. How do healers/healees form new conceptions of health and disease. How does this relate to reinscriptions of the body and discourses of power?

Throughout this chapter I have flagged up that power is a central element of healing practice, this being the power that heals, the power to heal, and perceptions of being healed. As part of this we have seen how there are multivalent discourses relating to, for example, the authority and authenticity of symbols, spirit guides and written knowledge. However, discourses of power also are intimately related to academic writing on the New Age and healing. Take for example, Wouter Hanegraaff's usage of Kleinman's theoretical distinction between illness and disease (as presented in Chapter Four of this book). This is summarized as follows.

> DISEASE refers to abnormalities in the structure and/or function of organs and organ systems; pathological states whether or not they are culturally recognised; the arena of the biomedical model.
>
> ILLNESS refers to a person's perception and experience of certain socially disvalued states including, but not limited to, disease (Kleinman in Hanegraaff, 1998: 42).

Hanegraaff regarded his academic appraisal of this definition in relation to healing to be more precise than emic evaluations of the same. However, I had found this definition to be problematic. For in the Scottish context, healers describe the 'dis-eased body' as being 'not at ease with itself'. Dis-ease is not, within healing frameworks, solely a pathological state. Rather, as we have seen, the dis-eased person is regarded as being 'out of harmony' with his or her spiritual path. This Brennan called the 'life task', while for Myss it was a 'sacred contract'. Being in a non-harmonious, un-balanced state was also related by healers to feelings of being out of control, de-valued and not at ease with the self.

Hanegraaff hence provides us with, in relation to the above definition, a useful example of how an academic may locate a medical anthropological interpretative framework 'over' emic evaluations and perceptions. For, as noted throughout this book, a person visiting a healer in the Scottish context is usually suffering physically and will have visited their medical practitioner and have found his or her treatment in some way lacking. They may have been 'cured' by the medical practitioner of some acute symptoms – these indicating some pathological malfunction, to use Kleinman's terminology – but they still will not feel healed. And as 'some kinds of sickness episodes also perform an ontological role – communicating and affirming important ideas about the real world' (Young cited in McClain 1989: 8), then how these episodes are dealt with can also tell us a lot about gendered ideas of health, healing and 'being at ease with one's self'. But let us return, for the moment, to an evaluation of *curing*, bio-medical models of health.

From a bio-medical perspective the treatment of disease is predominantly concerned with the curing of bodies and minds so enabling the person to return to society where he or she can usefully contribute to that system. Throughout the curing process the medical practitioner's knowledge is generally located 'over' that of the patient. And this is why sociologists of medicine and medical practice find a Foucauldian analysis of power 'particularly useful in understanding the functions of the medical profession and the related spheres of psychiatry' (Turner 1997: xi). I would however, like to reiterate here that this book is not a project in applying Foucauldian thought. Rather, I am interested in how sociologists of medicine and ethnographers of alternative religions engage with Foucault in relation to the dynamics of power and the body and the applicability of these perspectives to New Age healing practices.

As I observed in Chapter Three, Foucault sees power as operating at the local micro level where it may be typically disguised in the social system and embodied in day-to-day practices. Power, for Foucault, was not to be regarded as coming from a central point from which 'secondary and descendant forms would emanate' (Foucault 1994: 163). Rather power's 'condition of possibility' (Foucault 1994: 163) lies in fluid, unequal, unstable, local force relations, where it is continually produced and exercised in innumerable day-to-day interactions. In the clinic, hospital or medical setting this will be through the practices of doctors, social workers and other medical professionals all of whom will, in their discursive evaluations of the patient, 'produce identities or roles [for that patient]…these identities…then become the object and focus of medicalisation and normalisation' (Turner 1997: xii). For power is always exercised with a set of aims and objectives (Foucault 1994: 164). This, as far as healing practitioners would be concerned, would very much relate to bio-medical approaches to health negating 'the spiritual' as a factor that influences health. Hence, the healers I have met would agree, I feel, with Diane Treacy-Cole when she states that, 'One might rightly ask whether the dismissal of religion/spirituality from consideration [as a factor that influences health] serves the interests of the patient, or merely serves the self-interest of academic medicine' (2001: 141).

Sociologist Brian Turner states that the medical sociology inspired by Foucault is now highly critical of the power dynamics of the medical institution. For professionals in this field 'discipline individuals and exercise surveillance over everyday life in such a way that actions are both constrained and produced by them'

(Turner 1997: xiv). The patient is observed from a position of medical rationality where the 'sovereign power of the empirical gaze' (Foucault 1989: xv) holds sway. S/he is held in a dependent position awaiting the doctor's signification of disease and treatment of the same. Throughout the patient's course of treatment, and particularly at the time of their discharge, there may also be put forward 'lifestyle choices' to enable a 'healthy life'. Adherence to these 'choices' depends on the patient's belief in the authority of medical knowledge as truth and in the 'moral authority' of the medical professional based on institutional training. Hence, as Turner proposes, 'medicine and religion exercise a hegemonic authority because their coercive character is often disguised and masked by their normative involvement in the troubles and problems of individuals. They are coercive, normative and voluntary' (1997: xiv).

As I have observed throughout this book, New Agers often resist the hegemonic authority of medical institutions. This often relates to the perception that the 'medicalised body' is depersonalized and powerless. Of equal significance, however, is the belief that bio-medical institutions have difficulty in acknowledging and treating conditions 'that are not purely biophysical in manifestation and cause' (McGuire 1998: 203). Correspondingly, psychosomatic disease may be signified as less, by the medical professionals, with religious/spiritual belief being regarded as outwith the realm of medical intervention. Hence, the body becomes the domain of medical surveillance and the soul/spiritual—the church. For New Agers, this is highly problematic in that holism holds centre court in all evaluations of health and well-being as does a wish to, for some, find a higher synthesis of science and spirituality. However, medical science's exclusion of the spiritual as a factor in ill health may now be changing. For as Diane Treacy-Cole has found, there is also an increasing number of bio-medical practitioners interested in the possible connections between spiritual/religious beliefs and medicine.

She also proposes that it is science, and not religion or theology, which is setting the agenda for investigations into health and spirituality. Scientific and medical researchers are now 'willing, and increasingly able, to explore the new frontier of mind/body/spirit interrelations. Spirituality and healing in medicine is no longer a mere curiosity, but has become something of a demand. Medicine and religion are entering a new dynamic of mutual respect and

enquiry' (2001: 148). Now this is a thought provoking statement.
For 'Despite opposition from a not insignificant number of medical
researchers, Levin, Benson, Koenig and their colleagues have
identified and are substantiating their observations [on the
relatedness of spirituality and healing to health] following sound
scientific methodology' (Treacy-Cole 2001: 145). Benson, for
example, was at time of writing, MD of Harvard University Medical
School. He states that following twenty years of medical research,

> More and more I have become convinced that our bodies are wired to
> benefit from exercising not just our muscles but our rich human inner
> core—our belief, values, thoughts and feelings. I was reluctant to
> explore these factors because philosophers and scientists have, through
> the ages, considered them intangible and unmeasurable, making any
> study of them "unscientific" (Benson 1996: 50).

But explore them he does. Benson has also organized twice yearly
symposia under the wing of the Harvard Medical School from 1995,
topics including the 'physiological, neurological and psychological
effects of healing resulting from spirituality, and the power and
biology of belief' (Treacy-Cole 2001: 144). Much of this research is
based on a bottom up collection of evidence—that is 'researchers'
contact with individuals whose health has been positively affected
by religion or spirituality' (Treacy-Cole 2001: 144). Hence as Foucault
has proposed, power's 'conditions of possibility' (Foucault 1994:
164) lies in fluid, unequal, unstable, local force relations where it is
continually produced and exercised in innumerable day to day
interactions. The individual believer forces the system as a whole
to take a look at its long held rationalist presumptions, claims to
truth and the power that goes hand in hand with such authorised
truths.

Now Treacy-Cole also raises a further couple of interesting
points. She proposes that, while medical researchers are interested
in spirituality and health, mainstream Protestant Christian religious
denominations are predominantly not. Yet even here, we find a
bottom up power dynamic. For the Right Revd John Perry, Bishop
of Chelmsford and Chair of the Churches Council for Health and
Healing, states that there has been 'a considerable growth in interest
in healing inside and outside the church in the last twenty years'
(Treacy-Cole 2001: 147). I would argue that this relates very much
to a critique of the perceived loss of instrumental function *in relation
to healing* in the mainstream Church. For mainstream Protestant

churches still 'pay lip service' to healing services, favouring rather
a twentieth century theology which accepts the view 'that no
supernatural agency could break through natural law. The notion
of wellness being wired into biology had not yet been mooted'
(Treacy-Cole 2001: 146). Treacy-Cole hence observes that,

> The affirmations of growth in Christian spirituality and healing today
> still come from outside the churches and the academy [academic study
> of religion]. The public concessions made by the spokes*men* [italics
> original] quoted are not substantiated, an omission all the more glaring
> in contrast to the increased body of evidence presented by researchers
> in spirituality and healing in medicine (Treacy-Cole 2001: 148)

It would be interesting to note whether the absence of women's
voices in positions of authority in the church is reflected in those
that are attending and demanding healing services. It would also
be useful to reflect on where women are going specifically to find
such healing ministries. For McGuire found faith healing a significant
feature of Pentecostal (working-class), neo-pentecostal (middle-
class) and charismatic Christian healing groups (predominantly
middle-class) in America. It has, however, been outwith the remit
of this particular research to engage with Scottish, Christian healing
groups – this would be valuable ethnographic research for the
future. So let us now return briefly to bio-medical evaluations of
health and critiques of the same, before we return to specific
examples of energetic conceptions of health and dis-ease and how
these relate to power.

For Mary Daly, once a woman enters a bio-medical setting she
becomes the victim of violent and oppressive patriarchal practice.
'Reduced to a state of an empty vessel/vassal, the victim focuses
desperately upon physical symptoms, therapeutically misinterpreted
memories, and "appearance" frantically consuming medication [and]
counsel' (1991:233). She further argues that women pursue ideals
of 'man-made femininity, the normal state of feminitude' (1991:
231). This perspective may be related to Margaret Shildrick's
evaluation of women, power and medicine as introduced in Chapter
Three of this book. Shildrick argues that 'all women are positioned
vis-à-vis an idealised body ideal' (1997: 55). Daly and Shildrick both
state that this ideal of the 'perfect body' is unattainable which, for
Daly, is particularly damaging to women in that it 'swallows up the
remnants of naturally wild femaleness' (1997: 55). Therefore both
of these writers examine the micro-politics of power in the medical

setting and examine how these are played out on the woman's body in relation to, for example, elective cosmetic surgery, weight control and reproductive technologies. This is a huge area of investigation in its own right. The point I want to flag up here is that the objectifying gaze of medical institutions aims to produce a disciplined individual who engages in her own bodily surveillance. She works on herself to be healthy and tries to fulfil man-made ideals of 'correct' forms of behaviour. Her body is hence the site of power and the location for struggles over power. This is related to medical, political and governmental and religious institutions all of which promote idealized images of 'what it is to be a woman', and ideologies of the active healthy agent. Responsibility for the same is hence thrown back on to the woman herself. She must self-discipline so that she maintains a healthy, working, body.

Shildrick also proposes that women may complicitly support bio-medical and societal strategies of normalization 'over' their bodies with the acceptance and promotion of some forms of health care, these being seen as beneficial by women for women. Hence, bio-medical surveillance may be found in the ultrasound of pregnancy or the triannual check for the elderly woman. However, as I have already observed, once women recognize such strategies of normalization are occurring (as with the New Age woman refusing to comply to scientific, rationalistic, bio-medical definitions of the body, emotions and health) then devalued identities can be dissolved in favour of new constructions of holistic embodiment. So let us build up a simple representational picture here of how a woman may become a healer and feel re-empowered. For the purposes of clarity let us call her Jacqui. I shall then relate Jacqui's journey into healing to discourses of power and authority.

> Jacqui is a thirty-five year old woman who has longterm persistent digestive trouble. She has been repeatedly assessed by her doctor and has been prescribed a longterm course of pain relief, though no official diagnosis has been made. These drugs, and her condition, leave her feeling lacking in energy. This is highly problematic as she has two school age children and works full-time in health care. She feels that her partner, though helpful, doesn't really understand how limited in life she now feels.
>
> Jacqui has a long held interest in spirituality and healing. She has read many books on the same. She is concerned about the longterm potential side effects of drug use and the masking of symptoms with pain relief. She feels that her health condition is not being treated

seriously by bio-medical professionals. Correspondingly she feels trivialized and anxious. She decides to "go alternative" as nothing else has worked.

She turns to a healer recommended by a female friend. This healer works from a position that the body is an energetic entity. Jacqui is comfortable with this way of representing the body as she has read of chakras and has tried acupuncture. The healer, having assessed her energetic state promotes a new lifestyle regime of eating organic natural foods, meditation, yoga (when possible) and Indian head massage. The healer then commences with Jacqui a course of energetic healing work. She explains to her that while her pain might not be removed in entirety, she should feel significant improvements in discomfort and tiredness and should be able to progressively reduce or discontinue her drug intake. A level of trust is built up between the two women who feel they can relate to each other on more equal terms. Jacqui becomes aware that healing is not necessarily about the removal of "symptoms" in totality (though this may occur). Through practical experience she begins to value other ways of appraising her state of health. As new aetiologies of health are constructed, she begins to feel part of her own healing process. She feels that she is being really listened to and that her problems are of genuine importance. She is no longer just a "chronic medical condition".

Jacqui finds the emphasis on the interlinking of her mind, body and spirituality to the energetic whole empowering. She feels less isolated and "disabled" as she is beginning to feel connected (following healing sessions and meditational practice) to "all that is". The emphasis on holism also enables her to feel that power is located within for she is a spiritual, energetic being. She is engaged in a project of redefining herself.

She decides to learn to become a healer herself. For, as she has been made aware, everyone has the ability to heal. Her levels of pain are now greatly reduced and sometimes absent. She feels that being a healer will provide her with some supplementary income so that she has more independence. She also takes healing practice back to her previous work situation. Primarily, however, Jacqui wants to help others as she has been helped. She wants to put into practice her experiential awareness of herself as energetic being. For she feels that she can actively engage with these "new" frameworks of being and transform her life. She feels empowered. A whole new world of possibilities has opened up to her in her continued self-effort and reconnection to God/dess within. She feels at ease and has a new sense of self-authority.

In the above picture we should note several significant features. First, Jacqui has felt trivialized and isolated in that her doctor has attempted to treat her pain but doesn't appreciate her suffering. Jacqui needs to find some meaning for this suffering and wants to feel more in control of her own health. As McGuire puts it 'Rational medicine had no time and no place for the patient's need for meaning and order or even recognition as a person (rather than a case [of digestive trouble]' (1994: 241). When she visits the healer, the meaning of her illness is made clear within a holistic framework. She trusts the healer because she now feels a part of her own healing process. For the bio-medical 'power over' dynamic has been broken down in favour of one where Jacqui feels that she is a valued part of the energetically connected 'world as a whole'. She feels empowered. She has hence engaged in a project of personal redefinition and reclamation of her embodied being.

Jacqui's sense of connectedness is increased with continuing contact with other healers. She now relates the state of her health to her own holistic development and wishes to learn how to help others. As she becomes more effective at healing she feels transformed. She feels this is her path for life. She is no longer suffering, for her world has meaning and order.

I am now going to relate this representational image of a woman's journey into healing back to the third chapter of this book where I presented ethnographic material relating to workshops on the energetic body. In particular, I am going to refer to Barbara Ann Brennan's conceptions of health and disease. For I feel that questions need to be raised about the potentiality for the playing out of power in relation to 'seeing levels of the aura'. Foucault shall also be related to this enquiry.

At Helen Stott's workshops, these being based on Barbara Ann Brennan's *Hands of Light*, emphasis was placed on 'the body as energetic' and feeling this for oneself through experiential practice. This promotion of 'trying it out for yourself' is central to all types of healing practice in Scotland as we have seen, with a corresponding downplaying in the need for 'belief' for healing to work. The human body was described in these workshops as having a dense physical core 'around which' were the auric layers, these being 'tied in' to the chakras. Brennan states that it is possible for people *like Jacqui* to learn to see the aura by moving into High Sense Perception. Once one can see or feel the aura (for many healers tend to use their hands to sense energy flowing in the body), a transformatory shift in perception takes place. I found this out for myself. One is left with a sense of considerable wonder when you begin to appreciate that there is more to the human body than has been described within scientific paradigms.

However I would like to draw out a couple of points here with regard to Brennan's description of disease interpretation in the aura. First, she proposed, 'It is essential that we deal with the deeper meaning of our illnesses. We need to ask, what does this illness mean to me? What can I learn from this illness?' (1987: 7). Brennan also stated that if we wish to return to health we need to get back in touch with 'the spark of divinity within' (1987: 7), by changing our personal lives and ridding them of 'the source that caused the disease in the first place' (1987: 7). *For Jacqui, this means that she needs to get back in touch with her 'spiritual nature' and bring healing into her life on a practical level.*

I noted in Chapter Four, how for Brennan this 'allowing of one's process to evolve' was part of an evolutionary path where through the making of personal life changes, one would enable reconnection to the divine with a corresponding removal of dis-ease from the physical body. *For Jacqui, this would mean a whole new diet regime, daily meditation and self work on the energetic body.* However, one wonders how radical feminist Mary Daly would regard the sort of self-help therapy as promoted by Brennan. Would she regard it as just another example of a woman being told to get back in touch with the divine spark by a therapist who also feels the need to psychologise (patriarchal) her evaluations of being human? Would she regard Brennan as yet another example of a 'token woman' (1991: 8) whose mind had been bound and deceived, so that she thinks she is free 'but in reality is chained and possessed' (1991: 8), *and that she is correspondingly leading Jacqui down a similar path?*

Might she agree with a Foucauldian interpretation of Brennan 'as therapist', in that when she emphasizes that the 'sufferer' should take personal responsibility for the self, she is promoting a particular type of ideology tied to 'governmental' conceptualizations of the autonomous, active agent. *Here Jacqui is obliged to be healthy so that work can be done (as wife and mother and in the public sphere) so that 'goods' may be produced for the marketplace.* For, as Brennan might say, it is morally good to work and be healthy and I have the expert knowledge (culturally derived) to help (for a price) you on your path. Your life will be better if you listen to me (as expert) for I can tell you how to think about your 'self'. I will shape your self-perceptions.

Foucault argues that 'All the practices by which the subject is defined and transformed are accompanied by the formation of certain types of knowledge' (1980: 160) which, in the West, tend to be scientific in form. He further states that, in the 'scientific west', 'one of the main moral obligations for any subject is to know oneself, to tell the truth about oneself, and to constitute oneself as an object knowledge both for other people and oneself' (1980: 160). Therefore we need to find out 'which techniques and practices form the Western concept of the subject, giving it its characteristic split of truth and error, freedom and constraint' (Foucault 1980: 161). Brennan's discourse above sounds, potentially, to me like a technology of the self. Foucault describes technologies or techniques of the self in the following manner:

> I think, in all societies whatever they are...[one will find] techniques which permit individuals to effect, by their own means, a certain number of operations on their own bodies, on their own souls, on their own thoughts, on their own conduct, and this in a manner to transform themselves, modify themselves, and to attain a certain state of perfection, of happiness, of purity, of supernatural power, and so on (1980: 162).

Might, then, Brennan's 'technology of the self' also be related to a form of pastoral power? Let me relate this possibility to the writing of Sarah Nettleton for she draws on the work of Foucault in relation to governing the risky self. Nettleton points out that since the eighteenth century governmental mentality has been primarily concerned with the economic and social health and well being of the individual—its subjects. Foucault proposes that governmental activity prioritises the gathering of data about its subjects, the population. Hence data is gathered on employment, health, disease, birth and death etc. These institutional activities are in turn complemented by the individual subject engaging in 'practices of the self or self government. Individuals shape their own lives as well as react to the influences and actions of others' (Nettleton 1997: 210).

However, as I noted above, how an individual shapes his or her own life and produces a sense of self–identity is intimately tied in to cultural constructs. 'These are patterns that he finds in his culture and which are proposed, suggested and imposed on him by his culture, his society, his group' (Foucault 1988: 11). Therefore in order to govern its subjects, the state collects data, measures health, gains knowledge of the population so that these can be 'helped' to be healthy, happy and productive.

Foucault however, also identifies a transformation in power relationships with the development of power techniques oriented towards individuals rather than the centralized state. 'If the state is the political form of a centralized and centralizing power, let us call pastorship the individualizing power' (Foucault 1979: 136). Foucault states that within the early Christian context this pastoral power — as pastorship — had four particular characteristics which Nettleton usefully summarizes in the following manner,

> it assures individual salvation; it does not command sacrifice (like royal power) but must also be prepared to make sacrifices for subjects; it looks after each and every individual for his or her own life; and it exercises the need to know people's minds, souls, secrets and details of their actions (1997: 211).

Foucault argues that this form of pastoral power cannot be exercised without 'knowing the insides of people's minds, without exploring their souls, without making them reveal their innermost secrets. It implies a knowledge of the conscience and how to direct it' (1982: 783). This is tied in to 'experts' enabling the person to know him or herself. As again Nettleton usefully summarizes, 'Government has increasingly come to rely on these "technologies of the self" to shape and enhance the capacities of individuals. The subjects of government within this context are autonomous, independent and self reliant' (Nettleton 1997: 212).

It might, therefore, be rather easy to regard some aspects of New Age healing as a contemporary form of pastoral power. Let us return to Kleinman's categorization of disease as a starting point here. Kleinman states that disease 'refers to pathological states whether or not they are culturally recognized…[while] illness refers to a person's perceptions and experience of certain socially disvalued states including but not limited to disease' (in Hanegraaff 1998: 42). One could argue that in the healing context, dis-ease is a person's perceptions of a disvalued state now pathologized; this being culturally recognized. For within healing frameworks, as we have seen, there are very specific ideas of what it is to be healthy and whole. Pastoral power might now be disguised at the micro level in day-to-day practice. This might be observed in statements such as Brennan's 'it is essential that we deal with the deeper meaning of our illness' where the nature of dis-ease is signified' (1987: 18). For healers such as Brennan do need to know the inside of healees' minds and 'souls'. To this one might add another layer however, in that Brennan *et al.* also need to know the 'inside of people's auras'. And as the healee is told that that these cannot be hidden from the healer, and that deception is not possible, then it brings a whole new dimension to the surveillance of the human body. This 'need to know' then, might not be too dissimilar from earlier Christian traditions of the same.

It might also be the case that many healers want to produce the new identity of 'the healer' in their subjects. This new identity 'as healer' is seen to be tied into higher power, with 'techniques of individualisation' (Nettleton 1997: 211) being downplayed in favour of the philosophy, 'we are all part of one interconnected whole'. For within healing frameworks it is often posited that there is no such thing as an individual. This, one is told, is a purely ego-driven fallacy that must be ignored. New Age healing hence could then be regarded as a contemporary form of medicalisation.

However, Nettleton also argues that psychological theories (and Brennan locates the human being within this sort of framework) and practices 'have contributed to the reconfiguration of the individual, or subject, from being a relatively "docile", passive recipient of advice and health care to one who possesses the capacity for self control, responsibility, rationality and enterprise' (1997: 213-14). Within these fields experts 'must also seek out the subjective truth of a body capable of consciousness. Accordingly risk [health risks that the individual can insure against] is determined not only by one's personal circumstances but also one's personal capacities' (1997: 214). These capacities are, in the area of health, of particular importance in relation to the person's ability to take preventative steps with regard to illness. Hence, a person should take self-responsibility for his or her lifestyle and 'master the self'. Failure to do this through lack of self-control means that the individual is at risk from 'his or herself'. 'Such notions of the self reliant and enterprising self are of course reflected in the New Right, but its conditions of possibility are to be located more in the activities of the "experts" of the human condition' (1997: 214). In turn, individuals must draw from 'expert' knowledge so that they can 'assess their futures and take control of their biography' (Nettleton 1997: 215).

Risk factors such as unhealthy lifestyles become diseases in themselves and as such can be cured. Experts provide 'truths' about how one should live one's life as an active agent and hence also have an ethical dimension, for we can choose to be 'healthy' or 'unhealthy'. To be healthy is to be admired. And in the fields of complementary health, there are many providers of expert advice to choose from to enable the development of this sort of subjectivity.

> Power is exercised over free subjects. And only in so far as they are free. By this we mean individual or collective subjects who are faced with a field of possibilities in which several ways of behaving, several reactions and diverse compartments, may be realized (Foucault 1982: 790).

So where does this leave our composite woman, Jacqui. Well, she now finds herself in a position where she has to take responsibility for her life and her health and work on her life task. Dis-ease will now be regarded as being related to states of energetic imbalance, these being displayed in the aura and chakras. In turn, she will have been told that, 'We all create disease to some extent in our physical bodies. If you look back at the original cause, it is always based on forgetting who we are. As long as we believe that we must be separated in order to individuate, we will continue to create disease' (Brennan 1987: 145). She will also have been advised that pain is in fact a learning tool and not just a physical state. Pain will manifest if we 'ignore what we know we want or need to do...Pain teaches us to ask for help and healing and is, therefore, a key to the education of the soul' (Brennan 1987: 145). And she will be locked in to a system of continual self-surveillance where she is the cause of her own health or dis-ease. She will, initially at least, return to the expert healer and 'confess'. She will literally reveal the hidden truths of herself by displaying them in her aura. The trained healer will have privileged access to these truths as she is in a state of 'higher spiritual development'.

However, Jacqui will also have the option to move away from a Brennan type of evaluation of her body. She will most probably continue to adhere to 'the body as energetic' but she may learn new healing practices (such as Reiki) with different conceptualizations of the same. She may read Diane Stein and subscribe to a Goddess centred approach to healing self and others. She may redefine her identity as of the Goddess. Whatever way she chooses to develop 'her self' she will be doing so in a position of active agency. She will be implicitly critiquing rationalized bio-medical evaluations of her bodily state. She will have rejected Christian notions of her body as 'sinful' and will regard the same as a valuable vessel for growth and self transformation. She will have learnt to listen to her body. Hence as Meredith McGuire states,

> Much alternative healing promotes a qualitatively different perspective from that of the rationalized dominant culture. Many alternative healing approaches encourage a reflective and reflexive attitude toward oneself, one's body, and emotional and social life. They affirm the right and power of the individual to choose the quality of experience of body and emotions, to choose how to achieve health and healing, to choose and assert identity. They also promote a holistic perspective, a strong sense of connectedness with one's body and with other persons. If successful, such transformations of self could have far reaching consequences for the sociocultural and politico-economic spheres in modern society (1998: 257).

I shall turn now to my final question,

> 4. *Are New Age women engaged in a politics of reclamation with regard to healing practice and theologies of the same? How does this relate to the corresponding development of new and empowered identities 'as healer'?*

In this final part of the chapter I am going to argue, in conclusion, that New Age women *are* engaged in a politic of reclamation and that this has interesting parallels with Goddess, Wiccan and feminist Witchcraft spiritualities on two counts: first, because these women critique the exclusion of women's religious experiences—including healing—by patriarchal world religions; second, in that all of these women subscribe to a holistic worldview rather than to mechanistic rationalized accounts of human existence as found within scientific and bio-medical approaches to health. Hence, these women have developed—and continue to develop—important ideas about the 'real world' based on their own experiential practice.

I shall construct this concluding section in the following manner. First, I will note briefly some of the tensions to be found between science and healing. This I shall draw from Jeanne Achterberg's examination of the historical role of the feminine in Western healing traditions. And I shall revisit Diane Treacy-Cole's evaluation of the contemporary relationships between science, healing and medicine. These I shall then relate to spiritual feminists' critiques as noted above and my own ethnographic material. In this way I will 'complete the circle' and show how women are active agents in healing practice and are not subsumed in entirety under patriarchal systems. For women do healing work within fluid 'fields of force' (Foucault 1980).

Science and Healing

Jeanne Achterberg states that:

> Women have always been healers. Cultural myths from around the world describe a time when only women knew the secrets of life and death, and they alone could practice the magical art of healing. In crises and calamity, or so some of the stories go, women's revered position as keepers of the sacred wisdom was deliberately and forcibly wrested away from them. At other places and in other eras, women's legal right to practice the healing vocations was gradually eroded by changing mores and religious dogma (1990: 1).

She continues that this interest in healing may be seen in the contemporary health care system where, in the United States at least, over eighty percent of workers are women (1990: 1). This trend is also apparent in the UK, although I would argue, one must not forget that these same women are primarily located in the nursing and caring professions and are outnumbered at higher medical and teaching levels by men. Even so, healing (rather than curing) does still take place officially and unofficially in such settings with, for example, nurses being trained in therapeutic touch[8] and Reiki practitioners healing in the hospital setting. So let us commence with a necessarily brief review of the historical exclusion of healing from bio-medical health settings with the rise of rationalistic science. For representations of this form of science as 'the pinnacle of scientific evolution' are explicitly critiqued by many New Age healers.

Ziaddin Sardar states that Western science has represented itself as being 'the apex of science' (2000: 53) in relation to truth and efficiency. It has done this by not recognizing other 'civilizational or cultural sciences' (2000: 53). He proposes that science has 'maintained its monopoly in four basic ways' (2000: 53). First, the

> ...conventional Western history of science...denied the achievements of non-Western cultures as real science, dismissed them as superstition, myth and folklore. Second, the histories of non-Western science were largely written out of the general history of science. Third, it rewrote the history of the origins of European civilization to make it self-

8. See Hedges and Beckford's material in Chapter Three of this book.

generating... Fourth, through conquest and colonialization, Europe appropriated the sciences of other civilizations, suppressed the knowledge of their origins, and recycled them as Western (Sardar 2000: 53-54).

This meant for example that Islamic, Chinese and Indian sciences were subsumed or excluded, which many New Agers see as a significant loss. Correspondingly, they have appropriated elements of such sciences (and philosophies) and have incorporated them into their own healing ontologies as we have seen. For all of these non-Western systems have well-developed notions of the relationships of, for example, spiritual practice to health. However, of particular significance to this book is the fact that this 'real Western science' has also excluded women and denounced 'the earth as spiritual'. For by the seventeenth century men of science 'believed there were divine purposes in nature but held that they should play no role in the scientific account' (Barbour 1990: 28). And theoretical structures were set in place that continued to deny women a place within the fields of science and medicine. These were supported by the belief that 'men were superior to women [and of the mind, while] women were closer to the earth. [Hence] woman...was enslaved by the seventeenth-century metaphor linking her to nature, instead of being enthroned by it, as she had been much earlier' (Achterberg, 1990: 103). This positioning was to be found, for example, in the writing of Francis Bacon who also argued that 'Nature could be known through its association with the feminine, and mastery and domination must occur if civilization was to progress' (Achterberg, 1990: 103). Hence, 'In a patriarchal society, the exploitation of women and nature have a common ideological root' (Barbour 1990: 149).

Achterberg also reflects on another significant consequence of the Scientific Revolution. For it was not solely mind (man) and matter (woman) that were rendered apart and located in a power hierarchy. Spirit 'was conceptually eliminated from matter' (Barbour 1990: 149). leading to a denial of the body as sacred.

> Hence medicine no longer regarded itself as working in the sacred spaces where fellow humans find themselves in pain and peril, and where transcendence is so highly desired (Achterberg 1990: 103).

As we have seen, this positioning is heavily critiqued by New Agers and all those who hold holistic standpoints. For from these perspectives, all elements of humanity and nature are intimately spiritual. Nature is sacred. Health is reflected in the levels of energetic balance and connectedness. The embodied state is a sacred state. I shall return to these points shortly. For I have picked out here the key 'elements' that women engage with in a politic of reclamation. But let me briefly return to Sardar. Sardar argues that scientists have now got to confront 'new realities'. For, he proposes, we are moving in to a 'post-normal' phase in which, to use the words of Ravetz and Funtowicz[9] 'facts are uncertain, values in dispute, stakes high, and decisions urgent' (in Sardar 2000: 63).

> Post-normal science requires science to expand its boundaries to include different validation processes, perspectives, and types of knowledge. Thus, post-normal science becomes a dialogue among all stakeholders in a problem, from scientists themselves to social scientists, journalists, activists and housewives, regardless of their formal qualifications or affiliations.
>
> This is the essential novelty of post-normal science. It inevitably leads to a democratization of science. It doesn't hand over research work to untrained personnel; rather it brings science out of the laboratory and into public debate where all can take part in discussing its social, political and cultural ramifications (Sardar 2000: 64-65).

As I noted earlier in this chapter, such a shift in thought may now be beginning to take place. For as Treacy-Cole has observed, scientists and medical researchers are starting to investigate the affects of spirituality on health, this 'attracting attention from medical practitioners, those working outside of conventional medicine, and religious professionals from across a wide spectrum of traditions' (2001: 139). On the other side of the coin, New Agers are drawing from various sciences and philosophies and bringing healing practices into mainstream bio-medical settings. There is a sort of democratization (and appropriation) of practice even if Western science still appears to hold the key 'power card' in relation to the legitimization of healing practice in the bio-medical setting. As Ross states:

> On the one hand, the devotion to alternative, non-rationalistic belief systems places New Age thought outside the hierarchical structure of cultural capital observed by the legitimated scientific culture. On the

9. See Funcowicz, S. and Ravetz, J., 'Three Types of Risk assessment and the emergence of Post-Normal Science', in Krimsky, S. and D. Golding (eds.), *Social Theories of Risk* (Westport, Connecticut: Prager, 1992).

other hand, the New Age commitment to transforming science into a more humanistic and holistic enterprise involves taking on, to some degree, the structure of deference to authority that governs the institutional system of rationalist cultural capital (Ross 1991: 26-27).

Therefore as Foucault has argued, power's 'condition of possibility...[lies in] the moving substrate of force relations which, by virtue of their inequality, constantly engender [local and unstable] states of power' (1994: 163).

However, we would do well to remember that Western science still, as a whole, favours a predominantly androcentric perspective. Correspondingly, feminist critiques engage with science at all levels in relation to, for example, equal access for women to science education and employment, the focus of research projects and funding for the same, and male biases in theoretical standpoints and data interpretation (Barbour 1990: 147-48). Barbour also observes that the dualisms 'so pervasive in Western thought: mind/ body, reason/emotion, objectivity/subjectivity, domination/ submission, impersonal/personal, power/love' (1990: 147-48), where the first element is culturally defined as male, the second female, are also to be found in the scientific sphere. For here 'mind, reason, objectivity, domination, impersonality, power' (1990: 147-48) hold sway. Barbour sees no point, however, in reversing such dualisms and favouring 'the feminine' for this, he argues, will lead to equal imbalances and the perpetuation of dichotomisations (1990: 147-48).

And yet within New Age and Goddess 'philosophies' just such a reversal is promoted as we have seen. This does not mean, however, that the masculine is 'negated'. Both masculine and feminine are needed to 'make up a balanced whole'. And there is another major difference in relation to the location of power. Within New Age circles, *power* and *love* are often regarded as being one and the same. For example, Reiki Master Hiroshi Doi emphasizes that Reiki is intimately tied to 'the wave of love'. For love is 'the life energy emanating from the higher consciousness and spreading outwards in all directions equally' (Doi 2000: 28). Therefore when Reiki practitioners heal self and others, 'love as power' may be cited as the medium for this occurrence.

But let us return to science and spirituality for the moment. I drew in earlier Treacy-Cole's observation that science may be becoming more interested in the connections between belief, spirituality and health. I feel that a hermeneutics of suspicion ought to be applied here. For, not wishing to state the obvious, if women dominate in New Age spiritual healing practice—with, in the case of Reiki, male codification of theology and a perceived need to evaluate healing scientifically—and if science itself is interested in healing practice, (science being full of gender laden assumptions) then where does this leave women? For it does appear that this 'scientific interest' has a lot to do with containment, management and organization of democratized healing under the scientific umbrella. Further, as scientific empiricism is based on capitalist foundations, which go hand in hand with industry, pharmaceutical companies and technologies which may be damaging to individuals and all aspects of the environment, then why would New Age women healers wish to work within such overarching paradigms? Why not become Wiccan or a feminist witch? Why be accused of being 'fluffy', in that, as one female Druid observed,

> New Agers think that the universe is this great and marvellous place. There are marvellous parts, but there are many horrible things. Expressing nothing but white light, positivity and love is just not realistic at all. That is fluffy.[10]

However, I would argue that New Age women *are* subversively engaging with science and bio-medical approaches to health. They do this on several levels which have parallels with Goddess and feminist critiques of the suppression of women's religious experiences by patriarchal world religions. It is to these resistances that I turn next.

Powerful Healers

For women of the Goddess, power resides in the sacralized body where the Goddess is imminent. As Susan Greenwood observes in relation to Feminist Witchcraft, it has a holistic emphasis on the unification of the goddess with individuals on all levels of being as part of the universal whole. This holistic emphasis is common in all magical cosmologies and, as we have seen, in New Age cosmologies (though the Goddess may not be invoked in the latter).

Greenwood also proposes that the practice of feminist Witchcraft cannot be separated from the politics of the same. For emphasis is

---

10. This drawn from an interview as carried out by PhD candidate Aislinn Jones of Stirling University Religious Studies Department. April 2000, Glasgow.

placed on the reclamation and reinvention of historical traditions 'of a golden, matrifocal age whose mythology reveres women and Nature, before urban cultures of conquest with their patriarchal religions divided spirit from matter, shattering the former symbiotic wholeness with their emphasis on a divine force outside the world' (Greenwood 2000: 136). Hence these women actively critique patriarchal paradigms and, through ritual, attempt to reconnect with pre-patriarchal states of existence, while healing the 'wounds of patriarchy' (Greenwood 2000: 136) both at individual and planetary levels. Feminist Witchcraft is, hence, according to Greenwood, a 'transformatory politics' (Greenwood 2000: 136). So too, I would argue, is New Age healing. Rand, for example, emphasizes Reiki's potentiality for 'bringing world peace' (1990: 269) through its unifying and transformatory nature.

> Because Reiki is spiritual, yet not a religion, it has attracted students from all religious and spiritual backgrounds. Catholic priests and nuns practice Reiki. Jews, Protestants, Muslims, Hindus and Buddhists practice Reiki. Jains, Zoroastrinists, Taoists, and Shintoists practice Reiki. Wiccans, shamans, native people, and those on independent spiritual paths practice Reiki. Those in virtually all religious groups are attracted to the practice of Reiki. An important reason is that Reiki gives each person an immediate experience of the divine. Reiki places more people directly in contact with the higher power (regardless of the name one may call it) and provides direct experience of the higher power's grace and compassion. Reiki is thus helping unite all people of the world regardless of religious or ethnic background (Rand 2001: 269).

There is another key theme that underpins feminist, Witchcraft and New Age thought. For emphasis is also placed on finding 'a coherent and stable self' (Greenwood 2000: 137) in the face of postmodern 'fragmentation and discontinuity' (Greenwood 2000: 137). This search is reflected in New Age circles and may be seen, for example, in the increasing array of self-help and spirituality books and materials—these appealing to people on 'independent spiritual paths' (Rand 2001: 269). Treacy-Cole draws from publishers' responses in relation to this increased demand. These are informative. For publishers suggest that the book buying public feel that 'religion has become ghettoised....being only for academics or committed believers' (2001: 137). Hence, there is increasing demand for material that can enable the solitary searcher to re-find a sense of spiritual tradition and community, this search often being grounded in personal experiences of transformation, growth and health (2001: 137). This is not a new phenomenon however. Robert Fuller has documented the historical roots of such searching in relation to health and spirituality in the American context.

> The concept of metaphysical linking of the individual's inner mind with a higher cosmic power pointedly addresses the societal dis-ease that accompanied the dawn of modern American culture. Urbanization, industrialization, immigration, and the splintering of any theological consensus around which national life might revolve all jarred the American loose from traditional sources of stability (Fuller 1989: 63).

Correspondingly, individuals began to search, in the nineteenth and twentieth centuries, for sources of help with psychosomatic and stress related illnesses. And here a paradox arose. For the 'demands which a pluralistic society places upon a person to be inner-directed' and to draw upon 'higher healing energies' (1989: 64-5) could not be effectively addressed by the individual. For what were these inner sources of authority? Unable to find such inner reserves, the individual was forced to look 'without' – to medicine and the church for answers (1989: 64-5). However, 'the nation's "official religion" like its "official medicine", had little to offer those afflicted with nervous exhaustion [this also relating to stress induced illness]. A cultural niche was thus opened in which metaphysically inclined healing systems might flourish, and flourish they have' (Fuller 1989: 65).

> In the contemporary period little has changed. For there are, as we have seen, a multiplicity of healing practices all of which attribute dis-ease to metaphysical causes and which appeal to middle and upper educated classes. "These alternative healing systems appear to be expressions of an unsatisfied spiritual hunger rather than signs of desperation among the poor or ill-educated" (Fuller 1989: 91).

This searching for wholeness is, I would argue, part and parcel of a project of re-claiming the *embodied* self as empowered. For women, this means a re-valuing of their bodies as sacred mediums for active agency. 'Bodily experience is the very essence of feminist spirituality and is seen as the locus of women's power. The body is thus the source of self-affirmation and identity' (Greenwood 2000: 139). What we have in the contemporary setting then, is a continuing breaking down of 'theological consensus [with regard to] traditional sources of stability' (Fuller 1989: 63) and an ongoing critique of 'science as truth' as we have seen. This means that women healers are engaged in a parallel project of re-claiming their bodies from rationalistic, mechanistic bio-medical designations of 'health' and in asserting the validity of their own 'religious' experiences. They do this so that they may develop 'functionally useful ways of understanding [the] world' (Fuller 1989: 115) as 'whole' women. As healing work progresses, the individual chooses which elements of 'metaphysical causation' to embrace and which to discard. Science and bio-medical approaches to health are not rejected in totality but are located alongside other interpretative mediums. Similarly, elements of mainstream religiosity are appropriated—such as the Jesus as healer motif—and are integrated into personally developed experiential practice. The 'seeker' eclectically picks and mixes aspects that *work* and which provide senses of meaning and belonging.

For example, within Goddess spiritualities, emphasis is placed on the central significance of thealogies. This means that female divinity, the*a*, replaces male representations of the same and space is made for women to re-define themselves outwith of, for example, Christian theological representations of women. This we saw with Reiki teacher Diane Stein and her location of Reiki as 'a gift from the Goddess'. This shift is made in part to move on from Christian representations of the woman's body as 'fallen, corrupt and of the flesh'. For within the Christian tradition women's symbolic resources are often 'multiple and contradictory' (Scott 1986: 1067) as represented in Eve [virgin and temptress] and Mary [virgin and Madonna]. This means that women have historically been located in relation to 'myths of light [men/God] and dark [women/ Goddess], purification [men/male priests/doctors] and pollution, [menstruating women], innocence [Adam] and corruption [Eve]' (Scott 1986: 1067). These representations are expressed within religious doctrine and 'typically take the form of a fixed binary opposition, categorically and unequivocally asserting the meaning of male and female, masculine and feminine' (Scott 1986: 1067). Little room appears to be left for women to grow into whole, integrated, sexual and spiritual, empowered adults.

However, Goddess thealogies do contest such fixed assertions and do provide empowering symbolic resource pools for women to experience their bodies as sacred. For 'Many of the goddesses from ancient and contemporary times have been reclaimed and adopted by modern Western women as symbols of creativity and healing, liberation and empowerment' (Puttick 1997: 201). Hence space is also made for women to break away from traditional, patriarchal, representations of what the female body is 'supposed to be' (virginal daughter, wife, mother) so that women can explore what women 'want to be' (strong, independent and valued in their own right) enabling a move (metaphorically at least) from male promoted 'positions of dependence'.

Yet, as Puttick also states, drawing from the work of Ursula King, questions must be asked in relation to the *actual* power of women of the Goddess in society. For women are still subject to male power in the social and religious spheres. Hence, while men may worship the Goddess, this may ultimately also rest on male projection and superimposition of 'divine beauty and grace on the most seemingly unworthy of mortal women' (King 1989: 125) or on the denigration of women while still worshipping the divine feminine (King 1989: 125). This sort of tension may also be found in ritual practice. Helen Berger states that, 'The efforts to create gender equality [among Neo-Pagans and Wiccans] do not, however, mean that sexism has been obliterated (Berger 1999: 46). As one of her female Neo-Pagan interviewees asserted, 'I think half the men who get involved with Pagan/Wiccan stuff do it as a ploy to get laid. And the other half are trying to prove that they're better "Witches" than women. Poor babies' (Berger 1999: 46). One does wonder if these sorts of tensions are raising their heads in Reikian practice. For it does appear that certain aforementioned male Reiki writers are trying to appear 'better healers' than their female counterparts while systematically developing new 'more powerful' forms of Reiki practice: such as William Rand's Kahuna Reiki, Walter Lubeck's Rainbow Reiki and Frank Petters 'true' Usui Reiki – particularly when all of these new forms require additional training by the Masters themselves at not insignificant financial costs.

Hence, further questions ought to be asked in relation to the perceived status and authority of New Age teachers such as Petter, Lubeck and Rand. For these writers might be engaged in cultivating a sense of dependence from their students, as they are key sources of 'information' on Reiki theology and practice. They are also 'part and parcel' of the esoteric healing messages they deliver in that they produce 'new' worldviews for students to learn.

Tanice Foltz has examined such leadership in relation to a Kahuna (Hawaiian energetic healer) named Kali in the American context. She observes that, 'Kali has been extremely successful in introducing his students to a new way of looking at the world, and in obtaining their commitment to his reality. As the disseminator of the healing knowledge, Kali is considered the source and catalyst of the student's growth and transformation' (Foltz 1994: 119). However, Foltz also argues that this process is democratized in that students progressively learn to heal for themselves. 'This results in "a diffusion and effusion of superordinate power, available to all to recharge their spirituality and to transform their daily lives"' (Lopez in Foltz 1994: 119). This democratization is to be found, as we have seen, throughout Scottish healing circles. It also occurs among women of the Goddess, for one may learn to be, for example, a Witch even if one is self taught rather than initiated into a coven— though debates are also to be found about the need for formal training in Wiccan circles (Berger 2000: 105).

Therefore I would still argue that there are multiple spaces for women to work as active healing agents within New Age circles, and that fluidity of practice—and the centrality of one's own religious experience—is liberating for women. For as McGuire has noted in relation to healing in the American context, though individuals engaged collectively in healing rituals where 'symbols of power and order' (1998: 244) were pervasive, they also 'simultaneously sought privately experienced self-transformation and self validation' (1998: 244). They developed their 'own alternative world images [such as Stein's "Goddess spiral"]—and these were reflected in their ideas and values defined as "health", sources of healing power, individual responsibility, and the nature of self and self-transcendence. These world images were emphatically holistic—beyond the sense of mind body holism, to an insistence of all aspects of the cosmos' (1998: 244).

I have provided a number of examples of forms of holism within this book as it is indeed the central theme underlying all forms of energetic healing. For example, I briefly noted that healers may learn to 'dowse' energetic pathways and utilize this interpretative medium as confirmation of their ability to work as active healing agents. Therefore in learning to dowse and read how one's energetic being is affected by, for example, earth energies, the individual is provided with visible proof of cosmic connectedness that has long historical roots.[11] Connectedness to the earth is hence re-presented as a natural part of human existence in that 'human consciousness meets and dialogues with the Spirit of the Earth' (GO 2002). Health is hence intimately tied to the earth as part of the cosmos whole.

One will also find re-valuations of intuition being promoted in dowsing ontologies—this being common in all New Age thought as we have seen. For example, John MacManaway of the Westbank Centre, where I took part in two weekend workshops entitled 'Dowsing for Health' informed us that 'intuition is often regarded in a derogatory manner as women's stuff which needs to be crushed by male logical and rational explanations' this positioning being based on long held misogynist values. However, the Macmanaways *et al* regarded intuitive abilities as the cornerstone of healing and dowsing work. Intuition is a gift to be nurtured. It is hence a valuable tool that all humans have for 'self-growth through holistic connectedness'. Note how Barbour relates this to gender. '*Holistic thinking* is not limited to women, but it appears that in our culture women may be more sensitive than men to connections, contexts, and interdependencies and more attuned to development, co-operation, and symbiosis. There may be a biological basis for some of these gender differences, but they are mainly attributable to cultural patterns of socialization' (1990: 150 [italics original]). I am sure that women would be pleased to note that they have been so successfully socialized, in that they can now continue to do, in healing practice, what they have always known has worked—touch, intuition, loving care and compassion for self and others as part of an interconnected whole! For experiences of 'connectedness' are eminently empowering. Barrett draws from Carol Christ to describe this in relation to feminist Goddess ritual work. 'Common to women's rituals is the experience of immanence and transcendence. Women's spirituality rituals seek to allow women an experience of connection to the life force within all living things' (Christ 1987). 'Through this experience, many women feel that their rituals set a standard of how life should feel outside of the ritual circle' (Barrett 2000: 187). This is equally applicable to Reiki, where all group gatherings are ended by 'sending energy round the circle', and to

11. Workshops are held at The Salisbury Centre in Edinburgh where one can practice dowsing and, in the garden, visibly see how a person's aura expands or contracts once standing on ley lines (earth energy pathways).

individual healing practice. For *healing is connection* to cosmic power, all that is, love, the Goddess etc. Healing rituals are about also, in Wiccan practice as in New Age work, effecting change, both at individual (as part of 'the whole') and global levels as we have seen.

Which brings us back to the central underlying theme of this book, 'what it is to be healed'. Eller states that,

> Healing is a metaphor for any form of self-transformation, whether emotional, physical or mental. It is the name given to the overall effort to gain self knowledge and marshal personal power (Eller 1993: 10).

This personal power may be seen as 'of the Goddess' or as love, ki, prana etc. and resides within the individual. Being healed is not an end result but an ongoing transformation of self-to-society relationship. Healing is an embodied experience. It is about becoming a balanced energetic whole. To be healed is to free oneself from long held mores and societal constraints. For women, this means re-valuing their bodies positively as sacred mediums for growth. It is about re-valuing receptivity as empowering. For being 'open to the Goddess' or being open energetically (as in the chakras) enables one to be healthy and whole. On a practical level, emphasis is placed on the fact that there are alternatives to bio-medical and mainstream religious designations of being human as we have seen. New models are individually developed based on experiential practice, where the sacred becomes re-embodied and the self empowered. For women, this is active engagement in a politics of reclamation. For they reclaim 'from such institutions as religion and therapy the powers and tactics which were rightfully our own to begin with, and which have been warped and watered down after having been stolen by patriarchy' (Daly 1991: 282-83). Women question curing models of health and bring healing to medical settings. Women ask for healing services and rituals in the mainstream churches. Women demand acknowledgement as active healing agents. They network with other healers and 'work' locally and globally. They reject the centrality of striving for material gain as a lifelong task. They honour the masculine and the feminine divine in self and others and critique dualistic divisions. They acknowledge that healing is a process that involves not just the health of the individual's molecular and energetic body, but also 'the integrity of community, the environment, and concerns for the spirit' (Achterberg 1990: 193).

The woman healer no longer passively conforms to predetermined gender roles but actively engages in her own self-definition. She has 'learnt to see the world anew and name and shape it differently' (King 1989: 2). Woman as healer has re-claimed her voice and she demands to be heard. Hers is a voice of 'protest and promise' (King 1989).

Appendix A

Primary 'New Age' Sources (in alphabetical order)

FRW1:   Fiona's Workbook for 1st Degree Reiki, 2000.

FRW2:   Fiona's Workbook for 2nd Degree Reiki, 2000.

GO: 'Mid-Atlantic Geomancy', www.geomancy.org, 2002.

PWM: Petter Workshop Manual, 'Reiki Techniques', 2001.

NFSH: National Federation of Spiritual Healers Leaflet, 2000.

RICRT: William Rand, International Centre for Reiki Training, www.reiki.org, 2001.

SC1:   Salisbury Centre Brochure, Spring, 2001.

SC2:   Salisbury Centre Brochure, Summer, 2003.

WMH: Helen Stott Workshop Manual, 2001.

Appendix B

Questionnaire for Frank Arjava Petter's 'Reiki Techniques' Workshop

I am currently researching 'healing' at the University of Stirling, Department of Religious Studies for my PhD. As Reiki is a central focus of my research I am very interested in trying to build up a clearer picture of the networks of practitioners in Scotland. It would therefore be extremely helpful to me if you could spare a few minutes in this workshop to answer a few simple questions, answers to which will be treated in strictest confidence. However, if you prefer *not* to answer a specific question that's absolutely fine.

If I could speak to you at a later date in a little more depth could you please also give me a contact number.

1. What is your first name and gender? .... M/F

2. Tel. No: ....

3. What is your home location, town, county? ....

4. How long have you been involved with Reiki? ....
   ....
   ....

5. What drew you to this healing practice? ....
   ....
   ....

6. What do you perceive to be its primary benefits? ie. self-healing, healing others, global transformation ....
   ....
   ....

7. Any further comments you wish to make, please add here ....
   ....
   ....

Thank you very much for your assistance.

BIBLIOGRAPHY

Achterberg, J. *Woman as Healer* (Boston: Shambala Publications,1990).

Agar, M.H. *The Professional Stranger* (San Diego, New York, London: Academic Press, 1996, 2nd edn).

Albanese, C. *America: Religions and Religion* (Belmont, CA: Wordsworth, 1999, 3rd edn).

Aldridge, D. *Spirituality, Healing and Medicine* (London and Philadelphia: Jessica Kingsley Publishers, 2000).

Andrews, T. *The Healers' Manual* (Minnesota: Llewellyn Publications,1994).

Aponte, H.J. 'Love, the Spiritual Wellspring of Forgiveness: An Example of Spirituality in Therapy', *Journal of Family Therapy*, 20.1, (1998), pp. 37-58.

Asad, T. 'The Concept of Cultural Translation in British Social Anthropology', in Clifford, J. and G. Marcus (eds.), *Writing Culture* (Berkeley, Los Angeles, London: University of California Press, 1986).

Asad, T. 'Agency and Pain: an Exploration' in *Culture and Religion*, 2003.

Barbour, I. *Religion and Science* (San Francisco: HarperSanFrancisco, 1990).

Barrett, R. R. 'The Power of Ritual' in W. Griffin (ed.), *Daughters of the Goddess* (Lanham, MD: AltaMira Press, 2000).

Bax, K. The 'Eclipse of Folk Medicine in Western Society' in *Sociology of Health & Illness* 13. 1, (1991).

Beck, U., Giddens, A. & Lash, S. (eds.) *Reflexive Modernization* (Cambridge: Polity Press, 1994).

Beckford, J. 'Religion, Modernity and Post-Modernity' in B. R. Wilson (ed.), *Religion, Contemporary Issues* (London: Bellew, 1992).

Bednarowski, M.F. 'The New Age Movement and Feminist Spirituality' in Lewis, J. & J. G. Melton (eds.), *Perspectives of the New Age* (New York: State University Press of New York, 1992).

Bell, C. *Ritual Theory, Ritual Practice* (New York and Oxford: Oxford University Press, 1992).

Benson, H. *Timeless Healing*, (New York: Scribner,1996).

Berger, H. A. *A Community of Witches* (Columbia, University of South Carolina Press, 1999).

Bloom, William (ed.) *The New Age* (London: Rider, 1991).

Bohm, D. *Wholeness and the Implicit Order* (London: Routledge, 1980).

Boyarin, D. 'Gender' in *Critical Terms for Religious Studies* (Chicago: University of Chicago Press, 1998).

Braude, A. *Radical Spirits* (Boston: Beacon Press, 1989).

Brennan, B. A. *Hands of Light* (Toronto, New York, London: Bantam Books, 1988).

Brown, M. *The Channelling Zone* (Cambridge, MA and London: Harvard University Press, 1997).

Bruce, S. *Religion In Modern Britain* (New York and Oxford: Oxford University Press, 1995).

Butler, J. *Bodies That Matter* (London and New York: Routledge,1993).

_____ *Gender Trouble*, (London and New York, Routledge, 1990).

Buckman, R. and Sabbagh, K. *Magic or Medicine* (London, Sydney and Auckland: Pan Books, 1994).

Campbell, C. 'The Cult, The Cultic Milieu and Secularisation', *A Sociological Yearbook of Religion in Britain* 5 (London: SCM Press, 1972).

Campbell, J. *Traveller in Space: In Search of Female Identity in Tibetan Buddhism* (London: The Athlone Press, 1996).

Cant, S. and Calnan, M. 'On the Margins of the Medical Marketplace? An Exploratory Study of Alternative Practitioner's Perceptions', *Sociology of Health and Illness*, 13.1, (1991).

Cant, S. and Sharma, U. *Complementary and Alternative Medicine* (London and New York: Free Association Books,1996).

Capra, F. *The Tao of Physics* (Berkeley, CA: Shambala Publications, 1995).

Carrette, J.R. 'Post-structuralism and the Psychology of Religion' in Diane Jonte Pace and William Parsons (eds.), *Religion and Psychology* (London and New York: Routledge, 2001).

Carrette, J.R.(ed.) *Religion and Culture by Michel Foucault* (Manchester: Manchester University Press, 1999).

Christ, C.P. *Laughter of Aphrodite* (New York: Harper and Row, 1978).

_____ *Diving Deep and Surfacing* (Boston: Beacon Press, 1980).

Christ, C. and Plaskow, J. (eds.) *Womanspirit Rising* (San Francisco: Harper Collins, 1992).

Clifford, J. *Routes* (Cambridge MA: Harvard University Press, 1997).

Clifford, J. and Marcus, G. *Writing Culture* (Berkeley, LA, London: University of California Press, 1986).

Code, L. (ed.) *Encyclopedia of Feminist Theories* (London and New York: Routledge, 2000).

Corrywright, D. *Theoretical and Empirical Investigations into New Age Spiritualities* (Bern: Peter Lang Ag, European Academic Publishers, 2003).

Craib, I. *Modern Social Theory: From Parsons to Habermas*, (London: Harvester Wheatsheaf, 1992, 2nd edn).

Crowley, V. 'Healing in Wicca' in W. Griffin (ed.), *Daughters of the Goddesss* (Lanham, MD: AltaMira Press, 2000).

Csordas, T.J. The Rhetoric of Transformation in Ritual Healing, *Culture, Medicine and Psychiatry*, 7, (1983), pp. 333-75.

Daly, M. *Gyn/Ecology* (London: The Women's Press, 1991).

Davies, C. A. *Reflexive Ethnography* (London and New York: Routledge, 1999).

Davis, K. 'Embody-ing Theory' in *Feminist Perspectives on the Body* (London: Sage Publications, 1997).

Doi, H. *Modern Reiki Methods for Healing* (British Columbia: Fraser Journal Publishing, 2000).

Drane, J. *What the New Age is Saying to the Church* (London: Marshall Pickering, 1991).

Eller, C. *Living in the Lap of the Goddess: The Feminist Spirituality Movement in America* (New York: Crossroads, 1993).

Feher, S. 'Who Holds the Cards? Women and New Age Astrology', in J. R. Lewis, and J.G. Melton (eds.), *Perspectives on the New Age* (Albany, N.Y: State University of New York Press, 1992).

Ferguson, D. S. *New Age Spirituality* (Louisville: John Knox Press, 1993).

Ferguson, M. *The Aquarian Conspiracy* (Los Angeles, CA: J.P. Tarcher Inc., 1980).

Fetterman, D. M. *Ethnography Step By Step* (Thousand Oaks, CA: Sage Publications, 1998).

Foltz, T. *Kahuna Healer: Learning to See with Ki* (New York: Garland, 1994).

_____ 'Thriving, Not Surviving' in W. Griffin (ed.), *Daughters of the Goddess* (Lanham: AltaMira Press, 2000).

Foster, G. M. and Anderson, B, G. *Medical Anthropology* (New York: John Wiley and Sons, 1978).

Foucault, M. *Discipline and Punish* (London: Penguin Books, 1977).

_____ *The History of Sexuality, Vol.1, An Introduction* (New York: Penguin, 1980).

_____ 'The Subject and Power', *Critical Enquiry*, 8: (1982), pp. 777-95.

_____ 'Panopticism' in *The Foucault Reader*, Paul Rabinow (ed.; London: Penguin Books, 1984).

_____ In J. Storey, (ed.), 'Michael Foucault', Cultural Theory and Popular Culture: A Reader (London: Harvester Wheatsheaf, 1994).

_____ *The Birth of the Clinic: An Archaeology of Medical Perception* (London: Tavistock, 1996).

Fuller, R.C. *Alternative Medicine and American Religious Life* (New York and Oxford: Oxford University Press, 1989).

Garrett, C. 'Transcendental Meditation, Reiki and Yoga: Suffering, Ritual and Self Therapy', *Journal of Contemporary Religion*, 16.3, (2001).

Gerber, R. *Vibrational Medicine* (Santa Fe, New Mexico, Bear and Company, 1988).

Goulet, J.G. 'Dreams and Visions in Other Lifeworlds', in Young and Goulet (eds.), *Being Changed* (Canada: Broadview Press, 1994).

Gottschall, M. 'The Mutable Goddess' in W. Griffin (ed.), *Daughters of the Goddess* (Lanham, MD: AltaMira Press, 2000).

Greenwood, S. ''Feminist Witchcraft' in W. Griffin (ed.), *Daughters of the Goddess* (Lanham, MD: AltaMira Press, 2000).

Griffin, W. *Daughters of the Goddess* (Lanham, Maryland: AltaMira Press, 2000).

Gross, R. *Buddhism After Patriarchy* (Albany, NY: State University of New York Press, 1993).

_____ *Feminism and Religion: An Introduction*, (Boston: Beacon Press, 1996).

Grosz, E. *Volatile Bodies* (Bloomington: Indiana University Press, 1993).

Hall, M. *Practical Reiki* (London and California: Thorsons, 1997).

Hall, S. 'Notes on Deconstructing "the popular"' in *People's History and Socialist Theory*, (ed., R. Samuel; London: Routledge and Kegan Paul [reprinted in John Storey, 1994, *Cultural Theory and Popular Culture: A Reader*, London: Harvester Wheatsheaf, 1994).

Hammer, O. *Claiming Knowledge: Strategies of Epistemology from Theosophy to New Age* (Boston, MA: OSA; Leiden, Netherlands: Brill, 2000).

Hanegraaff, W. J. *New Age Religion and Western Culture* (New York, State University of New York Press, 1998).

_____ 'From the Devil's Gateway to the Goddess Within : The Image of the Witch in Neopaganism' in Joanne Pearson *Belief Beyond Boundaries: Wicca, New Age and Celtic Spirituality*, (Ashgate/Open University Press, 2002).

_____ *New Age Religion and Secularisation*, Numen, xlvii, No. 3, (2000).

Harvey, D. *The Power to Heal*, (Wellingborough:The Aquarian Press, 1983).

Hedges, E. and Beckford, J.A. 'Holism, Healing and the New Age' in S. Sutcliffe and M. Bowman, *Beyond New Age*, (Edinburgh: Edinburgh University Press, 2000).

Heelas, P. *The New Age Movement* (Oxford and Massachusetts: Blackwell Publishers Limited, 1996).

hooks, b. *Wounds of Passion: A Writing Life* (London: The Women's Press, 1997).

Horsfall, D. 'Black Holes in the Writing Process: Narratives of Speech and Silence' in H. Byrne-Armstrong, J. Higgs, and D. Horsfall (eds.), *Critical Moments in Qualitative Research*, (Oxford: Butterworth-Heinemann, 2001).

Isherwood, L. and McEwan, D. (eds.), *An A to Z of Feminist Theology* (Sheffield: Sheffield Academic Press, 1996).

_____ *Introducing Feminist Theology*, (Sheffield: Sheffield Academic Press, 1994).

Jacobs, J.L. 'Gender and Power in New Religious Movements' in J. Juschka (ed.), *Feminism and the Study of Religion* (London and New York: Continuum, 2001).

Jantzen, G. *Becoming Divine* (Manchester: Manchester University Press, 1998).

_____ *Gender, Power and Christian Mysticism*, (Cambridge and New York: Cambridge University Press, 1995).

Jenkins, R. *Pierre Bourdieu* (London and New York: Routledge, 1992).

Juschka, D.M. *Feminism in the Study of Religion* (London and New York: Continuum, 2001).

King, U. *Women and Spirituality* (London: Macmillan Education, 1989).

_____ *Religion and Gender* (Oxford: Blackwell, 1995).

King, U. and T. Beattie (eds.) *Spirituality and Society in the New Millenium* (Brighton: Sussex Academic Press, 2001).

Kleinman, A. The Comparative Studies of Health Systems and Medical Care, No. 3 (Berkeley, CA: University of California Press, 1980).

Kranenborg, R. 'The Presentation of the Essenes in Western Esotericism', *Journal of Contemporary Religion*, 13. 2, (1998).

Larner, C. *Enemies of God* (Baltimore: John Hopkins University Press, 1981).

Lemert, C. 'After the Crisis' in Steven Seidman (ed.), *Queer Theory/Sociology* (Oxford and Cambridge, MA: Blackwell Publishers, 1996).

Levin, J. S. 'Religion and Health: 'Is There an Association?', Is it Valid?' and 'Is it Causal? 'in *Social Science and Medicine* 38. 4 (1994).

Levi-Strauss, C. *Totenism* (London: Merlin Press, 1962).

Lewis, J. R., and Melton, J. G., *Perspectives on the New Age* (Albany, N.Y: State University of New York Press, 1992).

Lofland, J. *Doing Social Life*, (Hoboken, NJ: John Wiley and Sons, 1976).

Lubeck W., Petter F. and Rand W. *The Spirit of Reiki* (Twin Lakes, WI: Lotus Press, 2001).

Lubeck, W. *The Complete Reiki Handbook* (Twin Lakes, WI: Lotus Press, 1994).

_____ *Rainbow Reiki: Expanding the Reiki System with Powerful Spiritual Abilities* (Twin Lakes, WI: Lotus Press, 1996).

MacManaway, B. and Turcan, J. *Healing*; 'The Energy That Can Restore Health' (Wellingborough: Thorson Publications Ltd., 1983).

MacManaway, J. *Dowsing for Health* (London and New York: Anness Publishing Limited, 2001).

McClain, C.S. (ed.) *Women as Healers* (New Brunswick and London: Rutgers University Press, 1989).

McClenon, J. *Wondrous Healing* (DeKalb: Northern Illinois University Press, 2002).

McCutcheon, R. T. *The Discipline of Religion* (London: Routledge, 2003).

McGuire, M.B. *Ritual Healing in Suburban America* (New Brunswick: Rutgers University Press, 1998a).

_____ 'Religion and Healing', *in Wouter Hanegraaf, New Age Religion and Western Culture* (Albany, N.Y: State University of New York Press, 1998b).

_____ 'Gendered Spirituality and Quasi-Religious Ritual' in *Religion and Social Order*, 4, (1994), pp. 273-87.

_____ 'New-Old Directions in the Social Scientific Study of religion in J. Spickard, J. Landres, and B. McGuire (eds.), *Personal Knowledge and Beyond* (New York and London: New York University Press, 1992).

_____ 'Religion and the Body: Rematerializing the Human Body in the Social Sciences of Religion' in *Journal for the Scientific Study of Religion*, 29. 3 (1990), pp. 283-96.

McKee, J. Holistic Health And The Critique of Western Medicine, *Soc.Sci. Med*, 26. 8, (1988), pp. 775-84.

Mascia-Lees, F., Sharpe, P. and Cohen, C. 'The Postmodernist Turn in Anthropology', *Signs: Journal of Women in Culture and Society*, 15.11, (1989).

McNay, L. *Gender and Agency* (Cambridge and Oxford: Polity Press, 2000).

Melton, J. G. *New Age Almanac* (Detroit: Visible Ink Press, 1991).

_____ 'Reiki: The International Spread of a New Age Healing Movement' in *New Age Religion and Globalisation*, (Denmark: Aarhus University Press, 2002).

Micozza, M.S. (ed.) *Fundamentals of Complementary and Alternative Medicine* (New York: Churchill Livingstone, 1996).

Moore, H. L. *Feminism and Anthropology* (Oxford, Cambridge: Polity Press, 1988).

Moore, H. L. *A Passion For Difference* (Cambridge, Oxford: Polity Press, 1994).

Myss, C. 'Redefining the Healing Process' in William Bloom, *The New Age: An Anthology of Essential Writings* (London: Rider, 1991).

_____ *Anatomy of the Spirit*, (Toronto, New York, London: Bantam Books, 1997).

_____ *Sacred Contracts*, (New York: Harmony Books, 2002).

Needleman, J. *The New Religions* (Golden City, New York: Doubleday, 1970).

Neitz, M.J. 'In Goddess We Trust', in T. Robbins and D. Anthony (eds.), *In Gods We Trust* (New Brunswick, NJ: Transaction Press, 1990).

Nettleton, S. 'Governing the Risky Self: How to Become Healthy, Wealthy and Wise' in Peterson and Bunton (eds.), *Foucault Health and Medicine* (London and New York: Routledge, 1997).

Nye, M. *Religion, the Basics* (London and New York: Routledge, 2003).

Okely, J. and Calloway, H. *Anthropology and Autobiography* (London and New York: Routledge, 1992).

Okely, J. *Own and Other Culture* (London, New York: Routledge, 1996).

Oschman, J.L. 'Science and the Human Energy Field' in *Reiki News Magazine*, 1.3, (Winter 2002), Vision Publications.

Peterson, A. and Bunton, R. (eds.) *Foucault Health and Medicine* (London and New York: Routledge, 1997).

Partridge, C. 'Truth, Authority and Epistemological Individualism in New Age Thought' in *Journal of Contemporary Religion*, 14.1, (1999).

Petter, F. *Reiki Fire* (Twin Lakes, WI: Lotus Light Publications, 1997).

Puttick, E. *Women in New Religions* (London: McMillan Press, 1997).

Rabinow, M. *The Foucault Reader* (Middlesex and New York: Penguin, 1984).

Raphael, M. 'Monotheism in Contemporary Feminist Goddess Religion' in Deborah Sawyer and Diane Collier (eds.), *Is There a Future for Feminist Theology* (Sheffield: Sheffield Academic Press, 1999).

Rand, W. *Reiki, The Healing Touch* (Southfield, USA: Vision Publications, 2001).

Rand, William, Walter Lubeck and Frank Petter, *The Spirit of Reiki* (Twin Lakes, WI: Lotus Press, 2001).

Roman, S. *Spiritual Growth* (Tiburon, California: H.J. Kramer Inc., 1989).

Roof, W. C. *Spiritual Marketplace* (Princeton, N.J: Princeton University Press, 1999).

Rosaldo, M.Z. 'The Uses and Abuses of Anthropology; Reflections on Feminism and Cross-Cultural Understanding,' *Signs*, 5 (Spring 1980): p. 400.

Rose, S. 'An Examination of the New Age Movement: Who is Involved and What Constitutes its Spirituality?', in *Journal of Contemporary Religion, 13. 1, (1998).*

_____ 'New Age Women: Spearheading the Movement', in *Women's Studies*, 30 (2001), pp. 329-50.

Ross, A. *Strange Weather: Culture Science, and Technology in the Age of Limits* (London: Verso, 1991).

Sardar, Z. *Thomas Kuhn and the Science Wars* (Cambridge and New York: Icon Books UK and Totem Books US, 2000).

Schur, E. *The Awareness Trap: Self-Absorption Instead of Social Change* (New York: Quadrangle Books, 1976).

Scott, J. 'Gender, A Useful Category of Historical Analysis', *The American Historical Review*, 91, (December 1986), pp. 1053-75.

_____ 'Deconstructing Equality-Versus-Difference: Or, The Uses of Post-Structualist Theory for Feminism', in L. McDaniels and R. Pringle (eds.), *Defining Women* (Milton Keynes: Open University, Polity Press, 1992).

Scutt, J. *As a Woman Writing Women's Lives* (Melbourne: Artemis, 1992).

Sharma, U. 'Using Alternative Therapies: Marginal Medicine and Central Concerns', in B. Davey, A. Gray and C. Seele (eds.), *Health and Disease* (Buckingham: Open University Press, 1995).

_____ *Complementary Medicine Today* (London and New York: Routledge, 1995).

Sheldrake, R. A New Science of Life (Los Angeles, CA: J.P. Tarcher, 1982).

Shepherd McClain, C. (ed.) *Women as Healers*, (New Brunswick: Rutgers University Press, 1989).

Shildrick, M. *Leaky Bodies and Boundaries* (London and New York: Routledge, 1997).

Shuffrey, S. *Reiki, A Beginner's Guide* (London: Hodder and Stoughton, 1998).

Singer, J. *Androgyny* (York Beach, Maine: Nicols-Hays, 2000).

Sjoo, M. 'New Age and Patriarchy', *Religion Today*, 9. 3 (1994).

Spangler, D. 'The Movement Toward The Divine', in Ferguson (ed.), *New Age Spirituality,* (Louisville, KY: John Knox Press, 1993).

Spradley, J. *The Ethnographic Interview* (Austin, Texas: Holt, Rinehard and Winston Inc., 1979).

Spickard, J., Landres, J. and McGuire, B. (eds.) *Personal Knowledge and Beyond: Reshaping the Ethnography of Religion* (New York and London: New York University Press, 2002).

Starhawk in Bednarowski, Mary Farrell, 'The New Age Movement and Feminist Spirituality', Lewis and Melton (eds.) *Perspectives on the New Age* (Albany, N.Y: State University of New York Press, 1992).

Starr Sered, S. *Priestess, Mother, Sacred Sister* (Oxford: Oxford University Press, 1994).

Stein, D. *Essential Reiki* (California: Crossing Press, 1995).

_____ *The Women's Spirituality Book* (Woodbury, MN: Llewellyn Publications, 1987).

_____ *Stroking the Python*, (Woodbury, MN: Llewellyn Publications, 1987).

Stoller, P. *The Taste of Ethnographic Things* (Philadelphia, PA: University of Pennysylvania Press, 1989).

Storey, J. (ed.) 'Michel Foucault', *Cultural Theory and Popular Culture: A Reader* (London: Harvester Wheatsheaf, 1994).

Sullivan, R. 'Seeking an End to Text as Primary' in F. Reynolds and S. L. Burkhalte (eds.) *Beyond the Classics* (Otterup, Denmark: Scholars Press, 1990).

Sutcliffe, S. 'Seekers, Networks, and 'New Age', *Scottish Journal of Religious Studies* 18.2, (1997).

_____ *'New Age' in Britain: an Ethnographical and Historical Exploration,* unpublished PhD. Dissertation, The Open University, 1998.

_____ *Children of the New Age* (London and New York: Routledge, 2003).

Sutcliffe, S. and M. Bowman (eds.) *Beyond New Age* (Edinburgh: Edinburgh University Press, 2000).

Sutcliffe, S. (ed.) Journal of Culture and Religion, 4.1, (May 2003).

Tassano, F. The Power of Life or Death (London: Duckworth, 1995).

Thomas, T. 'Popular Religion' in J. Hinnels (ed.), *A New Dictionary of Religions* (London: Allan Lane, 1995).

Treacy Cole, D. 'Spirituality and Healing in a Scientific Age', in U. King and T. Beattie, *Spirituality and Society in the New Millenium* (Brighton: Sussex University Press, 2001).

Turner, B. 'From Governmentality to Risk, Some Reflections on Foucault's Contribution to Medical Sociology' in A. Peterson and R. Bunton (eds.), *Foucault, Health and Medicine* (London and New York: Routledge, 1997).

Tyler, D. 'At Risk of Maladjustment: The Problem of Child Mental Health' in A. Peterson and R. Bunton (eds.) *Foucault, Health and Medicine* (London and New York: Routledge, 1997).

Usui, M. and F. Petter, *The Original Reiki Handbook of Dr Mikao Usui* (Twin Lakes, WI: Lotus Press, 1999).

Van Hove, H. 'Higher Realities and the Inner Self: One Quest? Transcendence and the Significance of the Body in the New Age Circuit' in *Journal Of Contemporary Religion* 11. 2, (1996).

Walker, A. (ed.) *The Kingdom Within* (Forres, Scotland: Findhorn Press, 1994).

Waterhouse, H. 'Representing Western Buddhism:A United Kingdom Focus' in Gwilym Beckerlegge, *From Sacred Text to Internet* (Milton Keynes: Open University/Ashgate Press, 2001).

Wirth, D. P. 'The Significance of Belief and Expectancy Within the Spiritual Healing Encounter', *Soc. Sci. Med.* 41. 2 (1995), pp. 249-60.

Woodhead, L. and Heelas, P. *Religion in Modern Times* (Oxford: Blackwell Publishers, 2000).

Woolf, M. *A Thrice Told Tale* (Stanford, CA: Stanford University Press, 1992).

Yoder, D. 'Toward a Definition of Folk Religion', *Western Folklore* 33.1 (January 1974), p.14.

York, M. *The Emerging Network: A Sociology of the New Age and Neo-pagan Movements* (Lanham, MD: Rowan and Littlefield, 1995).

Young, A. *Justice and the Politics of Difference* (Princetown: Princetown University Press, 1990).

Young D. and J.G. Goulet, *Being Changed: The Anthropology of Extraordinary Experience* (Ontario: Broadview Press, 1994).

Index of Authors

Printed in the United Kingdom
by Lightning Source UK Ltd.
126927UK00001B/46-66/P